PROPHETIC CONFLICT AND YAHWISTIC TRADITION:
A SYNTHETIC STUDY OF TRUE AND FALSE PROPHECY
(JEREMIAH 26–29)

PROPHETIC CONFLICT AND YAHWISTIC TRADITION:
A SYNTHETIC STUDY OF TRUE AND FALSE PROPHECY
(JEREMIAH 26–29)

M. Sashi Jamir

GlossaHouse
Wilmore, KY
www.glossahouse.com

Prophetic Conflict and Yahwistic Tradition:
A Synthetic Study of True and False Prophecy (Jeremiah 26–29)

© GlossaHouse, LLC, 2016

All rights reserved. No part of this book may be reproduced or transmitted in any form or by any means, electronic or mechanical, including photocopying or recording, or by means of any information storage or retrieval system, except as may be expressly permitted by the 1976 Copyright Act or in writing from the publisher. Requests for permission should be addressed in writing to the following:
GlossaHouse, LLC
110 Callis Circle
Wilmore, KY 40390

Jamir, M. Sashi.
  Prophetic conflict and Yahwistic tradition : synthetic study of true and false prophecy (Jeremiah 26-29) / M. Sashi Jamir. – Wilmore, KY : GlossaHouse, ©2016.

   xvii, 278 pages ; 22 cm. -- (GlossaHouse dissertation series ; vol. 3)
   A revision of the author's Ph.D. dissertation, Asbury Theological Seminary, 2015.

   Includes bibliographical references (pages 231-264) and indexes.
   ISBN 9781942697213 (paperback)
   ISBN 9781942697220 (hardback)

   1. Bible. Jeremiah, XXVI-XXIX --Criticism, Interpretation, etc. 2. Bible. Jeremiah, XXVI-XXIX--Prophecies. 3. Prophecies--Biblical teaching. I. Title. II. Series.

BS1525.52.J354 2016   224/.206
Library of Congress Control Number: 2016954210

The fonts used to create this work are available from www.linguistsoftware.com/lgku.htm

Cover design by T. Michael W. Halcomb
Text layout and book design by Carl S. Sweatman
Volume Editor Carl S. Sweatman

GLOSSAHOUSE DISSERTATION SERIES

VOLUME 3

SERIES EDITORS

FREDRICK J. LONG
T. MICHAEL W. HALCOMB
CARL S. SWEATMAN

VOLUME EDITOR

CARL S. SWEATMAN

GLOSSAHOUSE DISSERTATION SERIES

The purpose and goal of the GlossaHouse Dissertation Series is to facilitate the creation and publication of innovative, affordable, and accessible scholarly resources—whether print or digital—that advance research in the areas of both ancient and modern texts and languages.

Temeim Ojala, Obala, Kenüngtsü, aser Jala ana atema

TABLE OF CONTENTS

ABBREVIATIONS	xi
PREFACE	xii–xvii
CHAPTER 1 Prophetic Conflict	1–38
CHAPTER 2 In Quest of a Hermeneutical Method	39–83

CHAPTER 3
    Yahwistic Tradition and Its Developments:
    A Critical Realist View
	84–123

CHAPTER 4
    The Socio-Economic and Political Context
    of the Ancient Israelite People in an
    Agrarian Society
	124–61

CHAPTER 5 Prophetic Conflict in Jeremiah 26–29	162–221
CHAPTER 6 Conclusions	222–30
BIBLIOGRAPHY	231–64
INDICES	265–78

Abbreviations

The abbreviations used throughout this thesis follow the standard established by the *SBL Handbook of Style*, 2nd edition (2014). Those employed that do not appear in the *Handbook* are (listed according to abbreviation):

DOTP	*Dictionary of the Old Testament Prophets*
DTIB	*Dictionary for Theological Interpretation of the Bible*
JPS	Jewish Publication Society
SBLSS	Society of Biblical Literature Symposium Series
SBTS	Sources for Biblical and Theological Study
SPT	Studies in Philosophical Theology
Thom	*The Thomist*

PREFACE

The aim of this dissertation is to demonstrate that ancient Israel had an adequate rubric in its Yahwistic tradition to distinguish between true and false prophecy. Generally, in Old Testament (OT) scholarship, it has been argued that ancient Israel simply did not have the capacity to discern between true and false prophecy. In fact, there is a tendency to reduce prophecy in the OT as mere *vaticinium ex eventu*. This notion has persisted partly because of an inadequate understanding and poorly conceived epistemology of divine revelation and history. Thus, in order to better construe divine revelation and its relation to tradition as *fidei depósitum*, the hermeneutic of critical realism is utilized. Critical realism espouses that knowledge is not about transmission of facts or information alone but, most importantly; it is about the transmission of authentic subjectivism. In other words, a critical analysis of subject matter such as revelation can lead to authentic knowledge. I argue that this revelation, in the case of ancient Israel, becomes the deposit of faith or tradition, and tradition in turn becomes the means of preserving revelation.

The study next explores the development of Yahwistic tradition and identifies some of its features. I argue that Yahwistic tradition did not oppose Israel's monarchy; instead, it insisted only that its monarchy should be a limited one. In other words, Israel's monarch should function within the ideals of the Yahwistic tradition. It is within this framework of Yahwistic tradition that ancient Israel prophecy should be studied. I then analyze the society of ancient Israel (Iron Age II) utilizing Gerhard Lenski and Patrick Nolan's macro-sociology of agrarian societies. This analysis was necessary for two reasons: first, prophecy, at its core, is sociological in nature; second, this analysis helps to paint the possible context within which the prophetic conflict existed. The study shows that the resources for survival were limited, and yet they were drained by the royal administration for its maintenance and self-aggrandizement. Interestingly, the prophets found themselves in the upper echelon of social stratification. Some of them were swayed by their greed for comfortable living and aided in institutionalizing the Yahwistic tradition. The institutionalized Yahwistic tradition paralyzed the minds of many Israelite kings and their supporters, causing them to be unreceptive to Yahweh's further revelation. All was not lost, however. I argue that there was a vestige in the עם־הארץ ("people of the land"), who aspired to see that the Yahwistic tradition was restored in the land. It is this עם־הארץ that supported the Yahwistic prophets and eventually became the key factor in identifying true prophecy.

This analysis is then used to understand the prophetic conflict as found in Jer 26-29. I argue that Jeremiah prophesied when he received revelation from Yahweh as well as by critically and imaginatively reading the received tradition. In other words, it was the covenant relationship between Israel and Yahweh that impacted the content of Jeremiah's prophecy. Hananiah, in contradistinction to Jeremiah, prophesied in relation to the institutionalized understanding of Yahwistic tradition and according to the influx of international politics. In an excursus, I also explore the criteria of adjudicating true and false prophecy as found in Deut 13:2-6 [Eng 13:1-5] and 18:21-22. The former articulates that a prophet or dreamer who gives a "wonder or sign" that comes to pass and uses that sign to lead the people to follow other gods is a false prophet (13:2-3). Such a prophet deserves capital punishment (v. 6). The latter asserts that a prophecy given in Yahweh's name must be fulfilled to be considered true (18:22). Both criteria are utilized by Jeremiah *mutatis mutandis* in his confrontation with the so-called false prophets. I argue that these criteria are not without meaning and value. However, they should not be interpreted as a fixed and final set of principles; rather, they should be evaluated in light of an evolving ancient Yahwistic tradition. It is only in such a synthetic study that one can relatively apprehend "a" scope whereby he or she can suggest that ancient Israel had a rubric for distinguishing between true and false prophecy in its Yahwistic tradition.

My interest in this topic developed out of a contextual concern. I come from Nagaland in Northeast India. Since Nagas, the ethnic people group of Nagaland, embraced Christianity in 1872, Nagaland has come to be known as a Christian-dominated state in an otherwise Hindu- populated country. Naga Christianity, however, suffers from nominalism or split-level Christianity. In other words, although the percentage of Christians is very high (c.90%), Christian values and norms are not translated into day-to-day political, social, and economic aspects of the state. Interestingly, there has been an increase in the growth of prophets and prophetesses and prophecy—the proclamation of messages allegedly received as divine revelation. Many prophets or local medicine men and women are involved in healing while others are engaged in identifying and fighting against evil spirits. Some are involved in soothsaying, some work only in close connection with high Christian bureaucrats, some as interpreters of dreams, and still others have managed to attract their own followers and form their own cult-like groups. Some of these practices are explicitly syncretistic in nature while others are not so obviously syncretistic. Such prophetic activity is the direct result of an improper understanding of Scripture, a lack of economic means, and the existence of other diverse religious traditions such as Hinduism.

My initial interest in the subject was deepened by a discussion I had with Dr. Lalsangkima Pachuau in the summer of 2011, which led me to take a course on the Old Testament prophets with Dr. John Oswalt. Although this dissertation does not address my contextual concern, it acts as a prolegomenon in gaining a perspective on the existential issue of true and false prophecy.

I want to express a deep thanks to my dissertation mentor, Dr. Bill Arnold, for guiding me diligently throughout the process of writing this dissertation. He gave me the liberty to explore my thoughts freely and provided wise suggestions when needed. His encouragements went a long way toward enabling me to focus and push myself to work harder. Without him, this dissertation would not have seen the light of day. I thank Dr. John Cook for his critical comments both during my dissertation proposal and toward the end of my dissertation, which made me think deeper about my own analysis. I also want to thank Dr. John Oswalt, my examiner, whose expert analysis of the Old Testament and its theology profoundly influenced my thoughts and construal of the ancient text. His probing questions and comments made during my defense also aided in making this dissertation tighter. Without the help of my two wonderful friends, Drs. Mark Awabdy and Michael Halcomb, this dissertation would not have been readable. Dr. Awabdy read and edited the whole first draft of my dissertation, and Dr. Halcomb edited part of my second draft. Thank you for generously investing your time and energy into this project. I am the only one responsible for any delinquencies in this paper.

I want to thank Asbury Theological Seminary for granting me a scholarship and stipend, allowing me to pursue my Ph.D. without which this venture would not have been possible. Many friends and well-wishers have supported me financially, spiritually, and emotionally through the process of this project: Mr. and Mrs. Meyi Aier, Mr. and Mrs. Omanson, Ms. Kristi Kappes, Dr. Joshua Lorin, Dr. and Mrs. Imli Jamir, Dr. and Mrs. Haralu, Drs. Allen and Denise Kjesbo, and my Sunday school group, Families of Faith, at

Beargrass Christian Church. Thank you! I would also like to acknowledge my first seminary educators who planted in me a deep passion to study God's word: Dr. and Mrs. Wati Aier, Dr. and Mrs. Zelhou Keyho, Drs. Cho-o and Lorin.

My mom and dad remain my inspiration. They have been my greatest supporters, and I thank them for their constant and unconditional love. I thank my siblings and my in-laws for their encouragements and unceasing prayers all through this journey. A pride of place goes to my best friend and talented wife, Dr. Ellen Jamir, who stood by me as my rock from the day I started applying for this program at Asbury until the day I defended my dissertation. She sacrificed her comfort and freedoms to make sure that I gave undivided attention to completing this program. My two loving daughters, Yusenti and Sayana, have endured this grinding process of research and writing with great discipline. On more than one occasion, they brought me joy, laughter, and inspiration. In the process of my work, they became enchanted by all the pictures printed on the covers of the books on my bookshelf! Their encouraging words of "Dad, you can finish this book" and frequent inquiry of "When are you finishing your work?" went a long way in teasing out my extra ounce of energy to see this project through.

Above all, I give all glory and honor to our living God. He did not only give me the vision to walk his path but also faithfully provided the means, strength, and perseverance to fulfill the vision he had sown in me.

כי גבר עלינו חסדו ואמת־יהוה לעולם הללו־יה

For great is his steadfast love toward us, and the truth of the LORD endures forever. Praise the LORD! (Ps 117:2)

Chapter 1
PROPHETIC CONFLICT

> *"If, therefore, someone is a prophet, he no doubt prophesies, but if someone prophesies he is not necessarily a prophet."*[1]

1.1. Introduction

The Masoretic Text (MT) does not use the term "false" to address any kind of נבא.[2] However, this does not mean that there was no prophetic conflict in ancient Israel's society. In fact, in some passages the attack by one prophet upon another is so harsh that the Septuagint (LXX) uses the noun ψευδοπροφήτης to translate נבא (Jer 6:13; 26:7, 8, 11, 16; 27:9; 28:1; 29:1, 8; Zech 13:2). The Old Testament (OT) also contains a number of instances where the classical prophets were involved in serious attacks against certain נבאם. This is especially clear when they use the word שׁקר.[3]

---

[1] Origen, *Commentary on the Gospel According to John* (trans. Ronald E. Heine; Washington, DC: Catholic University of America Press, 1986), 314.

[2] MT is the authoritative Hebrew text of the Tanakh for Rabbinic Judaism and is also the basis for translations of the Old Testament in most modern English Bible. The MT is represented in the *Biblica Hebraica Stuttgartensia*, which is based on the Leningrad Codex. For more information on MT see Bill T. Arnold, *Introduction to the Old Testament* (New York: Cambridge University Press, 2014), 26–28; Kenny E. Hillard, "Masoretic Text," n.p., *The Lexham Bible Dictionary of the Logos Bible*. Version 6. 2014.

[3] The verb שׁקר occurs six times in the Old Testament (Gen 21:23; Lev 19:11; 1 Sam 15:29; Pss 44:17; 89:33; Isa 63:8). Interestingly, it is strongly connected to contracts and covenants in the book of Genesis. In relation to this Seebass, Beyerle, and Grünwaldt assert that שׁקר means to "act deceptively" in contrast to "speak deceptively" (see Horst Seebass, Stefan Beyerle, and Klaus Grünwaldt, "שׁקר," *TDOT* 15:470–77). As a noun it is found 113 times and it

Hosea accuses prophets and priests for misleading people (Hos 4:5). Isaiah points out that both prophets and priests were indulging in strong drink, which disabled them when giving judgment (Isa 28:7). Micah states that some prophets prophesy for material gain (Mic 3:5–8). Zephaniah declares that the prophets in Jerusalem were insolent and treacherous men (Zeph 3:4). Jeremiah accuses prophets of speaking falsehood (Jer 6:13; 8:10; 14:14; 23:25; 27:10, 16; 28:15; 29:9), preaching peace (Jer 6:14; 8:11; 14:13; 23:17; 28:1–9), and not being sent by Yahweh (Jer 14:14; 23:21; 28:15; 29:9). Ezekiel charges the prophets for speaking false and empty oracles (Ezek 13:1–8; 22:28).

Although, the reasons for accusation among the prophets vary from spiritual (as in relationship with Yahweh) to moral (as in practical expression),[4] yet these events indicate that ancient Israel society did suffer from prophetic conflict.[5] The assertion that

---

does not connote a breach of a covenant or treaty; however, it always functions as the "objective determination of deception and falsity." Also it appears mostly in the legal (e.g., Deut 19:16–21) and cultic spheres (e.g., Ps 27:7–13). The noun form is found 37 times in Jeremiah, mostly in relation to prophetic conflict—an issue closely connected with the cultic sphere. Carpenter and Grisanti assert that this is because the prophet Jeremiah deals mostly with a broken relationship and covenant between God and Judah—see Eugene Carpenter and Michael A. Grisanti, "שקר," *NIDOTTE* 4:247–49. It should be noted that in Psalms שקר is related to evil and is considered the cause of lies. In its cognate forms, Mari *šikarum* relates to a breach of faith and old Aram *šqr* means to act treacherously in regard to a person or a covenant. To summarize, this word in Jeremiah provides a powerful meaning when understood in relation to covenant or tradition. Further, it also has a strong negative connotation.

[4] Spirituality and morality are complementary. In fact, prophecy cannot be simply separated from ethics.

[5] The issue of false prophecy is a key feature of prophetic communication in ancient Israel. It is well known that ancient communities in Mari (eighteenth century BCE) and Neo-Assyria (eighth century BCE) had prophetic traditions. However, unlike Israel's allegiance to Yahweh as the sole source of prophetic revelation, the prophets in Mari and Neo-Assyria claimed to have received their

ancient Israel suffered from prophetic conflict is also attested by the fact that OT provides criteria for dealing with the problems of true and false prophecy. In Deut 18:22, Moses states that one recognizes false prophecy when it does not become a reality. Deut 13:2–6 (13:1–5 [Eng.]) provides a concrete criterion, namely, a false prophet's announcement in the name of other gods rather than Yahweh. In Jer 28:8–9, Jeremiah avers that true prophets proclaim disaster whereas false prophets deliver a message of peace and prosperity.

So, then, if prophetic conflicts prevailed in the society of ancient Israel, the crucial question and that pertains to this present study is this: Could the Israelite distinguish between true and false prophecy? The way in which we answer this question entails historical and sociological studies of ancient Israelite society, such as analyzing Israel's prophetic conflict within her cultural context. However, such a study by nature is contentious because it involves hermeneutics.[6] Thus, it is imperative in this sort of study to

---

revelation from multiple deities. As such there is a lack of accusation for intentional falsehood in the latter prophetic traditions. Herbert B. Huffmon contends: "The biblical tradition thereby introduces the concept of 'false prophecy,' an accusation of intentional divinatory falsehood that does not occur in a similar fashion in the Mari and Neo-Assyrian texts. In these texts prophetic revelations may differ or even conflict with the interests of others, but they are not thereby judged to be from a source that is inherently or intentionally false" ("The Exclusivity of Divine Communication in Ancient Israel: False Prophecy in the Hebrew Bible and the Ancient Near East," in *Mediating between Heaven and Earth: Communication with the Divine in the Ancient Near East* [ed. C.L. Crouch, Jonathan Stökl, and Anna Elise Zernecke; LHB/OTS 566; London: T&T Clark, 2012], 68).

[6] Richard S. Hess points out that since 1990s there has been three dominant approaches in studying the historiography of ancient Israel. The first approach nullifies any historical value to the OT texts; the second approach, albeit does not discard the historicity of the OT, it opts to be critical at the orthodox way of reading the scripture; and finally, the third approach looks at OT historiography as a dovetail of history, literary, and ideology. See Richard S. Hess,

articulate a hermeneutic that provides a sympathetic hearing to the ancient text as well as treats the meaning of prophecy on its own terms. It has to be noted here that any hermeneutical lens utilized in such a study is done so as an attempt to understand the context of the prophetic conflict and the mindset of the ancient people, and not an argument that the ancient people had or required such hermeneutics to discern true and false prophecy.

Two additional preliminary comments must be made. First, the aforementioned criteria have generated interest among scholars concerned with the subject of true and false prophecy in the OT. At times these criteria appear to be unverifiable. One might argue that all true prophecies do not necessarily have to be fulfilled because some prophecies depend on the response of the audience. For instance, the prophecy of Jonah against Nineveh was not fulfilled because the Ninevites genuinely repented.[7] Sometimes prophecies are fulfilled after a prophet's lifetime. Deut 13:2–6 narrows down the debate of true and false prophecy since it centers on Yahweh's prophets alone. However, it remains a contentious criterion because both true and false prophets prophesy on Yahweh's behalf. Finally, Jer 28:8–9 only provides a contextual criterion. In other words, a true prophet, such as Isaiah who proclaimed that Judah will be restored by Yahweh, can also deliver a message of peace. The possibility of interpreting these criteria in more than one way contributes to the dilemma of discerning true and false prophecy. However, the most important task is to try and understand whether ancient Israelites had a capacity to understand these criteria and, if they did, how? Perhaps the answer lies in measuring these criteria

---

"Introduction: Foundations for a History of Israel," in *Ancient Israel's History: An Introduction to Issues and Sources* (ed. Bill T. Arnold and Richard S. Hess; Grand Rapids: Baker Academic, 2014), 1–22.

[7] See David Noel Freedman and Rebecca Frey, "False Prophecy is True," in *Inspired Speech: Prophecy in the Ancient Near East* (ed. John Kaltner and Louis Stulman; London: T&T Clark International, 2004), 82–87.

against a synthetic understanding of the background of ancient Israelite society and religious traditions.

Second, in order to understand the meaning of prophecy we must ask, *What is a prophet?* In general terms, a prophet is a spokesperson of a deity, someone who claims to receive messages directly from a god. Thus, divine revelation or at least one's claim to have received divine revelation, is a *sine qua non* of prophecy. Johannes Lindblom states, "[t]he special gift of a prophet is his ability to experience the divine in an original way and to receive revelations from the divine world."[8] While true, this definition of prophecy is quite vague. Divine revelation—the means and content of prophesy—is to be attested by the ethical expression of the prophet as well as by the community in which the prophet dwells. In other words, divine revelation is not random but occurs within community and tradition for a certain purpose. Thus, we can say divine revelation is sociological at its core. One of the sociological aspects of prophecy and divine revelation comes to the fore in the fact that every prophet has a support group and a network of followers. However, one has to be aware of the dynamics between the support group and its prophet. In some cases, it might be that prophets prophesy according to the needs and wishes of their support group; however, there might be cases where prophets prophesy according to the ideals or traditions under which both the prophets and their support groups are accountable. In other words, the latter kind of prophecy does not necessarily stem from the wishes of a support group or a desire simply to gratify that group.

Anthropological and sociological studies of ancient Israelite prophecy and the comparative study of ancient Near Eastern (ANE) prophecies (such as prophecies from Israel, Mari, Neo-Assyria, Neo-Babylonia, and Arabia) have illuminated the

---

[8] J. Lindblom, *Prophecy in Ancient Israel* (Philadelphia: Muhlenberg, 1962), 1.

phenomenon of prophetic movements throughout human society and throughout millennia.⁹ Moreover, cross-cultural studies of prophecies, which analyze contemporary prophetic movement in conjunction with ancient prophetic movement, might contribute to the understanding of biblical prophecy.¹⁰ More directly relevant are

---

⁹ See esp. Thomas W. Overholt, *Prophecy in Cross-Cultural perspective: A Sourcebook for Biblical Researchers* (ed. Burke O. Long; SBLSBS 17; Atlanta: Scholars Press, 1986); idem, *Cultural Anthropology and the Old Testament* (Minneapolis: Fortress, 1996); Lester L. Grabbe, *Priests, Prophets, Diviners, Sages: A Socio-Historical Study of Religious Specialists in Ancient Israel* (Valley Forge: Trinity, 1995); idem, "Shaman, Preacher, or Spirit Medium?: The Israelite Prophet in the Light of Anthropological Models," in *Prophecy and Prophets in Ancient Israel: Proceedings of the Oxford Old Testament Seminar* (ed. John Day; New York: T&T Clark, 2010), 117–32. Robert R. Wilson, *Prophecy and Society in Ancient Israel* (Philadelphia: Fortress, 1989); Martti Nissinen, *Prophets and Prophecy in the Ancient Near East* (SBLWAW 12; Atlanta: Society of Biblical Literature, 2003); Martti Nissinen, ed., *Prophecy in its Ancient Near Eastern Context: Mesopotamian, Biblical, and Arabian Perspectives* (SBLSS 13; Atlanta: Society of Biblical Literature, 2000); Matthijs J. De Jong, *Isaiah among the Ancient Near Eastern Prophets: A Comparative Study of the Earliest Stages of the Isaiah Tradition and the Neo-Assyrian Prophecies* (Leiden: Brill, 2007); J.J.M. Roberts, *The Bible and the Ancient Near East: Collected Essays* (Winona Lake, IN: Eisenbrauns, 2002), 157–253.

¹⁰ Grabbe, De Long, Wilson, and Overholt in their respective works (see footnote 9 above) have compared contemporary prophetic phenomena with that of ancient Israel's prophecy. However, for models of cautious comparative studies, see Shemaryahu Talmon, "The 'Comparative Method' in Biblical Interpretation: Principles and Problems," in *Congress Volume Göttingen* (ed. Walther Zimmerli; VTSup 29; Leiden: Brill, 1978), 320–56; repr. in *Essential Papers on Israel and the Ancient Near East* (ed. Frederick E. Greenspahn; New York: New York University Press, 1991), 381–419. Talmon argues for a "holistic approach" which gives priority to inner-biblical exegesis and only then to cross-cultural analysis of close historical and geographical proximity. William W. Hallo also proposes a "contextual approach" in doing comparative studies. He calls interpreters to pay close attention to both the similarities and differences in any comparative study—see Hallo, "Compare and Contrast: The Contextual Approach to Biblical Literature," in *Bible in the Light of Cuneiform*

comparative studies of the ANE prophetic movements, which shed light on understanding biblical prophecy because of the close parameters in time and space. Even then, the comparative studies should transcend mere identification of prophetic phenomenology by acknowledging and construing the varying traditions across the peoples of the ANE.[11]

To reiterate, a prophet is someone who receives divine revelation from a deity for his or her community. It is imperative to inquire at this juncture: Whose prophet? Which deity? What community? For ancient Israel, this deity is Yahweh and so the prophets are Yahweh's prophets and the community is an agrarian one. Alongside these inquiries it is vital to recognize, in order to construe ancient Israel's prophetic conflict and its subsequent discernment, that the divine aspect of prophecy (transcendence) is inextricably tied to history (immanence).

Literature (ed. William W. Hallo, Bruce William Jones, and Gerald L. Mattingly; New York: Edwin Mellen, 1990), 1–30.

[11] Grabbe espouses the view that there cannot be a chasm between Israel's prophets and her neighboring prophets. For instance, he believes that both Israel's prophets as well as non-Israelite prophets experienced trance and ecstasy and they all performed divination (see *Priests, Prophets, and Sages*, 116–18). Grabbe is, of course, partially correct, however, it is also true that Israelites were prohibited to indulge in divination (Lev 19:31; 20:6; Deut 18:10–13; 1 Chr 10:13–14). D.L. Petersen argued that ecstasy and trance is not characteristic of Israelite prophecy—see *The Roles of Israel's Prophets* (JSOTSup 17; Sheffield: JSOT, 1981). Such comparative studies also have the tendency to label Israel's prophets as intermediaries (see Wilson, *Prophecy and Society*, 27–28). However, there is a difference between a mediator or an intermediary on the one hand, and prophets on the other. A prophet is first and foremost a mouthpiece for God. Of course, there are times when a prophet plays an intermediary role by inquiring the deity on behalf of individual or group. However, this is not exclusively a prophetic role—see Ben Witherington, *Jesus the Seer: The Progress of Prophecy* (Peabody, MA: Hendrickson, 1999), 10.

1.2. Literature Review

The subject of true and false prophecy has generated great attention from the early Christian period to the present.[12] However, the intention of this literature review is not to provide an exhaustive history of interpretation on the matter of true and false prophecy. It is undertaken rather to investigate and demonstrate how the issue at hand has been interpreted from certain *a priori* concepts of hermeneutics in accordance with the philosophical worldview of a given historical context.[13] In doing this, I intend first, to be informed by and to learn from my predecessors' works and, second, to navigate a fresh approach in interpreting true and false prophecy in the OT.

1.2.1. Broad History of Biblical Interpretation

I will provide a survey of the research of the interpretation of true and false prophecy among OT scholars within the broader framework of the history of interpretation. Biblical studies, as a discipline, can be roughly divided along the time line of pre-critical, critical, and post-critical periods.[14] In order to remain

---

[12] R.W.L. Moberly points out that this subject is treated marginally either in a few paragraphs of an entire book or only a single chapter—see *Prophecy and Discernment* (Cambridge: Cambridge University Press, 2006), 14. Moreover, in the last quarter of the twentieth century there has been a steady decline of interest in this subject matter. See Seth B. Tarrer, *Reading with the Faithful: Interpretation of True and False Prophecy in the Book of Jeremiah from Ancient Times to Modern* (JTISup 6; Winona Lake, IN: Eisenbrauns, 2013), 158.

[13] Tarrer explores the history of the interpretation of the study of true and false prophecy beginning from early church (c. 345 CE) to the present time. However, his study is purely a descriptive study with an aim to "function as a hermeneutical guide" (*Reading with the Faithful*, 2).

[14] N.T. Wright classifies the time line into four sections by splitting the critical period into two subsets. The four trajectories are: pre-critical, historical, theological, and postmodern—see *The New Testament and the People of God* (Minneapolis: Fortress, 1992), 6–11.

focused on the issue I would, in line with N.T. Wright, consider the pre-critical period as a period prior to the Enlightenment of the eighteenth century; the critical period as a period that provided major emphasis on the philosophy of the Enlightenment; and the post-critical period as the most recent time, wherein philosophy of the Enlightenment is crumbling.[15]

During the early part of the pre-critical period, also known as the patristic period, interpretation of the Bible was generally divided into two camps: the Alexandrian and the Antiochene.[16] Conventionally, and rather generally, it is held that the former favored allegorical interpretation whereas the latter emphasized literal interpretation of the text. However, scholars such as John J. O'Keefe, David Dawson, and Frances M. Young have cogently argued that allegorical and literal interpretations were utilized by both Alexandrian and Antiochene camps.[17] One common factor

---

[15] *Ibid.*, 7.

[16] Jean-Louis Ska points out that there are, in fact, three camps namely, Alexandrian, Antiochene, and Syrian. The Syrian school of interpretation was vastly influenced by the Semitic world and is liturgical in nature. See Ska, *Introduction to Reading the Pentateuch* (trans. Sr. Pascale Dominique; Winona Lake, IN: Eisenbrauns, 2006), 97.

[17] O'Keefe, Dawson, and Young who have independently argued that both Alexandrian and Antiochene schools apply typology and allegory when it is required in their interpretations. In other words, the issue is more of emphasis rather than bifurcation of orientation. This argument is in contradistinction to the conventional division of the Alexandrian school as a strictly allegorical approach to interpretation and the Antiochene as strictly literal. See, John J. O'Keefe, "'A Letter that Killeth': Toward a Reassessment of Antiochene Exegesis, or Diodore, Theodore, and Theodoret on the Psalms," *JECS* 8 (2000): 83–104; David Dawson, *Allegorical Readers and Cultural Revision in Ancient Alexandria* (Berkley: University of California Press, 1992); Frances M. Young, *Biblical Exegesis and the Formation of Christian Culture* (Cambridge: Cambridge University Press, 1997), 152–60.

across the vast and diverse pre-critical period of interpretation was that doctrinal studies directed Bible reading.[18]

Critical hermeneutics have been by far the most dominant form of interpretation, beginning from the European *Aufklärung* to somewhere around the 1960s.[19] Critical hermeneutics were vastly informed by the epistemology of the Enlightenment era, which considers human reason as the highest order in the universe and demands human rationality to be empirical, objective, and neutral. Biblical studies during this time were predominantly historical in nature. That is, OT study was reduced to a historical study of religion—*Religionsgeschichtliche Schule*—that centered on the study of Ancient Israel's historical reconstruction and saw her religion as devoid of any metaphysical reality.[20]

It was in 1919, with the publication of Karl Barth's *Der Römerbrief*, that scholars of the OT began to show once again a theological interest in the study of the Bible. However, it was not a case of returning to the pre-critical era but one wherein history and theology together engaged OT studies. The hermeneutics of this period are represented by the works of Albrecht Alt, Martin Noth, Gerhard von Rad, and Walther Eichrodt in Germany, and William Foxwell Albright and his followers in North America. This period is also popularly known as the biblical theology movement. It has

---

[18] In his 1787 inaugural address at the University of Altdorf, Johann Philipp Gabler made a complete distinction between dogmatic and biblical theology and the right definition of their goals. This was, indeed, watershed moment in the history of biblical interpretation.

[19] It has to be mentioned that the Enlightenment did not come about overnight. It was rather the product and culmination of many historical events and intellectuals. In fact, many observe the Enlightenment period had its genesis in the Renaissance period.

[20] For a general description of the hermeneutics of this period, see Walter Brueggemann, *Theology of the Old Testament: Testimony, Dispute, Advocacy* (Minneapolis: Fortress, 1997), 1–60; Leo G. Perdue, *The Collapse of History: Reconstructing Old Testament Theology* (Minneapolis: Fortress, 1994).

to be noted that this movement is one within the critical period. As such, the scholars of the so-called biblical theology movement found themselves either struggling to synthesize an Enlightenment understanding of history and theological articulation of faith, or forcefully engage in proving the biblical narrative as history utilizing archaeology.[21]

By the 1960s, the flaw of the enterprise of the biblical theology movement was slowly but surely diagnosed, and it was chiefly the works of James Barr and Brevard Childs that brought an end to this movement.[22] Subsequent to Childs and his canonical approach were newer interpretive avenues, such as structuralism, which ultimately gave way to post-structuralism and reader response criticism. However, it has to be noted that the dominant form of hermeneutics of the critical period was not completely uprooted. In fact, the hermeneutics of the critical period linger on even today and may surface strongly in certain contexts.[23]

In post-structural hermeneutics, one encounters that history— i.e., the center of critical hermeneutics—is no longer a common

---

[21] Cf. John Goldingay, *Approaches to Old Testament Interpretation* (Downers: InterVarsity, 1990), 66–96; Walter Brueggemann, *The Book that Breathes New Life: Scriptural Authority and Biblical Theology* (Minneapolis: Fortress, 2005); John N. Oswalt, *The Bible among the Myths: Unique Revelation or Just Ancient Literature?* (Grand Rapids: Zondervan, 2009), 139–40.

[22] James Barr, "Revelation through History in the Old Testament and in Modern Theology," *Int* 17 (1963): 193–205; idem, *The Semantics of Biblical Language* (Oxford: Oxford University Press, 1961); Brevard Childs, *Biblical Theology in Crisis* (Philadelphia: Westminster, 1970).

[23] George Stocking, *The Ethnographer's Magic and Other Essays in the History of Anthropology* (Madison: University of Wisconsin Press, 1992), 342–61; see also Ferdinand E. Deist's work whose argument suggests that such switch of paradigm is not overnight, "The Prophets: Are We Heading for a Paradigm Switch?," in *"The Place is Too Small for Us": The Israelite Prophets in Recent Scholarship* (ed. Robert P. Gordon; Winona Lake, IN: Eisenbrauns, 1995), 582–99.

denominator either for textual interpretation or for the canon. Instead, the reader is empowered as the determiner of meaning. It is within this broader history and framework of biblical studies that I will attempt to evaluate the scholarly discussions of true and false prophecy.

1.2.2. Critical Framework of Biblical Interpretation

In the pre-critical era, hermeneutics was generally driven by the New Testament (NT) as the grid for interpreting the issue of true and false prophecy. A positive aspect of this approach was the affirmation of the revelation from God. However, from the beginning of the seventeenth century, naturalism began to take precedence over revelation. This is reflected in the works of Thomas Hobbes (1588–1679) and Benedict de Spinoza (1632–1677). Hobbes undermined faith in the discernment of true and false prophecy and argued that a person can only distinguish a true from false prophecy through reason.[24] In the same vein, Spinoza argued that all prophecy needed to be natural knowledge which was accessible to human reason. But, the fact that biblical prophecy was exclusive only for some meant scriptural prophecy "exclude(s) natural knowledge."[25]

Such a trajectory of historical emphasis, however, became the underlying hermeneutic of the eighteenth and nineteenth centuries. Within this paradigm, OT prophets were made out to be exceptional and creative geniuses who articulated the law and transformed ancient Israel's religion from a cultic religion into an

---

[24] Thomas Hobbes, *Leviathan* (ed. J.C.A Gaskin; Oxford: Oxford University Press, 1998), 36.20. Tarrer states: "Reason, Hobbes teaches, over and against an appeal to divine revelation, is the safer way to apprehend and discern truth" (*The Reading with the Faithful*, 73).

[25] Benedict de Spinoza, *Theological-Political Treatise* (trans. Samuel Shirley; Indianapolis: Hackett, 2001), 9.

ethical monotheism.[26] This understanding has deep ramifications for the study of true and false prophecy. It made the prophets the masters of traditions—the creators of Israelite religion. Wellhausen wrote:

> It belongs to the notion of prophecy, of true revelation, that Jehovah, overlooking all the mass media of ordinances and institutions, communicates Himself to the individual, the called one, in whom that mysterious and irreducible rapport in which the deity stands with man clothes itself with energy. Apart from the prophets, in *abstracto*, there is no revelation; it lives in his divine-human ego.[27]

The fact that every individual prophet was the owner of his or her religious experience made it difficult to demarcate any prophecy as true or false. Simply put, there were no parameters to apprehend the prophetic conflict. Thus Bernhard Duhm asserts that Jeremiah (in the context of his debate with Hananiah) might have had a

---

[26] John H. Hayes comments that the nineteenth century scholars viewed the prophets as "innovators and initiators of major new impetuses in the religion of Israel. Addressing their contemporaries with moral earnestness, with ethical principles, with anticultic emphases, and with individualistic perspectives, the prophets proclaimed the ethical over against the cultic, the individual as opposed to the communal, the internal versus the external, the universal in opposition to the national, monotheism instead of polytheism, and the historical in place of the natural. The prophets were often viewed as reforming theologians and brave individualists proclaiming the primacy of morality and the indispensability of a personal relation with God" (*An Introduction to Old Testament Study* [Nashville: Abingdon, 1991], 253). See also Robert P. Gordon, "A Story of Two Paradigm Shifts," in *"The Place is Too Small for Us": The Israelite Prophets in Recent Scholarship* (ed. Robert P. Gordon; SBTS 5; Winona Lake, IN: Eisenbrauns, 1995), 3–28.

[27] Julius Wellhausen, *Prolegomena to the History of Israel* (trans. J.S. Black and A. Menzies; Edinburgh: A&C Black, 1885), 398.

problem identifying Deutero-Isaiah as a true prophet because he was prophesying a message of peace.[28] Similarly, Abraham Kuenen argues that it is unfair to label the opponents of the canonical prophets as false.[29] This view construes divine revelation as ahistorical. Kuenen postulates that attributing prophecy as the act of supernatural revelation means to "allow ourselves to be deprived of the belief in God's presence in history."[30] In other words, revelation is not concrete history and therefore, prophecy based on revelation is inconceivable.

In the era of the biblical theology movement, there was an attempt to understand divine revelation within history. However as stated above, one has to keep in mind how history—presumably objective and neutral—was made to dance with metaphysics in this era. To begin, we briefly analyze Gerhard von Rad's work on this subject of true and false prophecy. Although von Rad followed the clarion call of Barth in making biblical study relevant for ecclesiology, his work on OT theology faced sharp criticism for his struggle to construe Israel's *Heilsgeschichte* within the scholarly historical reconstruction of Israel. Childs opines:

> Von Rad begins his theology by separating off the "real history" of Israel, reconstructed much after the fashion of M. Noth, from his own kerygmatic approach (3–102). He

---

[28] Bernhard Duhm, *Das Buch Jeremia, vol II* (KHC; Tübingen: Mohr Siebeck, 1901), 225.

[29] Abraham Kuenen, *De Profeten en de Profetie onder Isräel: Historisch-dogmatische studie* (2 vols.; Leiden: P. Engels, 1875), 2:581; ET: *The Prophets and Prophecy in Israel: An Historical and Critical Enquiry* (trans. Adam Milroy; London: Longmans, Green, and Co., 1877).

[30] Kuenen, *De Profeten*, 585. William McKane similarly, but with a slight twist, argues that attributing prophecy to the supernatural realm dehumanizes the prophets—see *A Late Harvest: Reflections on the Old Testament* (Edinburgh: T&T Clark, 1995).

then confesses his inability to reconcile Israel's "confessional history" with that reconstructed by modern critical scholarship (107), which is at least a frank, if inadequate, statement of the problem.... The subtle dialectal reason between Israel's inner and outer history which at places is so stunningly espoused, is seriously undercut.[31]

This criticism of von Rad has to be kept alive even as one analyzes his argument for the discerning of true and false prophecy. Besides this, one should also keep track of his hermeneutic of traditio-historical criticism.[32]

---

[31] Brevard Childs, *Biblical Theology of the Old and New Testaments: Theological Reflection on the Christian Bible* (Minneapolis: Fortress, 1993), 103; similarly Barr also criticizes von Rad: "The cleft between history as it really happened (if we may be permitted that phrase!) and the history as it is told in the Old Testament is probably a matter of importance for any Old Testament theology; but for one who insists on history as a central guiding category, and at the same time insists on the re-telling of the history as Israel itself told it, the problem becomes extremely severe. And it is this point more than any other that has suffered criticism from von Rad's critics" (*The Concept of Biblical Theology: An Old Testament Perspective* [Minneapolis: Fortress, 1999], 35). However there is truth when Brueggemann argues that von Rad was not interested in "verifiable facticity, but in the power of generative imagination to think and utter 'outside the box.'" Brueggemann continues, "Such generative imagination, of course, has a hard time with modernists. However, it does seem clear that, were von Rad's intention transposed into the categories of our own time, he would have a large company of allies in his claim for understanding "history" differently" (*The Book that Breathes New Life*, 80).

[32] Von Rad states, that Israel's faith was an achievement of a complex tradition process. He identifies the earliest "credo recitals" of Israel faith in Deut 6:20–24; 26:5–6; and Josh 24:1–13. This credo, von Rad argues, was not only elaborated in the unfolding of Israel's tradition but also new traditions such as the creation materials of Gen 1–11, the later development of the ancestral materials of Gen 12–50, and finally the independent Sinai material. This development at first took shape in the cultic centers but later, because of Israel's

Von Rad, in line with Kuenen, called for an objective and neutral reading of the conflict among the prophets.[33] He argued that it was not easy to distinguish between true and false prophets. For instance, he points out that both Jeremiah (see ch. 28) and Micaiah ben Imlah (see 1 Kgs 22) could not label their opponents as false prophets.[34] As such, von Rad concluded that discernment could be achieved only by judging the message of the prophets. In other words, the message of the true prophet concerns judgment whereas the message of the false prophet concerns weal.[35] This understanding led him to conclude that Deuteronomy might have been a product of the so-called false prophets because it conveys the message of forgiveness and protection toward Israel in spite of her mistakes.[36]

Von Rad further points out that Deuteronomy portrays prophets as institutional intermediaries who interceded between Yahweh and the people.[37] In other words the so-called false prophet might have been a cult or institutional prophet. In distinction from this Deuteronomic (D) cult prophet, von Rad argues that the Elohist (E) was interested in seeing the prophet as a free charismatic individual.[38] In other words, a true prophet is someone removed from a formal cult. Here von Rad, apart from bifurcating the cult prophet as false and the non-cult prophet as true, is navigating into

---

growth as nation and hence secularization, the recital was taken out of the context of worship and became simply a national epic recital, perhaps in a way to preserve her identity in the world. See *Old Testament Theology* (2 vols.; San Francisco: Harper and Row, 1962, 1965), 187–90.

[33] Gerhard von Rad, "Die Falschen Propheten," *ZAW* 51 (1933): 109–20.

[34] *Ibid.*, 109.

[35] *Ibid.*, 112.

[36] In fact von Rad implies that both Deuteronomy and Nahum bear the tenets of false prophecy (*ibid.*, 117).

[37] *Ibid.*, 113.

[38] *Ibid.*, 115.

the fabric of the sociology of competing traditions—i.e., the Davidic-Zion (D) and the Mosaic (E) traditions. Von Rad, in his interpretation of Jer 28, interprets the false prophet (Hananiah) to be over-confident of the future and dismissive of God's actions. A true prophet (Jeremiah), however, is tentative about his prophecy because he provides the space for Yahweh to act within history.[39]

Von Rad's understanding of true and false prophecy is dictated by his understanding of tradition-historical criticism. In spite of his attempt to distance himself from the enterprise of the *Religionsgeschichte Schule*, von Rad appears to still be entangled within the scheme of developmentalism. In other words, the act of telling and re-telling of Israel's core belief was an open-ended enterprise.[40] In the end, von Rad suggests that there are no criteria to differentiate true or false prophets, but only that a prophet can understand the transcendental experience and expression of another prophet.

Von Rad's construal was further elaborated by scholars such as Martin Buber, Gottfried Quell, James L. Crenshaw, and James A. Sanders. It is interesting to note that in post-von Rad scholarship, many have denied the possibility of distinguishing true and false prophecy.[41] Buber, in his study of Jer 28 asserts that false prophecy proclaimed the right theological message at the wrong time.[42] He further points out that Hananiah took Isaiah's message of peace as a timeless truth that would not alter as times and situations

---

[39] *Ibid.*, 119.

[40] See footnote 27.

[41] As Moberly rightly asserts: "the overall tenor of such scholarly work as has been produced has been negative as to the possibility of valid criteria of discernment" (*Prophecy and Discernment*, 8).

[42] Martin Buber, "False Prophets (Jeremiah 28)," in *Biblical Humanism: Eighteen Studies* (ed. Nahum N. Glatzer; London: Macdonald, 1968), 166–71.

changed.[43] By utilizing Isaiah's message as a dogma, Hananiah fell into the pit of falsehood.

Quell argued that no distinction between true and false prophets can be ascertained since a true or false prophecy depended upon the people's subjective opinions.[44] By this, Quell was already anticipating the later sociological analysis that discerned instances of true and false prophecy.[45] Quell argues that it is incorrect to project biased moralistic judgment on a prophet and label him as deceptive. In light of this, Quell asserts that Hananiah in Jer 28 is not a false prophet any more than Jeremiah is a true prophet. Thus, Quell states that since the adjudication process between true and false prophets depends on the subjective opinion of the people, this problem is unsolvable. Apart from that, the fact that prophets claim their authority from the divine makes the prophetic conflicts incomprehensible. Only a prophet who is possessed by a divine spirit can ascertain a true or false prophet.

Quell's views also influenced James Crenshaw. In his monograph, *Prophetic Conflict*, Crenshaw investigates the conflict between Israel's true and false prophets and its impact on the history of Israelite religion.[46] Crenshaw believes that "[p]rophetic conflict is inevitable, growing out of the nature of prophecy itself."[47] The ground for such an understanding stems from the notion that human beings, with all their limitations, do not have the ability to comprehend the sovereign divine purpose.

---

[43] *Ibid.*, 167.

[44] See Gottfried Quell, *Wahre und Falsche Propheten: Versuch einer Interpretation* (BFCT 46.1; Guetersloh: C. Bertelsmann Verlag, 1952).

[45] *Ibid.*, 13. This point is given an elaborate treatment by Robert Wilson and Burke O. Long from a social, anthropological perspective. I will discuss their works briefly below.

[46] James Crenshaw, *Prophetic Conflict: Its Effect upon Israelite Religion* (BZAW 124; Berlin: de Gruyter, 1971).

[47] *Ibid.*, 3.

Crenshaw considers three areas in order to closely analyze Israel's prophetic conflicts: the *vox populi* of Israel, the criteria for prophetic validation, and the demonic side of YHWH.[48] Crenshaw contends that YHWH is unpredictable and acts in a mysterious and demonic fashion with the prophets (cf. 1 Kgs 13; 2 Kgs 22).[49] He concludes that it is not possible to comprehend the prophetic conflict. The incomprehensible manner of conflict finally led the apocalyptic and wisdom movements to consume Israel's prophetic movement.

Crenshaw has dealt a negative blow to the study of the distinction between true and false prophecy. His arguments, however, are shrouded with ambiguity. In fact, the part where Crenshaw indulges in deconstructing the criteria is the weakest link in his monograph. At times it appears as though Crenshaw is not seriously considering the literary and historical contexts of the passages. For example, in his attempt to explain the point that false prophets stole oracles (Jer 23:30), Crenshaw argues both that Jeremiah himself depended upon (or stole) the messages of Micah and also that Isaiah depended upon Amos. Crenshaw also asserts that the prophets cannot be distinguished in terms of morality. He cites the example of Hosea's marriage to Gomer, a prostitute. However, Hosea's action has to be understood within his overall message and context. Hosea's marriage to Gomer and the naming of his children pointedly address the context of northern Israel in the eighth century BCE—a context filled with corruption (cf. Mic 2–3). Hosea's actions, devoid of his message, might be labeled as a moral lapse, but his message qualifies his action. It would be difficult to argue that Hosea's actions are blatant immorality.

In the end, Crenshaw's argument for the prophetic conflict rests on two factors: (1) the prophets' emphasis on history, both in

---

[48] *Ibid.*, 23–90
[49] *Ibid.*, 77–90.

terms of the fulfillment of the prediction and on the disagreement among the prophets in interpreting the historical situations, and (2) divine mystery. Crenshaw has managed to completely dichotomize prophetic conflict into history and metaphysics, putting the issue of false prophecy beyond comprehension.

James A. Sanders regards prophetic conflict from a canonical perspective within the larger framework of von Rad's diachronic hermeneutics of tradition-historical criticism.[50] Sanders' argument is that the judgment of true and false prophecy should be understood from the perspective of the canonization process.[51] For Sanders, canon has the character of both stability and adaptability. In other words, an old tradition may take on a new vibrant meaning in a new historical context.[52] Likewise, true and false prophecies cannot be adjudicated by relying on certain fixed criteria. Rather, true and false prophecies can be ascertained by analyzing how the prophets re-interpret the tradition according to the given historical situation and need.[53] Sanders thus asserts that the conflict between true and false prophecies can be understood fully by analyzing three major factors: ancient traditions (i.e., texts), situations (i.e., contexts), and hermeneutics.[54]

---

[50] Tarrer avers, "The tradition-historical criticism embodied by von Rad would be succeeded and subsumed into Old Testament studies' emerging field of canon-criticism" (*Reading with the Faithful*, 141).

[51] James A. Sanders, "Hermeneutics in True and False Prophecy," in *Canon and Authority: Essays in Old Testament Religion and Theology* (ed. George W. Coats and Burke O. Long; Philadelphia: Fortress, 1977), 21–41.

[52] *Ibid.*, 28; also see James A. Sanders, "Adaptable for Life: The Nature and Function of Canon," in *Magnalia Dei, The Mighty Acts of God: Essays on the Bible and Archaeology in Memory of G. Ernest Wright* (ed. Frank Moore Cross, Werner E. Lemke, and Patrick D. Miller, Jr; Garden City: Doubleday & Company, 1976), 531–60.

[53] Sanders, "Hermeneutics in True and False Prophecy," 28.

[54] *Ibid.*, 21.

Sanders, basing his claims on Buber's argument that a prophet is someone who could read "history," states that one of the marks of a true prophet is the ability to hear the word of God afresh, even when the historical-cultural situation has changed.[55] Sanders points out that the process of applying the text to a context is called hermeneutics. He observes the debates between the prophets and argues that the form of prophecy employed by false prophets was the same as that of the true prophets. However, Sanders argues that the notion of monotheism is crucial for prophetic hermeneutics. False prophets, in proclaiming Israel's election, reject other nations whereas true prophets, in proclaiming the same, affirm that YHWH is the God of the universe. In doing this, Sanders believes that the true prophets were slowly moving toward monotheism.

Sanders' framework of adjudicating true and false prophecy is reasonable and has much to commend it. However, his emphasis on hermeneutics has the tendency to limit the aspect of divine revelation in prophecy. Not that context and text are unimportant, but one must not rule out *a priori* that the origin of Israel's prophecy was divine revelation. If von Rad's interpretation of true and false prophecy was constrained by his understanding of traditio-historical criticism, then in Sanders' hermeneutic of monotheism one may envisage a trajectory of von Rad's approach. Sanders' construal of the development of canon is sociologically insightful, especially in terms of how a community's tradition develops.

However, a second thought is required when the adjudication of true and false prophecy is positioned within the concept of canonical development. Prophecy is deeper than merely interpreting texts, traditions, and contexts, since elders or priests in

---

[55] Buber, *On the Bible*, 166–71.

the community may perform such a task.⁵⁶ Prophecy at its core depends on revelation from God and a fine distinction exists between revelation and inspiration. A prophet is someone who receives revelation from God whereas an interpreter might not necessarily receive revelation but may simply be inspired by something.⁵⁷ Of course, this does not readily resolve the problem at hand, but understanding this distinction will allow one to remain focused on divine revelation in prophecy.

Another problem with Sanders' position is his understanding of canon. It is so flexible that the process of canonization itself might become another complicated issue, similar to that of distinguishing the true and false prophecy.⁵⁸ Sanders argues that Hananiah, in his controversy with Jeremiah, depended on the message of Isaiah—that YHWH was going to restore Judah. Sanders points out that the

---

⁵⁶ Hopi (a federally recognized tribe of indigenous Native American people) prophecy is said to adhere strictly to a hermeneutic of the myth, although, it contains prediction. See Lester L. Grabbe, "Ancient Near Eastern Prophecy from an Anthropological Perspective," in *Prophecy in its Ancient Near Eastern Context: Mesopotamian, Biblical, and Arabian Perspectives* (ed. Marti Nissinen; Atlanta: Society of Biblical Literature, 2000), 13–32.

⁵⁷ William J. Abraham argues that God's revelations, such as the Exodus event, Israel's prophetic ministry, and finally, the special revelation in Jesus Christ, are irreducible. These revelations of God reveal God's mighty acts and his behavior. The authority of the Bible depends on these revelations. The concept of inspiration on the other hand relates to someone being inspired by the revelations. Subsequently, in the case of the biblical writers, they were moved to write the Scripture. Since the inspired ones are humans and humans are fallible, Abraham concludes that the Holy Scripture contains errors, but not to the extent that it may misguide believers. It has to be understood that the matrix of Abraham's discussion is within the debate of biblical inerrancy—see *The Divine Inspiration of Holy Scripture* (Oxford: Oxford University Press, 1981).

⁵⁸ Sanders argues that the account of Abraham and Isaac in Gen 22 in the old tradition was about child sacrifice, but for the later Israelites during the exilic time it had a theological implication of hope, in spite of their trying circumstances—see "Adaptable of Life," 551.

problem with Hananiah is that he applies Isaiah's message as if it were a fixed tradition or dogma instead of re-interpreting it according to the context. However, it is clear that Sanders' expression is shaped by his understanding of a dynamic canon—i.e., older traditions being superseded by newer traditions. It should be noted that Isaiah's message is based on the understanding of YHWH as a faithful God, which one might take as relevant within any given context. The problem with Hananiah is not about interpretation of the tradition, but incomplete or bad Yahwistic theology.

Quell's contention that true or false prophecy depends upon the opinion of the people finds an elaborate treatment in the works of Burke O. Long and Robert R. Wilson.[59] Long opines that in the study of the prophetic conflicts the "social, non-theological dimensions of the prophets' conflicts were largely, if not entirely, overlooked."[60] This deficiency is addressed independently by both Long and Wilson. They utilize sociological and anthropological methodology in analyzing Israel's prophetic conflict. Before studying the biblical prophetic conflicts, both Long and Wilson explore the phenomenology of prophetic conflict across different societies. Long insightfully investigates the social, political, and economic issues in order to situate in history the prophetic conflict

---

[59] Burke O. Long, "Social Dimensions of Prophetic Conflict," in *"The Place is Too Small for Us": The Israelite Prophets in Recent Scholarship* (ed. Robert P. Gordon; SBTS 5; Winona Lake, IN: Eisenbrauns, 1995), 308–31; Robert R. Wilson, "Interpreting Israel's Religion: An Anthropological Perspective on the Problem of False Prophecy," in *"The Place is Too Small for Us": The Israelite Prophets in Recent Scholarship* (ed. Robert P. Gordon; SBTS 5; Winona Lake, IN: Eisenbrauns, 1995), 332–44.

[60] Long, "Social Dimensions of Prophetic Conflict," 309.

in the book of Jeremiah.[61] However, he concludes that prophetic conflicts are anything but theological.[62]

Wilson argues that in a society where prophetic movement is encouraged, the prophet is required to have a group of people supporting him, otherwise his prophecies might not be seriously considered. In this way the community plays a vital role in distinguishing true and false prophecies. As Wilson argues: "Societies recognize individuals as true prophets because their words and deeds fit stereotypical patterns of prophetic behavior."[63] He further contends that prophets can be divided into central and peripheral prophets. The peripheral prophets enable those of low status to improve and even to restructure the whole society, whereas the central prophets work to maintain the status quo.

Thus Wilson utilizes these findings in analyzing Jer 28–29. He argues that Jeremiah is a peripheral prophet from the Ephraimite tradition and that Hananiah is a central prophet from the Judean tradition.[64] The Ephraimite tradition holds to Deuteronomistic theology, and the Judean tradition endorses Jerusalemite royal theology. In other words, on this reading, the clash between Jeremiah and Hananiah is an ideological one.[65] The discrepancy

---

[61] *Ibid.*, 317–28.

[62] Long avers that, "[a]nthropological studies help us realize that conflict is a vital element in prophetic activity, and that it is both deeper and broader than disputes over religious beliefs" (*ibid.*, 328).

[63] Wilson, "Interpreting Israel's Religion," 339.

[64] For more detail information about the Ephraimite and Judean traditions see Robert R. Wilson, *Prophecy and Society in Ancient Israel* (Philadelphia: Fortress, 1980). It has to be noted that Wilson himself is aware of his weak construction of the Jerusalemite royal tradition (*ibid.*, 253). Moreover Long contends that Jeremiah might not have been a peripheral prophet—see "Social Dimensions of Prophetic Conflict," 325.

[65] Long argues that "From anthropology we gain a wider range of questions, a heightened sense of the relative place of ideology (or theology)" ("Social Dimensions of Prophetic Conflict," 310).

between Jeremiah and Hananiah is not about true or false prophecies. Rather, it is a conflict between two ideological groups. Wilson's argument, however, is one-sided. Brueggemann states that, "[t]he social matrix of Israel includes theological Yahwism rooted in Moses. Thus one could study the prophets of Israel in Wilson's way and never grasp the radical social vision, nor the claims for authority of that vision. That is, everything can be reduced to the self-serving needs of the marginal ones."[66] Brueggemann's critique exposes the missing emphasis of both Long's and Wilson's otherwise useful contributions on the issue of prophetic conflicts.

So far I have surveyed the scholarship on true and false prophecy focusing particularly on showing how history and divine revelation were generally considered either antithetical or made to dance an awkward tango. To counter this shortcoming, Childs proposed a new approach known as canonical criticism.[67] Canonical criticism (and new literary criticism) in biblical studies arose partly as a frustration with the historical critical method.[68]

---

[66] Walter Brueggemann, "The Social Matrix of Israel's Prophecy," *Int* 35.3 (1981): 290–93.

[67] It has to be mentioned that Childs' canon approach was not an isolated development. As noted above, James Barr has also articulated the discrepancies of the historical-critical method. Besides, Childs' own Yale school was developing the post-liberal hermeneutics prominently under Hans Fei and George Lindbeck. Moreover, new literary criticism was beginning to emerge as a tool to investigate the biblical text. All these approaches overlap and interrelate with one another and all these approaches critique the historical-critical method of the Enlightenment.

[68] Brevard S. Childs, *Old Testament Theology in a Canonical Context* (Philadelphia: Fortress, 1985); idem, *Introduction to the Old Testament as Scripture* (Philadelphia: Fortress, 1979); R.N. Whybray, *The Making of the Pentateuch: A Methodological Study* (JSOTSup 53; Sheffield: Sheffield University Press, 1987); Adele Berlin, *Poetic Interpretation and Biblical*

These approaches focus on the final form of the text, scrutinizing the intricacies of the literary structure as well as concentrating on the community that gave shape to the biblical canon. However, the danger of these approaches is that while concentrating on the text, there is the tendency to push history to the periphery.[69]

We turn now to survey Childs' work on Jer 28 concerning true and false prophecy and we will emphasize two of his important conclusions.[70] Childs rightly contends that prophetic conflicts arise from the fact that both true and false prophets employ "thus saith the Lord" and appeal to that very authority.[71] He reconsiders the reading of Jer 28 and focuses on verse 6. When Hananiah rejected Jeremiah's message and proclaimed a speedy return of all the vessels of YHWH's house from Babylon (vv. 2–3), Jeremiah, instead of denouncing him, receded into the background. It is only later in vv. 15–16 that we see Jeremiah coming back to pronounce judgment on Hananiah for misleading the people. This is the point that intrigues Childs. He argues that Jeremiah came back only when he received YHWH's message of judgment towards Hananiah. Jeremiah's receding into the background in vv. 2–3

Narrative (Sheffield: Almond, 1983), 111–34; Robert Alter, *The Art of Biblical Narrative* (New York: Basic Books, 2011).

[69] For instance, Whybray in critiquing the form and tradition-historical methods in the study of Pentateuch, concludes that the Pentateuch is more or less a fictitious literary creation of a sixth century BCE author—see *The Making of the Pentateuch*, 221–42; although cf. Childs, who differs greatly from Whybray. Still in his argument of true and false prophecy in the book of Jeremiah, Childs concludes that the distinction of the messages of Jeremiah and Hananiah as true and false prophets was possible because of the hindsight advantage of the exilic community. Otherwise it would not be possible for the pre-exilic community. See Childs, *Old Testament Theology*, 138–39. For further criticism of Childs' approach, see John Barton, *Reading the Old Testament: Method in Biblical Study* (Louisville: John Knox, 1996), 77–88.

[70] Childs, *Old Testament Theology*, 133–44.

[71] *Ibid.*, 133.

suggests that Hananiah's message partly convinced him of a speedy return. Thus, using this point, Childs argues that true prophecy has nothing to do with reading the historical times and events correctly.[72] Rather, true prophecy is solely confirmed by God.[73] This is Childs' first conclusion toward understanding true and false prophecy. He completely locates the source of prophecy in the divine.[74] He therefore provides a helpful corrective, while at the same time he displaces his predecessors' emphasis on history.

Childs' second conclusion comes to the fore when he critiques Sanders. He asserts that the canon does not function as Sanders proposes—i.e., the hermeneutical triangle of text, context, and hermeneutics. For Childs, the canon is already in its final form. Therefore, Jer 28 provides additional criteria to determine true and false prophecy. By doing this, Childs is critiquing Sanders' view of the canon as dynamic. For Sanders, the overarching concept that guided the hermeneutical triangle of the true prophet was the concept of monotheism. In other words, Sanders looks at the prophetic conflict as part of the canonizing process. In contrast to that Childs argues that the prophetic conflict in Jeremiah is already taken as an authoritative text by the exilic and post-exilic community to adjudicate between true and false prophets. He thus concludes that pre-exilic Israel could not discern the prophetic conflicts whatsoever. It is only the exilic and post-exilic Judahites who came to realize that Jeremiah was a true prophet and thus canonized his prophecy.

---

[72] This point is contra von Rad, Buber, and Sanders whose approaches Childs critiques as existential (*ibid.*, 135).

[73] This is in conjunction with W. Zimmerli, "Der Wahrheitserweis Jahwes nach der Botschaft der beiden Exilspropheten," in *Tradition and Situation* (ed. E. Würthwein and O. Kaiser; Göttingen: Vandenhoeck & Ruprecht, 1963), 133–51.

[74] Childs, *Old Testament Theology,* 136.

Gerald T. Sheppard, a student of Childs, concurs with his teacher on the canonical level.[75] However, he avers that prophetic conflicts have to be understood on two levels: historical and canonical, and this distinction of levels is necessary to navigate the arguments of Sanders and Childs. However, Sheppard's argument of the historical serves only to enhance the conclusions of scholars who have applied socio-scientific methods chiefly because he uses them to guide his argument. He asserts, "[t]he criteria for evaluating an instance of 'prophecy' makes sense only from within the domain of a socially defined support group and its marginal sympathizers, with their own recognized 'true' prophets and idiosyncratic role expectations…. The criteria could and did change overtime and through social circumstance."[76]

This leads us to James E. Brenneman, who applies postmodern hermeneutics to study the canonization process with prophetic conflicts as the governing paradigm.[77] As a student of Sanders, Brenneman concurs with his teacher but also furthers the original argument. Brenneman truly embraces the postmodern agenda of plurality, textual contradictions, and readers as those determining meaning.[78] One of his main contentions is that true meaning can only be found in contradictions. He critiques Childs for his understanding of the canon as a fixed entity and affirms Sanders' notion of the canonical process. He contends that, "Childs' argument rests on the assumption that it is the text as scripture, and

---

[75] Gerald T. Sheppard, "True and False Prophecy within Scripture," in *Canon, Theology, and Old Testament Interpretation: Essays in Honor of Brevard S. Childs* (ed. Gene M. Tucker, David L. Petersen, and Robert R. Wilson; Philadelphia: Fortress, 1988), 262–84.

[76] *Ibid.*, 267.

[77] James E. Brenneman, *Canons in Conflict: Negotiating Texts in True and False Prophecy* (Oxford: Oxford University Press, 1997).

[78] *Ibid.*, 13–51.

not its readers that provides the primary role for theological continuity."[79]

However, Brenneman also stretches Sanders' view of the canonical process and places the locus of meaning within the community of believers.[80] He states, "[t]hat the truly essential bearer of theological continuity between generations has always been the living breathing readers of sacred scripture. In that sense, the believing community is the keeper of the flame of continuity."[81] He asserts that the only criterion to adjudicate the contradictions of the text within the community is ethic. As a Mennonite believer he asserts that non-violence should be the rubric for this adjudication.

With this understanding in place, Brenneman observes the contradictory message of Isaiah-Micah (Isa 2:4; Mic 4:3) and Joel (Joel 4:10) concerning the transformation of swords into plowshares and plowshares into swords. In this contradiction he avers that the present communities of believers should choose Isaiah as a true prophet because of his non-violent message and reject Joel as a false prophet. He states, "I reject Joel 4:9–17 as true prophecy and would argue that in time, if not yet, its voice will become, in functional terms, as canonically marginalized as other 'texts of terror' are increasingly becoming (on women) or have already become (on slavery). Could it be that future generations will consider the question of sacred violence in the name of

---

[79] *Ibid.*, 90.

[80] *Ibid.*, 90. Brenneman avers that any canon, whether sacred or non-sacred, is a result of the status-quo which means a canon in itself has oppressive power. Therefore he postulates that, "any canon that does not contain within it the seeds of its own deconstruction will become a tool of ideological and political brutality" (*ibid.*, 139). Indeed, Sanders does not advocate such a notion but his understanding of canon enables such an interpretation.

[81] *Ibid.*, 90

Yahweh as canonically closed, functionally if not formally?"[82] With Brenneman the pendulum swings from history to reader. The ideal approach should be one that considers a reasonable epistemology such as history or literature instead of resting the authority fully within the community.

1.2.3. Recent Developments in the Research

Matthijs J. De Jong has written an article on the fallacy of true and false prophecy in Jer 28:8–9.[83] He argues that the conventional understanding of the message of true prophet as judgment and false prophet as weal is incorrect. One underlying principle that guides his argument is that there is a distinction between Israel's and Judah's prophecy as a socio-historical phenomenon and the scribal depiction of prophecy in the biblical literature.[84] He articulates this contention through comparative and exegetical study. In the former he argues that all the ANE prophets were involved in directing, blessing, admonishing, and even judging the kings. By contrast, in biblical prophecy, true prophets are depicted in opposition to the status quo. To De Jong, this is a later scribal reflection.

For instance, he points out concerning Jeremiah, "[t]he later revision of the early traditions decisively re-shaped the 'prophecies' of Jeremiah, by interpreting the disasters as Yahweh's punishment of the sins of Judah."[85] Thus, to categorize the true prophet as judgment preacher and the false prophet as weal proponent is unfounded. In the exegetical study he analyzes the text to show that Jeremiah is not a doom preacher (Jer 28:8). De Jong asks the question, "doom and peace for whom?"[86] He replies

---

[82] *Ibid.*, 141.
[83] Matthijs De Jong, "The Fallacy of 'True and False' in Prophecy Illustrated by Jer 28:8–9," *JHS* 12 (2012): 1–29.
[84] *Ibid.*, 4.
[85] *Ibid.*, 5.
[86] *Ibid.*, 13.

by saying that the doom is for the foreign powers (v. 8). In opposition to Hananiah, however, Jeremiah was prophesying peace for a foreign nation (Babylon) and enjoining the Judean exiles to seek the welfare of Babylon for "in her peace will be your peace" (29:7).

Thus De Jong argues that both Jeremiah's and Hananiah's message toward Judah was about welfare: "Whereas Hananiah propagated 'survival through resistance,' Jeremiah propagated 'survival through submission.'"[87] Moreover, both Jeremiah and Hananiah proclaimed the common and usual prophetic practice, namely, to reveal divine revelation for the people so that they make the right decisions. Thus, Jeremiah did not prophesy a doom message for Judah, but rather pointed a direction through which Judah would experience shalom. De Jong argues that Jer 28:8–9 is one of the prophet's earliest traditions. The issue of prophet against prophet is a later deuteronomistic redaction and concludes that the issue of true and false prophecy is a case of *vaticinium ex eventu*.[88]

Marvin A. Sweeney argues that the distinction between true and false prophecy is a non-issue.[89] Sweeney, basing on the biblical criterion the concept that a true prophecy is always fulfilled in history, argues that some of the canonical prophets and their prophecies are potentially false. To show this, he points out how both Jeremiah and Hananiah were involved in some rereading of Isaiah's message. Sweeney argues that Jeremiah, as a pro-Babylonian prophet, was against the peace message of Isaiah (which Hananiah upheld). Sweeney goes on to argue that Isaiah was a false prophet because his prophecy of peace did not actually

---

[87] *Ibid.*, 20.

[88] *Ibid.*, 26.

[89] Marvin A. Sweeney, "The Truth in True and False Prophecy," in *Truth: Interdisciplinary Dialogues in a Pluralist Age* (ed. Christine Helmer and Kristin De Troyer; SPT 22; Leuven: Peeters, 2003), 9–26.

materialize with the downfall of Assyria as Neo-Babylonia took over Judah.

Armin Lange in his *habilitationsschrift* discusses the issue of true and false prophecy from the perspective of history, literary, and redaction-criticism.[90] Lange's work concentrates on how the inner-prophetic conflict of the pre-exilic community resulted in the rejection of all prophecy in the post-exilic and future generations and gave birth to the interpretations of the authoritative text.[91] He argues that the rejection of prophecy because of inner-prophetic conflict, in fact, began in the eighth century BCE. The Zion message of peace was no longer applicable after the fall and exile of Judah because of the actualization of the doom prophesy. Thus the oracles of doom began to replace the Zion ideology.[92]

Lange further notes that it was the DtrJer—the exilic editor of the book of Jeremiah—who made fulfillment a criterion of true prophecy after witnessing the fulfillment of Jeremiah's prophecy of the death of Hananiah.[93] Moreover, Lange argues that it is the work of DtrJer that labeled prophets who announced peace and hope as false prophets. As such, Haggai and Zechariah are considered false prophets.[94] However, in the end, according to Lange, the DtrJer did not find any concrete reason to adjudicate the prophetic conflicts that gave way to the retrospective exegesis of

---

[90] Armin Lange, *Vom prophetischen Wort zur prophetischen Tradition: Studien zur Traditions-und Redaktionsgeschichte innerprophetischer Konflikte in der Hebräischen Bibel* (FAT 34; Tübingen: Mohr Siebeck, 2002).

[91] "Die vorliegende Arbeit hat sich die Frage gestellt, wie sich aus den inner-prophetischen Konflikten der vorexilischen Zeit in nachexilischer Zeit eine Ablehnung aller gegenwartigen und zukunftigen Prophetie zugunsten der Auslegung autoritativer Texte entwickeln konnte, oder, anders gesagt, was den Anlab für die theologiegeschichtliche Bewegung vom Wort zur Auslegung gab" (*ibid.*, 309).

[92] See A.C. Hagedorn's review, *VT* 54 (2004): 283.

[93] Lange, *Vom prophetischen Wort*, 87.

[94] Citing from Tarrer, *Reading with the Faithful*, 167.

accumulated older prophecies.⁹⁵ In other words, on this view, the incomprehensibility of the prophetic conflict in history gave birth to interpretation of prophetic authoritative texts. Thus, "the process of replacing new revelation with written traditions of past revelation provided a major impulse for a larger process that eventually led to the canonization of Torah and Prophecy."⁹⁶

The works of Daniel Epp-Tiessen and Anthony C. Osuji have dealt independently with the issue of true and false prophecy from a synchronic perspective.⁹⁷ Both Epp-Tiessen and Osuji are critical of the inconclusive results of the historical critical method. As such, they focus on the literary text of the final form to analyze the subject of true and false prophecy. The former argues that Jer 23:9–29:23 is a concentric literary structure whereas the latter considers Jer 26–29 and analyzes it by utilizing narrative criticism. Moreover Osuji, *contra* Robert P. Carroll, portrays through narrative criticism that Jer 26–29 is a unit tied together by a common theme of true and false prophecy.⁹⁸ Osuji's theological conclusion on true and false prophecy resonates with Buber's and Childs' views when he argues that true prophecy involves humility, obedience and timeliness.⁹⁹ Epp-Tiessen arranges the text (Jer 23:9–29:23) in a concentric structure¹⁰⁰ and argues that the text

---

⁹⁵ Lange, *Vom prophetischen Wort*, 267–68—citing Tarrer, *Reading with the Faithful*, 168.

⁹⁶ Citing from Daniel Epp-Tiessen's review of Lange's work—see *Concerning the Prophets: True and False Prophecy in Jeremiah 23:9–29:32* (Eugene: Pickwick, 2012), 31,

⁹⁷ Epp-Tiessen, *Concerning the Prophets*; Anthony C. Osuji, *Where is the Truth?: Narrative Exegesis and the Question of True and False Prophecy in Jer 26:29 (MT)* (Leuven: Uitgeverij Peeters, 2010). Both these works were first written as dissertations.

⁹⁸ Osuji, *Where is the Truth?*, 263–321.

⁹⁹ *Ibid.*, 388–91.

¹⁰⁰ "A. 23:9–40: Condemnation of false prophets in general; B. 24:1–10: Jeremiah's true prophecy—a vision regarding exiles and non-exiles; C. 25:1–38:

(Jer 23–29) clearly indicates that Jeremiah is the true prophet without any nuances.[101] He further argues in section A (23:9–40) of his concentric structure that "immorality is one of the identifying features of false prophecy."[102] Epp-Tiessen's exegetical insights are commendable; however, his concentric structure of the text is criticized as superimposing.[103]

Walter Moberly provides an exegetical and theological argument for the discernment of true and false prophecy.[104] Moberly's work is different from most of the work being reviewed here because he takes the Bible on its own terms. In other words, Moberly accepts divine revelation as a legitimate source of true prophecy. He counters scholars such as Carroll, Brueggemann, Friethem, and Miller who argue that appeals to divine revelation for true prophecy are inadequate. As a result, it is not possible to distinguish between a true and a false prophecy.[105] Moberly, on the other hand, provides three criteria to distinguish true prophet from false namely: the morality of the prophet, the prophet's message of repentance, and the prophet's divine council.

In summary, the works of De Jong, Sweeney, and Lange are creative and thought provoking, but unfortunately their work only enhances the general opinion of their predecessors—i.e., the inability to distinguish between true and false prophecy. The

---

Jeremiah's true prophecy; D. 26:1–24: Proper and improper responses to true prophecy; C'. 27:1–28:17: Jeremiah's true prophecy; B'. 29:1–19 Jeremiah's true prophecy—a letter regarding exiles and non-exiles; A'. 29:30–32: Condemnation of specific false prophets." Quotation from Epp-Tiessen, *Concerning the Prophets*, 44.

[101] *Ibid.*, 39.
[102] *Ibid.*, 83, 105.
[103] See Kelvin Friebel, review of Epp-Tiessen, *Concerning the Prophets: True and False Prophecy in Jeremiah 23:9–29:32*, RBL (2013).
[104] Moberly, *Prophecy and Discernment*, 38.
[105] *Ibid.*, 70–82.

respective works of Epp-Teissen and Osuji advance Childs' conception of a proper methodology for biblical studies. Moberly's work is refreshing and provides a way forward for this perennial discussion of true and false prophecy.

1.3. Thesis Statement

The thesis of this study is to argue that ancient Israel had an adequate rubric in its Yahwistic tradition which enabled it to distinguish between true and false prophecy. The above discussion may suggest that ancient Israel simply did not have the capacity to discern between true and false prophecy. This notion has persisted partly because of an inadequate understanding and poorly conceived epistemology of divine revelation and history. The remedy for this, I believe, lies in a hermeneutic of critical realism. Critical realism is a hermeneutic that attempts to nurture both objectivity and subjectivity as the source of concrete knowledge. Ben F. Meyer argues that, "objectivity is not achieved by the flight from subjectivity nor by any and every cultivation of subjectivity but by an intense and persevering effort to exercise subjectivity attentively, intelligently, reasonably, and responsibly."[106] It is possible that a discussion between the epistemology of divine revelation and history will open the way for reading the Scripture afresh and provide a renewed perspective on the issue of true and false prophecy in the OT studies.

Closely connected to reorienting one's understanding of divine revelation is the importance of correctly construing a given tradition or religion and how it operates and shapes a society. This above literature review has shown that OT scholars have come to understand ancient Israel's traditions as diverse and constantly

---

[106] Ben F. Meyer, *Reality and Illusion in New Testament Scholarship: A Primer in Critical Realist Hermeneutics* (Collegeville: Liturgical, 1994), 4. See also Wright, *New Testament and the People of God*, 29–144.

evolving. Indeed, every tradition evolves and is partly diverse. However, many scholars have made it impossible to locate which tradition the prophets were utilizing in their prophecies. Moreover, the prophetic conflict is reduced to a mere ideological clash. A better construal of tradition or religion, along with their role in shaping a society and culture, might actually provide a clearer view on how the prophets utilized their tradition(s). The current investigation will assume that tradition and religion together serve as a framework within which a community lives and learns to express its experiences. This view stands in contrast with the perspective that religion and tradition are expressions of a community's experience. In other words, Israel's religion and tradition provided a framework for Israel's prophets to experience revelation and subsequently proclaim the same.

Thus, this study, relying on a synthetic analysis of ancient Israel informed by a hermeneutic of critical realism, explores the degree to which ancient Israel had the rubric to distinguish true from false prophecy. Synthetic analysis is the social, cultural, political, and theological study of ancient Israel in relation to adjudicating true and false prophecy. The research question addressed here is whether the Yahwistic tradition was the mark of true prophecy in ancient Israel. In other words, I want to know whether there is a need for any specific criteria for adjudicating among the prophets, or whether the authentic moral application of the Yahwistic tradition provides the standard for distinguishing a true prophet from the false one. The primary text for interpretation will be Jer 26–29 because it is here that the prophetic conflict reaches its climax.

1.4. Organization of this Study

The literature review has established that the argument as to whether the ancient Israelite had the capacity to adjudicate between true and false prophecy would need a better concept of epistemology which, in turn, would enable one to define divine revelation and its relation to tradition. Thus, the second chapter will deal with the articulation of an epistemology of critical realism through which a closer look at divine revelation and tradition will be undertaken.

The third chapter will examine the development of Yahwistic tradition, particularly its origin and features. This portion of the investigation will show how Israel's Yahwistic faith in essence was distinct from her other ANE neighbors. This will be done by taking into consideration the worldviews as depicted in Israelites' and Canaanites' religions.[107] Once the core of the Yahwistic tradition is navigated, it will prove beneficial to answer the question of what factors might have helped to foster false prophets and prophecies. I will argue that the Yahwistic tradition became blurred due to the installation of the monarchy. The monarchy was supposed to be a "limited monarchy."[108] In other words, YHWH was still to play a major role in the lives of Israel's day-to-day activities both nationally and internationally.[109] However, it was the inability of the kings to live within the tension of a "limited monarchy" and "monarchy in the model of other nations" (1 Sam 8:5) that twisted the worldview of Israel. This inability of the kings, both in the southern and north kingdoms, greatly affected the people who once lived within the Yahwistic tradition. This inability also twisted the theology of the *vox populi* as well as provided the right environment for the conflict of Israel prophets

In the fourth chapter, since ancient Israel was an agricultural society, Gerhard Lenski and Patrick Nolan's concept of macro-

---

[107] Yehezkel Kaufmann, *The Religion of Israel: From Its Beginnings to the Babylonian Exile* (trans. Moshe Greenberg; Chicago: University of Chicago Press, 1960); cf. Oswalt, *Bible Among the Myths*.

[108] Paul D. Hanson, *The People Called: The Growth of Community in the Bible* (New York: Harper & Row, 1986), 100.

[109] *Ibid.*, 100.

sociology of agricultural society will be utilized. Lenski and Nolan's concept is helpful for analyzing the socio-political aspects that might have contributed to the moral failure of some prophets.[110]

In the fifth chapter, Jer 26–29 will be used as a case study to show that a critical realism interpretation can indeed enable us to uncover the rubric whereby the Israelites were able to recognize true and false prophecy. I will end this study with a summary and several concluding remarks.

---

[110] Gerhard E. Lenski, *Power and Privilege: A Theory of Social Stratification* (Chapel Hill: University of North Carolina Press, 1984); Patrick Nolan & Gerhard Lenski, *Human Societies: An Introduction to Macrosociology* (Boulder: Paradigm Publishers, 2009). Some contemporary biblical scholars who have drawn from Lenski's works include Carol Meyers, Charles Carter, Marvin L. Chaney, Keith W. Whitelam, Richard A. Horsley, Anthony J. Saldarini, Patricia Dutcher-Walls, and S.L. Cook. However, Lenski's theory is not without critique. Walter J. Houston has provided an insightful critique on the application of Lenski's theory of agrarian society on ancient Israel's society— see "Exit the Oppressed Peasant? Rethinking the Background of Social Criticism in the Prophets," in *Prophecy and Prophets in Ancient Israel: Proceedings of the Oxford Old Testament Seminar* (ed. John Day; LHBOTS 531; New York: T&T Clark, 2010), 101–6.

Chapter 2
IN QUEST OF A HERMENEUTICAL METHOD

"Whatever exactly be the case here, my concern is that one is unlikely to make progress with understanding and evaluating the phenomenon of speech for God without recognizing, and successfully circumnavigating, the tips of some major icebergs that lurk in the sea of modern thought."[1]

2.1. Methodological Trajectory

The literature review in the previous chapter revealed three interconnected issues which needed to be addressed. First, the review showed that the interpretation of true and false prophecy in OT studies correlates with the epistemologies of human inquiry. This acknowledges and embraces the idea that we, as humans, are people of our own *Zeitgeist*. It also indicates that human epistemologies are not dogma, but are contested and constructed. Thus, it is imperative that we explore, assess, and acquire a sound epistemology that attempts to understand Scripture concretely by scrutinizing it rationally, reasonably, and responsibly.

Second, the literature review suggested that an investigation of this question would benefit from a more precise exploration of the development of ancient Israel's Yahwistic tradition. There is no denying the fact that the OT interpretation of true and false prophecy is not a simple straightforward description, as the review has shown (cf. von Rad, Sanders, and Wilson). The shades of grey area become prominent especially when the prophets of the same people group prophesy in the name of one God and yet offer opposing and contradictory messages. This calls for further investigation of ancient Israel's rich and complex tradition with

---

[1] Moberly, *Prophecy and Discernment*, 35.

this question in view. Ancient Israelite society, culture, and tradition did evolve as time elapsed. Many scholars have asked questions concerning Israel's tradition which I intend to assess (chapter 3), however, my task here will be to define tradition and analyze its evolution from a perspective of critical realism.

Finally, the literature review also suggested that the construal of God's revelation needs to be reconsidered in order to study the subject of true and false prophecy in the OT. Is God's revelation haphazard, unintelligible, and even shrouded with mystery? Or can God's revelation be reasonably construed? Is revelation different or similar from inspiration? Perhaps an understanding of God's revelation that espouses revelation as subjective human experience, yet inextricably connected with tradition is possible to define and would be beneficial to this latter question. Thus, epistemology, tradition, and revelation are interconnected issues in the study of true and false prophecy of the OT. Israel believed that their prophets received *revelation* from God which contributed in forming their *tradition*. This process can only be understood meaningfully when we approach it from an *epistemology* that holds both subjective experiences and objective data as legitimate means for authentic and concrete knowledge.

2.1.1. Proposing an Epistemology of Critical Realism

The Enlightenment and postmodern construal of knowledge have been the two prominent approaches used in the OT study of true and false prophecy. The Enlightenment construal is encapsulated by words such as neutral, empirical, and objective and, even though, there have been attempts to improvise its construal of knowledge, the improvisation remains within the form and not the core content of its epistemology (as shown above in the discussion of Enlightenment scholars and Biblical Theology movement). The postmodern construal places the authority of interpretation not with history or text but the reader or the community. In these approaches, the distinction of true and false prophecy is seriously obfuscated by emphasizing the inability of comprehending it in history. As an alternative to these approaches, I propose the epistemology of critical realism as the way forward in investigating the subject of true and false prophecy in the OT. It provides a *via media* between Enlightenment and postmodern approaches. Before explaining critical realism, I will briefly analyze the background of its development.

2.1.1.1. En Route to Critical Realism

The Renaissance period (fourteenth to seventeenth centuries) sowed the seed of modernity in Europe. It was a time of "rebirth," or "revival," of the classical Greek and Roman cultures. British philosopher and scientist Francis Bacon (1561–1625) played an important role in shaping the trajectory of modernity. Bacon believed that it was through science that humanity could rule over nature. Thus, for Bacon, knowledge was power[2]—a view that found rigorous support in Bacon's successors.

Along with the critical mind of the Renaissance during the eighteenth and nineteenth centuries—which is also popularly called the Enlightenment period—human reason and its ontology was lifted to an unprecedented height. Rene Descartes (1596–1650), the father of modern philosophy, was one of the champions of this period. His hermeneutic of doubt was the basis of all reason. According to Descartes, through doubting and reasoning, one gets to the authentic truth. His dictum *"Cogito ergo sum"* summarizes his philosophical agenda.[3] The human is the highest being because

---

[2] Stanley J. Grenz, *A Primer on Postmodernism* (Grand Rapids: Eerdmans, 1996), 59.

[3] Henry H. Knight III, *A Future for Truth: Evangelical Theology in a Postmodern World* (Nashville: Abingdon, 1997), 37–38.

he can think and reason; whatever cannot be reasoned by the human mind cannot be true.[4] Thus, a place for miracles in the Scripture could not be found.

Bacon's and Descartes' reasoning then gave rise to the notion that every truth must be scientifically and objectively proven. Auguste Comte (1798–1857) later articulated this notion as positivism.[5] Comte also provided a full-fledged understanding of evolutionary theory, one of the chief tenets of the Enlightenment thinking. According to Comte, scientific knowledge evolves through three successive states:

> The theological or fictitious, in which small numbers of isolated observations were linked by supernatural ideas; the metaphysical or abstract, in which a larger number of facts were linked to ideas conceived as personified abstractions; and the scientific or positive, in which great numbers of facts were connected by the smallest possible number of general laws, each in turn suggested or confirmed by facts.[6]

In other words, everything from nature to humanity evolves from simple or primitive to sophisticated entities.

The positivistic approach is often criticized as naïve realism because of its pictorial or representational mode of construal of knowledge. For instance, a positivist will argue that his sense data (the five senses) experiences objective "reality." However, such construal of knowledge can easily fall into the pit of parochialism or obscurantism. Moreover, and ironically, even though positivism

---

[4] *Ibid.*

[5] Paul G. Hiebert, *Missiological Implications of Epistemological Shifts: Affirming Truth in a Modern/Postmodern World* (Harrisburg: Trinity, 1999), 3.

[6] Citing from George W. Stocking, *Victorian Anthropology* (New York: Free, 1987), 28.

aspires for scientific and universalistic knowledge, it promotes antagonism between competing theories or principles. David Hume (1711–1776), based on this positivistic construal of knowledge, came to the logical conclusion that since human sense data cannot experience miracles or God's revelation they either do not exist or are false.[7]

Immanuel Kant (1724–1804), in a way, attempted to correct Hume's skepticism through his philosophy of transcendental idealism. Specifically, Kant distinguished between reality-in-itself (*noumenon*) and reality-as-it-appears (*phenomenon*). In other words, Kant argued that the "reality" exists but it is not within the boundary of human sense data. For Kant knowledge is the synthesis of the data derived from the five human senses and our ability to understand these data through in-built concepts in the mind.[8] This notion is called Kant's "Copernicus revolution." Kant placed the human mind in the center with all other elements around it.[9] For this Kant can be rightly called the first phenomenologist. Yet, Kant believed that there is a universal human concept of knowing which can be achieved through human rationality.[10]

Within this concept, Kant articulated that God exists but cannot be known because he is beyond the world and inactive in the world. Kant excluded both God and divine revelation from the realm of history and thus was a deist. Thus for Kant the only way to understand God is through human morality.[11] However, one has

---

[7] See Laurence W. Wood, *God and History: The Dialectical Tension of Faith and History in modern Thought* (Lexington: Emeth, 2005), 84–88.

[8] *Ibid.*, 94.

[9] Robert C. Solomon, *Continental Philosophy Since 1750: The Rise and Fall of the Self* (Oxford: Oxford University Press, 1988), 40.

[10] Grenz, *A Primer on Postmodernism*, 80.

[11] Immanuel Kant, *Critique of Practical Reason and Other Works on the Theory of Ethics* (trans. T.K. Abbott; London: Longmans, Green, and Co., 1927), 88.

to be careful here because Kant was not arguing that God is the foundation of human morality, rather it is the other way round. The fact that humans have the urge for moral living indicates that God does exist.[12] In the end, Kant's God is merely a human regulative idea. Such philosophy became a dominant underlying theme for protestant liberal scholarship.

This Enlightenment philosophy, which was characterized by elevating the individual/self over and against tradition or authority and its complete bifurcation of history and metaphysics, was the undercurrent that moved the work of many biblical scholars. This inability to comprehend the divine in a knowledgeable manner has ramifications for the study of the adjudication of true and false prophecy in OT scholarship.

Kant's philosophy gave way to the initial signs of postmodern philosophy, namely, relativism. Friedrich Nietzsche (1844–1900) advanced the idea that there is actually nothing beyond the human mind. Thus he eliminated Kant's noumenon realm in arguing that there is no true world and that everything is our own perspectival appearance or illusion.[13] According to Nietzsche, the human world is a mere illusion created and recreated continually by our creative works of art. As such, for him there is nothing behind or beyond the human web of illusion. However, even if Nietzsche argued that there is no objective truth, he insisted that a conceptual understanding of truth is necessary for humankind to survive.

Nietzsche attributed this creativity of the human mind to the "will to power." He argued that our understanding of truth and morality are not an outcome of our ability to comprehend the transcendent realm, but are the consequence of our "will to

---

[12] *Ibid.*, 89.

[13] Friedrich Nietzsche, "On Truth and Lie in an Extra-Moral Sense," in *The Portable Nietzsche* (ed. and trans. Walter Kaufmann; New York: Penguin Books, 1976), 44–46.

power."[14] This "will to power" is ideological in nature. In other words, the human mind and creativity function in such a way to fulfill their desires and wishes. As Stanley Grenz contends: "Nietzsche announced that Western culture had separated itself from the transcendent."[15]

Nietzsche's philosophy becomes the bedrock for postmodern understanding of knowledge. In fact, Michel Foucault (1926–1984), one of the earliest proponents of postmodernism, is called the truest twentieth century successor of Nietzsche.[16] Foucault completely rejected the Cartesian-Kantian self as the starting point of human knowing.[17] Instead he depended on Nietzsche's emphasis on relativity of reality. He argued for the preference of specific and particular rather than general and universal. Foucault points out three loopholes in the Enlightenment philosophy of knowledge, namely: the notion that reality exists beyond the human mind; knowledge as neutral and value free; and knowledge as universal.[18] In rejecting this, Foucault argues that knowledge is actually a human product and that it stems from the human struggle for power, which constitutes the world. Thus, for Foucault truth is an arbitrary construction of human knowledge.[19] This is the core of postmodern epistemology of knowledge and such epistemology, has radical implications for one's worldview. For instance, history

---

[14] Allan Megill, *Prophets of Extremity: Nietzsche, Heidegger, Foucault, Derrida* (Berkeley: University of California Press, 1985), 58–59.

[15] Grenz, *A Primer on Postmodernism*, 92.

[16] Merold Westphal, *Suspicion and Faith: The Religious Uses of Modern Atheism* (Grand Rapids: Eerdmans, 1993), 241.

[17] James Miller, *The Passion of Michel Foucault* (New York: Simon & Schuster, 1993).

[18] Sheldon S. Wolin, "On the Theory and Practice of Power," in *After Foucault: Humanistic Knowledge, Postmodern Challenges* (ed. Jonathan Arac; New Brunswick: Rutgers University Press, 1988), 179–202.

[19] Grenz, *A Primer on Postmodernism*, 132.

is viewed as fiction or ideological propagandistic literature; in literary criticism, meaning is envisaged not in the author or the text, but the reader and context;[20] ethical morality is no longer a set of authoritative principles, but relative according to any individual's construction.

2.1.1.2. Epistemology of Critical Realism

For a subject matter such as the adjudication of true and false prophecy, assuming the epistemologies of the Enlightenment or postmodernism have not been fruitful. The former with its outlook of naïve realism makes the distinction of true and false prophecy incomprehensible in history, whereas the latter with its emphasis on relativity eliminates any parameters for determining anything, let alone true and false prophecy. As an alternative to these two epistemologies, I propose the use of critical realism as a more fitting epistemology to address the complex subject of true and false prophecy in the OT. Critical realism is appropriate because it affirms that there is a "reality" beyond the human mind (hence realism), but this reality can be ascertained to a certain degree through educated dialogue (hence critical).

However, critical realism in its method is varied. In fact, there are four forms of critical realism: the early form was represented in the writings of R.W. Sellars, A.O. Lovejoy, and George Santayana in the early twentieth century;[21] the second was represented by scholars who are philosophers of science and religion such as Arthur Peacocke, Ian Barbour, and Wentzel van Huyssteen;[22] the

---

[20] Jacques Derrida, *Positions* (trans. Alan Bass; Chicago: University of Chicago Press, 1980), 28–29.

[21] For more information about this movement, see Durant Drake, et al., eds., *Essays in Critical Realism* (London: Macmillan, 1921).

[22] Arthur Peacocke, *Intimations of Reality: Critical Realism in Science and Religion* (Notre Dame: University of Notre Dame Press, 1984); idem, *Theology for a Scientific Age* (Minneapolis: Fortress, 1993), 11–19; Ian Barbour, *Myths,*

third was represented chiefly by the work of Roy Bashkar and his disciples;²³ finally, the fourth was associated with Bernard Lonergan, whose work has been applied to biblical study more directly by Meyer and indirectly by Wright.²⁴ All these forms are distinct in their origins and independent from one another and vary in emphasis.²⁵ However, there is a general framework within which they all strive to function, namely, their frustration with the positivistic assumption of naïve realism, yet without succumbing to the relativistic tendency of the epistemologies of the idealist and

---

Models and Paradigms: A Comparative Study in Science and Religion (New York: Harper & Row, 1974); Wentzel van Huyssteen, *Essays in Postfoundationalist Theology* (Grand Rapids: Eerdmans, 1997); idem, *The Realism of the Text: A Perspective on Biblical Authority* (Pretoria: University of Pretoria Press, 1987); idem, *The Shaping of Rationality* (Grand Rapids: Eerdmans, 1999); idem, *Theology and the Justification of Faith: Constructing Theories in Systematic Theology* (trans. H.F. Snijders; Grand Rapids: Eerdmans, 1989).

²³ Roy Bhaskar, *A Realist Theory of Science* (New York: Verso, 1997); idem, *The Possibility of Naturalism: A Philosophical Critique of the Contemporary Human Sciences* (Atlantic Highlands: Humanities, 1979); idem, *Scientific Realism and Human Emancipation* (New York: Verso, 1986); *Dialectic: The Pulse of Freedom* (New York: Verso, 1993). Cf. Andrew Collier, *Critical Realism: An Introduction to Roy Bhaskar's Philosophy* (New York: Verso, 1994); Margaret Archer, et al., eds., *Critical Realism: Essential Readings* (New York: Routledge, 1998).

²⁴ Both Meyer and Wright are NT scholars. In the OT field Sean McEvenue has applied Lonergan's approach in the area of hermeneutics. See Sean McEvenue, *Interpretation and Bible: Essays on Truth in Literature* (Collegeville: Liturgical Press, 1994); also Sean McEvenue and Ben F. Meyer eds., *Lonergan's Hermeneutics: Its Development and Application* (Washington: Catholic University Press, 1989).

²⁵ For their distinct emphasis, see appendix 2 ("Varieties of Critical Realism") of Donald L. Denton, *Historiography and Hermeneutics in Jesus Studies: An Examination of the Work of John Dominic Crossan and Ben F. Meyer* (London: T&T Clark, 2004).

phenomenologist.²⁶ In this study, I will focus on the fourth form of critical realism, which is represented by the approaches of Lonergan, Meyer, and Wright.

2.1.1.2.1. Bernard Lonergan

One of the chief and earliest proponents of the fourth form of critical realism is Bernard Lonergan (1904–1984), a Jesuit philosopher.²⁷ Lonergan was a Thomist who simply did not adopt the cognitive theory of Aquinas, but adapted it for his current contemporary matrix. He spent his initial scholastic years mastering Aquinas' works which he later contextualized.²⁸ He avers, "[Aquinas] remains a magnificent and venerable figure in the history of Catholic thought. He stands before us as a model, inviting us to do for our age what he did for his."²⁹

Lonergan's critical realism—or transcendental method—is an attempt to get beyond the empirical skepticism of Hume, the transcendental idealism of Kant, and post-Kantian relativism.³⁰ In other words, Lonergan's critical realism operates between the

---

²⁶ Thorsten Moritz, "Critical Realism," *DTIB* 147–50.

²⁷ Bernard Lonergan expounded his method of critical realism in two of his major works: *Insight: A study of Human Understanding* (London: Longmans, 1957); *Method in Theology* (New York: Herder and Herder, 1972).

²⁸ Lonergan wrote his doctoral dissertation on Thomas Aquinas entitled *Verbum: Word and Idea in Aquinas*.

²⁹ Bernard Lonergan, "The Future of Thomism," in *A Second Collection* (ed. W.F. Ryan and B.J. Tyrrell; Philadelphia: Westminster, 1974), 49–53. To contextualize classical Thomism for the modern era he outlined five points: 1) a shift from logic to method; 2) a shift from Aristotelian science to modern science; 3) a shift from "soul to subject;" 4) a shift from human nature to human history; 5) a shift from the reliance on 'first principles' to his transcendental method.

³⁰ Bernard Lonergan, "The Origins of Christian Realism," in *A Second Collection* (ed. W.F. Ryan and B.J. Tyrrell; Philadelphia: Westminster, 1974), 239.

extreme epistemologies of positivistic/naïve realism—i.e., idealism and relativism. He argues that both these epistemologies employ "picture thinking" in their analysis.[31] For the naïve realist, the real object is what the eyes see or the other senses experience, whereas for the idealist the real object is mental or intuition, in that the real object is mere appearance or phenomena. Against this, for Lonergan human knowledge is an amalgam of experience, understanding, and judgment. To arrive at any sort of knowledge without the process of experience, understanding, and judgment would mean pure reductionism. Theodore W. Nunez in explaining Lonergan's critical realism asserts, "Knowing, then, is not simply a matter of 'taking a good look'—that is, it is not an immediate intuition. Rather, it is a discursive process that involves experiencing and understanding and judging—the multileveled achievement of a critical realist."[32]

According to Lonergan, then, knowledge of the reality begins through the available human sense data (outer experience) and human consciousness (inner experience). It is in this first level that the human knower meets the indubitability of reality. This level inevitably leads to the stage of inquiry, such as asking the simple question, *what is it?* This question provides ideas, insight, or understanding. In the second level, the data of experience is summarized and analyzed to form meaningful insight. Finally, this insight goes through questions of reflection such as: "Is it? Is it so? Whether this or that?"[33]

---

[31] See Meyer, *Reality and Illusion*, 61–86; Dental, *Historiography and Hermeneutics*, 221.

[32] Theodore Nunez, "Rolston, Lonergan, and the Intrinsic Value of Nature," *JRE* 27 (1999): 121.

[33] Bernard Lonergan, *Collected Works of Bernard Lonergan: Understanding and Being* (ed. Elizabeth A. Morelli and Mark D. Morelli; 22 vols.; Toronto: University of Toronto Press, 1990), 5:111.

Joseph Flanagan, commenting on the importance of questioning in Lonergan's critical realism, states: "Questioning puts us in the paradoxical state in which we know and at the same time, know that we do not know."[34] In fact, as long as there are questions to inquire concerning any knowledge, knowledge remains conditional. It is only when all the possible questions are asked that a knowledge becomes unconditional.[35] Only through this reflection of judgment is knowledge authenticated. Thus, true knowledge is articulated and sustained through the process of experience, understanding, and judgment. Unlike critical realism, knowledge in naïve realism is based on sense data or experience, whereas in idealism human understanding itself is the basis of knowledge. However, the significant factor that discriminates critical realism from both empiricism and idealism is judgment.

For Lonergan, there are four elements of good judgment: (1) one needs to have the desire to pursue further knowledge; (2) one has to have a certain level of acquired expertise in a particular area; (3) one should be willing to self-correct in the process of learning; and (4) the possession of a good temperament that encourages one to dig deeper without rushing to rash conclusions.[36] This cognitional process of experience, understanding, and judgment appears trivial; however, it is not, as Donald L. Denton contends:

> It appears to be a rehearsal of what in our day is self-evident to common sense, that normally functioning human beings cognitively process data in order to understand. But in another respect it is not trivial because common sense would often short-circuit the understanding and judging operations, most often in the area of perception, and

---

[34] Joseph Flanagan, "Lonergan's Epistemology," *Thom* 36 (1972): 81.
[35] Lonergan, *Insight*, 277–78.
[36] *Ibid.*, 310–12.

assume that knowledge springs ready-made from data. In addition, most formal epistemologies overlook the roles of understanding and judgment.[37]

Lonergan asserts that these three levels of knowledge are the same for all human endeavors whether in science, math, or religion. In doing this, Lonergan bridges the chasm between science (which is conventionally considered to be objective study) and theology (which is conventionally considered to be subjective study). Thus, for Lonergan objectivity is but the authentic deliberation of the human knower which is encapsulated in the process of experience, understanding, and rational judgment. These are Lonergan's words about the process:

> Experience is inquiring into being. Intelligence is for thinking out being. But by judgment being is known. And in judgment what is known is known as being. Hence knowing is knowing being, yet known is never mere being, just as judgment is never mere yes apart from any question that "yes" answers.[38]

Subjectivity, for Lonergan, is the foundation of objectivity, although objectivity is prior, broader and exclusive to the human knower. It is here that the notion of horizon comes into play.

By horizon Lonergan means the context, experience, and understanding of the knower. Meyer states that horizon is the boundary between the "known unknown" and the "unknown unknown"—the known unknown is the range of questions one can raise but does not know the answer, whereas the unknown

---

[37] Denton, *Historiography and Hermeneutics in Jesus Studies*, 84.
[38] Lonergan, *Insight*, 381.

unknown is the question one does not know even to raise.[39] Lonergan concurs that the horizon of the human knower/subject, which varies from one knower to another, determines the degree of objectivity.[40] Thus, a knower should expand and enhance his or her horizon in order to achieve a higher degree of objectivity. This expansion of horizon is possible only in a person's pure desire to know. However, Lonergan asserts that there are human biases that hinder a human's pure desire to know, namely: desire of "oversight" rather than insight (which he calls dramatic); putting individual interest above that of the community; making community the base of knowledge at all cost; and general biases, especially making knowledge as seeing rather than knowledge as experience, understanding, and judgment.[41] While the general heuristic structure of the human knower is to strive for objective knowledge, there is a tendency for the knower to decline in knowledge through these biases.

Therefore, Lonergan argues that the human knower should experience conversion in three areas: intellectual, moral, and religious conversions. Intellectual conversion happens when the human knower engages in the dialectical process of experience, understanding, and judgment, instead of knowledge through seeing.[42] Moral conversion signifies a growth in the human knower that operates from the affirmation of the good and true value, instead of from selfish motives.[43] Finally, religious conversion signifies the reliance of the human knower on transcendent love and divine grace, which in turn enables the human knower to prefer the good and surmount biases to achieve full human

---

[39] Meyer, *Reality and Illusion*, 49.
[40] Bernard Lonergan, "The Subject," in *A Second Collection* (ed. W.F. Ryan and B.J. Tyrrell; Philadelphia: Westminster, 1974), 69.
[41] Lonergan, *Insight*, 214–51.
[42] Lonergan, *Method in Theology*, 238.
[43] *Ibid.*, 240.

knowledge.⁴⁴ The process of conversion is such that the later conversion sublates the earlier. In other words, moral sublates intellectual, religious sublates both moral and intellectual. This process brings one to a fuller realization of knowledge.

The process of subjective authenticity of the human knower (experience, understanding, and judgment) then leads to the truth or real object. For Lonergan truth or real object is not about the distinction of object and subject where object is the truth. Instead, objective truth is achieved through the subject's experience, intelligence, and rationality. Truth is an outcome of the knower's desire for pure knowledge. For Lonergan the criterion for truth is the process of reflection done virtually unconditioned in the affirmation of judgment.⁴⁵ He writes:

> Essentially, then, because the content of judgment is unconditioned, it is independent of the judging subject. Essentially, again, rational consciousness is what issues in a product that is independent of itself. Such is the meaning of absolute objectivity, and from it there follows a public or common terrain through which different subjects can and do communicate and agree.⁴⁶

In other words, while truth is the result of human cognition, it also transcends the human knower and becomes objective and public when the knower's reflection and judgment is performed unconditionally. It has to be clear here that when Lonergan emphasizes subjectivity, he is not falling into relativity; likewise, when he emphasizes the unconditional judgment he does not mean complete objectivity. It is this tension that has to be dealt with

---

⁴⁴ *Ibid.*
⁴⁵ See Meyer, *Reality and Illusion*, 85.
⁴⁶ Lonergan, *Insight*, 573.

intelligently, reasonably, and responsibly that produces a construal of critical realism. Lonergan's greatest contribution is his cognitive theory of human knowing. Lonergan not only provides an alternate epistemology in critical realism, but also articulates a cognitive theory of human knowing to express this epistemology. Lonergan provides a clear bridge between the objective and subjective through his cognitive theory of human knowing. Ontology and epistemology are bridged by the process of human understanding. In this way objective truth is not just about transmission of information, but the transmission of authentic subjectivity.

2.1.1.2.2. Ben F. Meyer

Meyer's work in New Testament (NT) studies is a reflection and application of Lonergan's transcendental method of critical realism. This is most notably seen in Meyer's *Reality and Illusion in New Testament Scholarship*, where he states explicitly that the position he presents is that of Lonergan's, with "no attempt to improve upon the master."[47] Here I will briefly illustrate Meyer's application of Lonergan in his study of the historical Jesus.[48]

---

[47] Meyer, *Reality and Illusion*, viii. Other works of Meyer that utilizes Lonergan's approach are: *The Aims of Jesus* (London: SCM, 1979); and *Critical Realism and New Testament* (Allison Park: Pickwick, 1989).

[48] McEvenue, an Old Testament scholar, has also utilized Lonergan's critical realism. However, I will mention McEvenue less often, only when needed, because his application of Lonergan and Meyer are basically identical. McEvenue writes, "My theory is in complete agreement with that of Ben Meyer. Interpretation has to begin with scholarship leading to a precise understanding of the intended meaning. Otherwise one has failed to be attentive to the text: one has not really read. This reading should bring one to an encounter with the author" ("Afterward," in *Lonergan's Hermeneutics: Its Development and Application* [ed. Sean McEvenue and Ben F. Meyer; Washington, DC: Catholic University of America Press, 1989], 158). McEvenue's chief argument is that Bible should be read as a literary piece and that apart from getting the authorial intention an interpreter should also pay close attention to elemental truths (i.e.,

Meyer argues that applying the cognitive theory of Lonergan, namely, the process of experience, understanding, and judgment will lead to the understanding of the real Jesus.[49] He contends that it is only by successfully answering the virtually unconditioned questions that one can know the object of knowledge.[50] For Meyer, as for Lonergan, the real is what is known when questions are responded to correctly.

Meyer further argues that Lonergan's method provides space for theologically motivated questions as a legitimate means in the quest of history. Consequently, "the history that is known in answer to those questions amounts to a changing historical framework for persisting theological truth."[51] In relation to Meyer's point of asking a question to get into the truth, McEvenue provides a solid example in his work on "The Rise of David Story."[52] McEvenue cogently argues that the rise of the David story (1 Sam 16–2 Sam 8) should be read with a compact mentality. In other words, in the ancient context religion, politics, and history were not adequately differentiated and so to read the rise of David as a story of a bloody assassinator and ideological manipulator (in

---

body language, tone of voice, facial expression) of the text (McEvenue, "Afterward," 158). McEvenue also utilizes Lonergan's eight specialties (i.e., research, interpretation, history, dialectic, foundations, doctrines, systematic and communication) in his biblical hermeneutics. The first four specialties deal specifically with exegesis of the text while the latter four relate to contemporary application. McEvenue states that biblical hermeneutics is incomplete without exegesis and application, but at the same time in order to be fruitful in this endeavor Lonergan's eight specialties have to be closely considered—see *Interpretation and Bible*, 113–22.

[49] Ben F. Meyer, *Christus Faber: The Master Builder and the House of God* (Allison Park: Pickwick, 1992), 3.

[50] Meyer, *Critical Realism*, 85–86.

[51] I am quoting here Denton's delineation of Meyer's use of theological questions in historical research—see *Historiography and Hermeneutics*, 87.

[52] McEvenue, *Interpretation and Bible*, 113–14.

relation to claiming divine authority for his action) is a "massive anachronism."[53] McEvenue also points out that the passage on the rise of David is redactional in nature.

However, to argue that the final form of the text is purely an outcome of the interpretation of the final redactor would mean that our modern interpretation is once again untrue to the compact mentality of the ancient authors. The ancient authors were at best expressing their religious experiences rather than articulating theological doctrines.[54] In order to avoid this problem, McEvenue contends that, "Interpretation, then, would need to reach into the historical, socio-cultural context to imagine creatively and feelingly the experience which was conveyed to the first readers of this story."[55] McEvenue, in other words, asserts that questions asked to the text should be those that shed light on the historical context of the first readers.

He further asserts that these questions include theological inquiry which is in turn triggered by one's acquired tradition. He therefore states: "These questions arise because my foundations include a heuristics of revelation and tradition: my knowledge of God is dependent on those who knew him before me, and specifically on the affirmations about God made by David and David's era. Were those people credible only because later ages lived through the culture they created, or were they worthy of belief in themselves?"[56] In sum, McEvenue appeals to take the OT context seriously, at the same time provides space for theological, subjective questions to be asked in order to intelligently understand the text.

---

[53] *Ibid.*, 114.
[54] *Ibid.*
[55] *Ibid.*
[56] *Ibid.*, 118.

Meyer also applies Lonergan's understanding of objectivity and subjectivity in his work, particularly in the understanding of history. Meyer points out that history in a positivistic perspective is understood incorrectly as purely objective. For him, a historian relies on the whole range of experience and understanding before coming to judgment. In this way, history is a matter of authentic subjectivity—an outcome of the subject's horizon.[57] Of course, this does not mean that Meyer's construal of history falls into relativism; rather it means that objectivity is mediated through a process of the subject's triad cognition—i.e., experience, understanding, and judgment.

Besides these, Meyer also applies Lonergan's understanding of horizon and conversion in his articulation of NT hermeneutics, specifically against an ideological reading of the text. Horizon refers to one's boundary of knowledge. There is no doubt that utilizing one's horizon in construing knowledge is valid; however, one's horizon can be enlarged and it can also change. The change takes place not merely by argument but by conversion from one horizon to another.[58] The underlying notion of this conversion is encapsulated in the pure desire to achieve authentic subjectivity.[59] Meyer suggests that intellectual, moral, and religious conversion is needed for understanding the profundity of the NT text.[60] Meyer states: "It may be that the problem of the interpreter is not met by resources such as encyclopedias, handbooks, Oxford Dictionaries of one kind or another, and that what is needed is neither information nor the solution of a problem but the cure of a blind-

---

[57] Meyer, *Critical Realism*, 141.
[58] Denton, *Historiography and Hermeneutics*, 91.
[59] Meyer, *Critical Realism*, 81.
[60] *Ibid.*, xiii.

spot which might be massive."⁶¹ The cure, Meyer argues, might be found in intellectual, moral, and religious conversions.

As segue to the next discussion, I mention Meyer's construal of biblical theology. Meyer argues that biblical theology should stem from both history and theology. In other words, biblical theology involves the reconstruction of religious institutions of ancient Israel and early Christianity, but biblical theology also means understanding and interpreting the ancient community as having a tacit homogeneous foundation of and for the modern Christian community.⁶² Historically, for Meyer, there has always been a division of emphasis between history and theology in the field of biblical theology. It is only in critical realism that both can be amicably conjoined to couch a vibrant, relevant biblical theology. Meyer states: "The task, then, is necessarily approached not under positivist or Neo-Kantian constraints but in the manner of critical realism; not from a dogma-free platform but from within commitment to historical Christianity."⁶³

2.1.1.2.3. N.T. Wright

Wright, in his first volume of the proposed six volumes *Christian Origins and the Question of God*, outlines his methodology, which is based on critical realism.⁶⁴ Wright is indirectly influenced by Lonergan through the work of Meyer. Wright's form of critical realism is eclectic in that it attempts to synthesize the positives of both Enlightenment and postmodern epistemologies of knowledge. Thus, Wright's critical realism primarily draws the positive aspects of both the positivist and

---

⁶¹ Meyer, *Reality and Illusion*, 92–93. See also McEvenue, *Interpretation and Bible*, 23–39.

⁶² Meyer, *Critical Realism*, 197.

⁶³ *Ibid.*, 208.

⁶⁴ Wright, *New Testament and the People of God*, 32–46.

phenomenologist. Moritz writes this about Wright's critical realism:

> Some of [his stance] sounds phenomenalistic and some of it positivistic. This is hardly surprising. For the phenomenalist too argues that knowledge is subjective and the positivist agrees with the critical realist about the separate reality of the object "out there." Some resemblance between critical realism and phenomenalism and with a chastened positivism cannot in the final analysis be avoided. Critical realism is precisely about combining the strengths of a variety of approaches.[65]

Unlike positivism and phenomenalism, where knowledge is considered a description of the relationship of object and subject, critical realism ascribes knowledge as a dialogue or conversation between human (not neutral) and event (not detached or meaningless object).[66] Thus, critical realism espouses relational epistemology where the knower is involved in the process of knowing, and objects can fully be grasped only in their relation to the knower. In other words, there is no distinction between subject

---

[65] Thorsten Moritz, "Critical but Real: Reflecting on N.T. Wright's Tool for the Task," in *Renewing Biblical Interpretation* (ed. Craig Bartholomew, Colin Greene, and Karl Möller; Grand Rapids: Zondervan, 2000), 179. However, it should be pointed out that Donald Denton and Quentin Quesnell have argued independently that Lonergan's critical realism is not necessarily a *via media* between positivism and phenomenalism as Wright's critical realism; instead Lonergan's critical realism combines and transcends the extremes of other epistemologies. See Denton, *Historiography and Hermeneutics*, 221; Quentin Quesnell, "Mutual Misunderstanding: The Dialectic of Contemporary Hermeneutics," in *Lonergan's Hermeneutics: Its Development and Application* (ed. Sean McEvenue and Ben F. Meyer; Washington, DC: Catholic University of America Press, 1989), 19–37.

[66] Wright, *New Testament and the People of God*, 44.

and object in construing knowledge as in positivism and phenomenalism; rather knowledge is a consequent of a unique interrelationship between subject and object. Wright contends: "To know is to be in a relation with the known, which means the 'knower' must be open to the possibility of the 'known' being other than had been expected or even desired, and must be prepared to respond accordingly, not merely to observe from a distance."[67]

How does this unique relationship between subject and object come about? Wright claims that this comes about through the perspective of stories and worldviews. Thorsten Moritz states that the originality of Wright's critical realism is his emphasis on story as the crucial factor in understanding the worldviews of the ancient people and their community.[68] For Wright, reality and knowledge are always shaped by the community's worldview, and the way to know the worldview is through the narrated stories of the community.[69] For him knowledge is not neutral, objective, and universal but all knowledge is specific and community oriented. Knowledge is found within the stories of the community as relevant and purposeful questions are inquired; at the same time knowledge is verified within these stories. Wright points out that it is wrong to think that "perception is prior to the grasping of larger realities" as positivist and phenomenologist imagine.[70] He further states that it is imperative for a positivist to realize that the so-called facts come already with theories attached and these theories are, in fact, the stories that provide framework for the facts to work as facts.[71]

---

[67] *Ibid.*, 45.
[68] Moritz, "Critical Realism," *DTIB* 147-50.
[69] Wright, *New Testament and the People of God*, 37.
[70] *Ibid.*, 43.
[71] *Ibid.*

To apply Wright's critical realism to OT studies means to understand the worldview and the stories of the biblical community which will in turn enable us to comprehend the reality and knowledge as postulated in the biblical text.

Before going any further, let us ask the question: does Wright's construal of knowledge as specific and community-oriented mean knowledge is private, exclusive, and relative? As discussed above, the answer would involve an epistemological conversion—i.e., from naïve realism to critical realism. Apart from that, Wright, in concurrence with Lonergan's cognitive theory, applies the process of questions, hypothesis, and verification to attend the objective truth.[72] When two competing and opposing stories confront each other, the only way to resolve this confrontation is to come up with an alternative story—a story that considers all the relevant data in a more meaningful and simpler outline.[73] In other words, it is not about a subject trying to articulate a detached object; rather the subject is trying to articulate the object as best as he or she can with the existing data.

Accordingly, Wright asserts it is through question that one forms the hypothesis. The question asked is not in a vacuum, rather it is formulated within the framework of stories and worldviews. A good hypothesis includes data, simple outlining of data, and finally making greater sense of the outlined data when faced with explaining the problem.[74] In verification, one must survey whether the existing data have been utilized carefully and responsibly, and whether the outlined data are simple and coherent.[75] It is through this process that knowledge is objectified. However, knowledge is not neutral, but as Wright says, "the proof of the pudding remains

---

[72] *Ibid.*, 42.
[73] *Ibid.*
[74] *Ibid.*, 42, 98–100
[75] *Ibid.*, 105–6

in the eating"—i.e., whether the hypothesis makes greater and better sense and whether the available data has been responsibly organized are the matters that count.[76]

This understanding of critical realism is utilized by Wright in studying the literature, history, and theology of the NT, which are, in fact, the three pillars in studying the biblical text. In his treatment of literature, he deals with ways to read the text. He begins by pointing out weaknesses of positivist/naïve realist, phenomenologist, and postmodernist. For instance, he argues that a positivist approaches the text with the notion that he is able to get to the objective meaning of the text which lies beyond the author and the text in the actual event. The phenomenologist approaches the text with a mindset that the meaning of the text is vested in the sense data of the author. The postmodernist approaches the text by concentrating not on the author and the event, but the reader himself. Wright argues that for a responsible reading all these three approaches should be included, which critical realism espouses. He writes:

> What we need, then, is a theory of reading which, at the reader/text stage, will do justice *both* to the fact that the reader is a particular human being *and* to the fact that the text is an entity on its own, not a plastic substance to be molded to the reader's whim. It must also do justice, at the text/author stage, *both* to the fact that the author intended certain things, *and* that the text may well contain in addition other things—echoes, evocations, structures, and the like—which were not present to the author's mind, and of course may well not be present to the reader's mind. We need a both-and theory of reading, not an either-or one.

---

[76] For a further discussion on Wright's critical realism and divine revelation, see below section 2.3.2 "Authentic Subjectivity Leads to Objective Knowledge."

> Similarly, we need a theory which will do justice, still at the text/author stage, *both* to the fact that texts, including biblical texts, do not normally represent the whole of the author's mind, even that bit to which they come closest, *and* to the fact that they nevertheless do normally tell us, and in principle tell us truly, quite a bit about him or her. Finally, we need to recognize, at the author/event stage, *both* that authors do not write without a point of view (they are humans, and look at things in particular ways and from particular angles) *and* that they really can speak and write about events and objects...which are not reducible to terms of their own state of mind.[77]

This hermeneutic is referred to by Wright as the hermeneutic of love where "the lover affirms the reality and the otherness of the beloved."[78] Wright's hermeneutic of love suggests that in reading, the relationship between the reader and the text/author should be signified by love, respect, and willingness to compromise for bringing transformation to the reading. Christopher McMahon writes about the hermeneutic of love: "This hermeneutical approach enables one to engage the literature in a critical realist manner—affirming the reality of the referent of the text, while at the same time, raising critical questions about possible and inevitable misunderstanding in the course of an ongoing conversation."[79]

---

[77] *Ibid.*, 62–63.

[78] The notion of hermeneutic of love is also found in the work of Anthony Thiselton, *New Horizons in Hermeneutics: The Theory and Practice of Transforming Biblical Reading* (Grand Rapids: Zondervan, 1992), 597–618.

[79] Christopher McMahon, "The Relevance of Historical Inquiry for the Christian Faith: A Comparative Study of the Historical Methodologies of J.P. Meier and N.T. Wright" (Ph.D. diss., Catholic University of America Press, 2003), 163.

Besides this ethical reading, Wright also indicates that literature expresses human worldviews or "better still, the telling of stories which bring worldviews into articulation."[80] Here Wright is making a point that one should acknowledge the worldview as postulated in the text rather than anachronistically imposing another worldview upon it. This also provides reason for Wright to look at the structure of the literature/story attentively because it is in the structure that the worldview is expressed and understanding this worldview will lead to the meaning of the text.[81]

Story, for Wright, is historical. It leads him to the analysis of history. For Wright, history is not merely about facts but history is always interpreted. Once again he points out the mistakes of the phenomenologist whose tendency is to deny the referent point by concentrating on the sense data of the author, whereas the positivist argues for the full access to the objectivity of referent. Against this, Wright argues that critical realism acknowledges the importance of knowing the referent but that this referent can be ascertained only through the study of subjective sense data. History is a science that attempts to articulate the referent of the story. However, articulating the historical event of the story does not mean seeking for a detached already-out-there object. But it is a matter of articulating the object/known by utilizing the data available for the subject/knower. Wright once again brings up the process of question, hypothesis, and verification in ascertaining the referent of the story. For Wright, the process of formulating hypothesis and verification leads to the search of historical knowledge.

Historical knowledge does not simply mean bare facts but it is an outcome of the reflection of the historian on the facts. Historical

---

[80] Wright, *New Testament and the People of God*, 65.
[81] *Ibid.*, 69.

knowledge, argues Wright, is the true task of the historian.[82] As he contends: "Historical knowledge is arrived at, like all knowledge, by the spiral of epistemology, in which the story-telling human community launches enquiries, forms provisional judgments about which stories are likely to be successful in answering those enquires, and then tests these judgments by further interaction with data."[83] Thus meaning stems from events through the story-building process of communal hypothesis and verification. An insightful point that Wright indicates within this process is that historians reading the event might overlook some evidences or might approach the event with complex hypothesis and, therefore, historians should co-operate with one another to get to the fuller picture.[84] History, thus, is not just the study of historical events or facts, but also the study of intentions, motivations, mindsets, and worldviews behind historical events in their historical context.[85]

Besides literature and history, one factor that defines and sustains a worldview is the theology of the community. In treating theology, Wright provides a fuller explanation of worldview: "worldviews are in fact, from one point of view, profoundly theological, and we must therefore examine the meaning of 'theology' within this context."[86] Wright declares that "worldviews have to do with the presuppositional, pre-cognitive stage of a culture or society. Whenever we find the ultimate concerns of human beings, we find worldviews."[87]

---

[82] *Ibid.*, 171.

[83] *Ibid.*, 109.

[84] *Ibid.*

[85] See Raymond Meyer, "An Evangelical Analysis of the Critical Realism and Corollary Hermeneutics of Bernard Lonergan with Application for Evangelical Hermeneutics" (Ph.D. diss., Southeastern Baptist Theological Seminary, 2007), 164.

[86] Wright, *New Testament and the People of God*, 109.

[87] *Ibid.*, 122.

Furthermore, according to Wright, worldviews function in four ways: worldviews provide the *stories* through which human beings view reality; worldviews enable humans to inquire basic *questions* that determine their existence; worldviews produce the *symbols* in and through which culture expresses itself; and worldviews comprise the *praxis* which form the action and behavior of culture.[88] Wright understands theology within these functions of worldviews. He writes: "Theology suggests certain ways of telling the story, explores certain ways of answering the questions, offers particular interpretations of the symbols, and suggests and critiques certain forms of praxis."[89] To neglect the importance of how theology functions within the framework of worldviews would result in misreading either the culture we dwell in or the culture we are investigating.

Next, Wright raises the question of whether or not theology or God-talk points to reality beyond space-time reality or is it simply about meta-language. He points out the positivist's tendency to objectify God simply on the basis of revelation, whereas the phenomenologist's tendency to either subjectively portray god according to his/her imagination/ideology or simply talk about revelation as god in action. Conversely, Wright suggests the holistic answer to this question lies in metaphor which is a mini-story in itself. Metaphors provide a way to look at reality, which cannot be reduced to terms of metaphor itself. Theology thus functions like a metaphor in its articulation of god.

Wright also points out that "metaphors and stories are in fact more basic within human consciousness than apparently 'factual' speech, and recognizing the essentially storied nature of god-talk is therefore no bar to asserting the reality of its referent."[90] The fact

---

[88] *Ibid.*, 123–24.
[89] *Ibid.*, 130.
[90] *Ibid.*, 129–30

that god-talk is intrinsic to human worldviews as expressed in the stories "suggest that we must, however critically, recognize the presence of something we may as well call 'revelation.'"[91] Wright's diagram of this discussion on god-talk is as follows:[92]

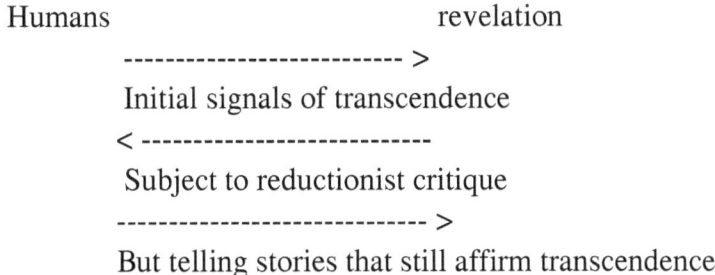

In the end, there is a god/referent ("realism") outside the subject, but the subject needs to be open to consider certain given worldview and stories of a community ("critical") in order to construe the reality of god. This whole issue of theology and its interrelationship with worldviews allows Wright to discuss subjective meta-language as a legitimate means to understand objective human truth.[93]

2.1.1.3. Summary

The Cognitive theory of Lonergan which is encapsulated in the process of experience, understanding, and judgment is, indeed, intrinsic to human nature. This theory of human understanding provides the necessary impetus to articulate and express the epistemology of critical realism, namely, authentic subjectivity as a legitimate means to objective knowledge. In fact, the epistemology

---

[91] *Ibid.*, 129.
[92] *Ibid.*
[93] For further discussion on worldview as "authentic subjectivism", see the section below 2.3.1 "Revelation as a Threshold Concept."

of critical realism makes no distinction between object and subject. It is completely different from positivism where the distinction of object and subject is eternally maintained. However, critical realism understands that objective knowledge cannot be attained without one's subjective experience, motivation, and worldview. Such epistemology opens up vistas for theological inquiries as an important and a necessary element in the quest of objective truth.

Understanding the role of horizon is imperative in any interpretation and construal of knowledge. Critical realism not only discusses the need for the enlargement of one's horizon but also for conversion of horizon. Closely related to the understanding of the dynamic of horizon is the acknowledgment that knowledge is specific and not universal. This implies understanding one's worldview as well as the worldview of the context under study. Insensitivity to one's worldview leads to distortion of truth and anachronism.

2.2. *Revelation as the Essence of the OT Prophecy*

Before examining the issue of revelation from the perspective of critical realism, I will first highlight how prophecy in the OT is inextricably tied to revelation. Jack R. Lundbom outlines some chief characteristics of Yahweh's prophet that signify the close relationship between prophecy and revelation.[94] First, Yahweh's prophet is someone who has received a divine call. In fact, the word נבא most likely means "one who is called."[95] The OT records

---

[94] Jack R. Lundbom, *The Hebrew Prophets: An Introduction* (Minneapolis: Fortress, 2010), 7–31.

[95] The etymology of נבא is still unsure. However, it is accepted today that this word is related to the Akkadian word *nabû(m)*, "to name, call." Yet still it is disputed as to whether the noun should be considered in the active as "speaker, proclaimer" or in the passive as "called one." J. Jeremias asserts that the latter is the correct understanding because: first, most of this word occurs in nominal form; second, the Akkadian congnate word also means "called"; finally, the verb

some of the divine callings of the prophets with longer descriptions—e.g., the divine call of Moses (Exod 3:4–6, 10), Isaiah (Isa 6:1–13), and Jeremiah (Jer 1:4–19). However, these examples are exceptional. In other words, other prophets might have experienced a divine calling but, perhaps, one that was not so dramatic and elaborate. For instance, in the case of Amos, his divine call was mentioned only in his confrontation with Amaziah, the priest (Amos 7:15). Thus, all Yahweh's prophets received divine revelation, but the manner in which they received the divine call varied.

Second, Yahweh's prophets spoke divine words.[96] The prophets did not simply speak their mind and heart, but they spoke according to the instruction of Yahweh. When Yahweh instructed Isaiah to cry along with Him, the prophet replied, "What shall I cry?" and Yahweh gave him the words (Isa 40:6). In fact, when Yahweh speaks, his prophets are compelled to deliver his words to his people. Amos says, "The Lion has roared; who will not fear? The Lord God has spoken; who can but prophesy?" (3:8). The prophets based the authority of their prophecy on Yahweh alone, and this is indicated in the phrase "Thus says the LORD," which occurs more than three hundred times.[97] John N. Oswalt points out that in the prophetic literature Yahweh is "not only the primary character; he is also the primary speaker, with much of the material said to have been received in verbal form directly from him."[98]

---

form of this word occurs in the reflexive and passive stems—see "נָבִיא" *TLOT* 2:697–710. See also H.P. Müller, "נָבִיא," *TDOT* 9:129–50; William F. Albright, *From the Stone Age to Christianity: Monotheism and the Historical Process* (New York: Doubleday, 1957), 303; G. Ernest Wright, "The Nations in Hebrew Prophecy," *Enc* 26.2 (1965): 225–37.

[96] *Ibid.*, 17–20.

[97] For instance, the phrase occurs 36 times in Isaiah, 149 times in Jeremiah, and 123 times in Ezekiel.

[98] John N. Oswalt, "God," *DOTP* 280–93.

Third, Yahweh's prophets possessed divine vision.[99] In other words, Yahweh's prophets discerned the signs of the times, which ordinary people could not perceive. The prophets were privy to future events. For instance, Amos had visions concerning the fall of northern kingdom (Amos 7–9); Jeremiah also saw the destruction of Judah in his vision (Jer 1:13–14). The prophets had such insight and foresight because they were filled with divine spirit (רוּחַ). In fact, the presence of divine spirit enabled Yahweh's prophets to engage in mighty works.

Lundbom also explains that one of the characteristics of Yahweh's prophets is spending time in prayer or conversing with Yahweh.[100] Perhaps, this is a way of strengthening the relationship within the divine council (cf. Jer 23:18). It is only because of such a close bond between Yahweh and his prophet that a prophet could be a prophet of Yahweh. It has to be mentioned that Yahweh can speak and reveal himself to anyone he chooses; however, it is unimaginable, for instance, for a prophet to receive perpetual revelation, unless, there is repentance followed by faithfulness in the life of the prophet. There is no doubt that God himself takes the initiative to communicate to his prophet; yet, once the prophet responds to the self-communication of God in repentance and faithfulness, a close proximity between God and the prophet is established. The above discussion demonstrates that prophecy in the OT is intrinsically related to divine revelation.

2.3. *Understanding Revelation and Tradition through Critical Realism*

If the content of prophecy is divine revelation, it is imperative to have a proper understanding of revelation so that we might envisage the meaning of it as postulated in Scripture. Critical

---

[99] Lundbom, *The Hebrew Prophets*, 20–24.
[100] *Ibid.*, 30.

realism and its construal of knowledge provide a unique platform to understanding divine revelation. Enlightenment epistemology has reduced the understanding of divine revelation to non-science that relates purely to human subjectivity; whereas, postmodern philosophy has exacerbated the understanding of divine revelation by curtailing ontology from human expression, thus, leaving the human as the sole owner of his or her own revelation. My goal here is to answer two pertinent questions: Is God's revelation haphazard, unintelligible and shrouded with mystery? Or can God's revelation be reasonably construed? The answers to these require the conversion from an Enlightenment understanding of knowledge to that of critical realism. It also entails an explanation of tradition and its role in mediating revelation.

The impact of Enlightenment epistemology on OT studies was the transformation of the latter to historical studies devoid of transcendental meaning. Enlightenment epistemology espouses scientific and objective inquiries as the only legitimate approach. Behind this approach is the underlying notion that an individual/self is *norma normans*, free from any tradition and authority.[101] Wright, as noted above, has shown in general how history should be understood. Moreover, Wright has articulated that history has a referential point, but at the same time he argues that history is a communal enterprise.

William J. Abraham also deals with the issue of the historical-critical-method as understood in the Enlightenment milieu and attempts to rehabilitate the method.[102] It is appropriate to consider the argument of Abraham because he deals predominantly with the work of Ernst Troeltsch whose work epitomizes the rationale

---

[101] See Colin E. Gunton, *A Brief Theology of Revelation: The 1993 Warfield Lectures* (Edinburgh: T&T Clark, 1995), 20–39.

[102] Abraham, *Divine Revelation*, 92–115.

behind the historical studies of the Enlightenment period.[103] Abraham argues that the historical-critical-method does not need to be criticized in a wholesale manner, but that it needs to be re-orientated. Thus, Abraham's argument functions in a critical realist fashion, though he does not specify his own hermeneutical praxis.

In order to reorient the historical method of the Enlightenment epistemology, Abraham outlines Troeltsch's argument. According to Troeltsch, historical methods are based on three pillars, namely: criticism, analogy, and correlation. Criticism is best understood as the preconceived skepticism towards sources; analogy is, more or less, defining the past using the present human experiences; and correlation means the causality (cause and effect) in history that is caused by natural forces or human agencies.[104] This understanding of the mechanism of history has prevailed in the humanities generally and OT historical studies in particular, resulting in either an obfuscated or suppressed notion of revelation.

The three pillars—criticism, analogy, and correlation—are unabashedly secular and there is no doubt these criteria are articulated to provide a scientific, unapologetic, and objective construal of knowledge.[105] Abraham critiques Troeltsch's criterion

---

[103] See R. Morgan, "Troeltsch and Christian Theology," in *Ernst Troeltsch: Writings on Theology and Religion* (ed. and trans. R. Morgan and M. Pye; Louisville: Westminster, 1990), 203–33.

[104] Citing from V. Philips Long, "Historiography of the Old Testament," in *The Faces of Old Testament Studies: A Survey of Contemporary Approaches* (ed. David W. Baker and Bill T. Arnold; Grand Rapids: Baker, 1999), 145–75.

[105] Troesltsch asserts, "In history, as in other things, purely theoretical knowledge is knowledge based upon general conceptions, and that signifies knowledge derived from causal conceptions. The sole task of history in its specifically theoretical aspect is to explain every movement, process, state and nexus of things by reference to the web of its causal relations. That is in a word, the whole function of purely scientific investigation" ("Historiography," in *Encyclopedia of Religion and Ethics* [ed. James Hastings; Edinburgh: T&T Clark, 1914], 6:716–23).

of criticism by arguing that since this criterion is based on being skeptical about the traditional sources, the historian's conclusion can only be in terms of probability which is constantly subject to new findings. Abraham also points out the weakness of Troesltch's analogy which is, basically, a concept of *a posteriori* reasoning. To a certain extent one might get to the "cause" through the study of "effect," especially, when the gap between effect and cause is narrow; however, when the gap is wide more speculations are inevitably entertained. Abraham further critiques the criterion of correlation by claiming that not all relationships between cause and effect are derived from natural law or human agency and so objectively verifiable.

As a way of reorienting Troeltsch's view, Abraham purports that the principle of criticism should not begin from skepticism but with an open-minded assessment.[106] As for the second criterion, Abraham points out that the analogy goes both ways: not only is the present projected to the past, but also the past informs and shapes the present.[107] Finally, Abraham articulates that the principle of correlation can be caused not only by natural law or human agency, but also by personal agency. Thus, Abraham could invoke the role of God and his relationship with his people within the framework of the historical-critical-method.[108] Abraham has cogently shown that history is not just about facts and numbers, but it is subjective. His work reinforces the critical realist construal of knowledge of Lonergan, Meyer, and Wright, as discussed above.

2.3.1. Revelation as a Threshold Concept

Critical realism acknowledges the specific contextual worldview of a given people group and community. Wright talks

---

[106] Abraham, *Divine Revelation*, 100.
[107] *Ibid.*, 109.
[108] *Ibid.*, 109–15.

about how stories can function as the window through which one can understand a given worldview. I would like to further the argument of Wright by saying that if stories articulate the worldview then, in the case of Israel, it is divine revelation that gave rise to stories. In other words, Yahweh's revelation "in" or "through" the Exodus, laws, and the prophetic messages were the foundation of Israel's worldview.

Abraham compares the experience of divine revelation to that of crossing the threshold.[109] According to him, once the prophet accepts the revelation of God, his or her perspective is completely changed so much so that it becomes the epistemological lens for the prophet.[110] Abraham calls this an epistemic change, and argues that it provides us the scope to study revelation as a legitimate and intelligible subject matter. He illustrates how a person standing at the door does not have the full view of the room, but when that person crosses the threshold he or she becomes fully aware of the entire room—e.g., its settings, the furniture, the full access to the house, and so on.[111]

Abraham further illustrates the concept of revelation as threshold by pointing to the experience of Paul's conversion. The total transformation that Paul went through is nothing less than breathtaking. The fact that Paul was transformed from being a persecutor to persecuted sums up his turnaround. The fascinating and crucial aspect of the transformation is that, this experience of crossing the threshold pierces through the inner most being of one's life. Paul's experience of divine revelation became the lens through which he viewed and interpreted everything. It became the basis for his theological claims. As Abraham asserts: "Crossing the

---

[109] Abraham, *Crossing the Threshold*, 79–94. Similarly, Gorringe considers revelation as displacement—see *Discerning Spirit*, 7–11.

[110] Abraham, *Crossing the Threshold*, 81.

[111] *Ibid.*, 86.

threshold of divine revelation is a massive cognitive and spiritual revolution."[112] This threshold concept of divine revelation provides us with a glimpse of how Yahweh's prophets might have been transformed. Moreover, this concept portrays how a worldview is formed or altered. The fact that the divine revelation causes one to formulate or alter worldviews indicates that divine revelation cannot be reduced to a mere subjective, unintelligent, absolute mystery that is irrelevant for any objective knowledge.

2.3.2. Authentic Subjectivity Leads to Objective Knowledge

The epistemology of critical realism allows us to look at revelation as authentic, objective knowledge. This does not mean that the concept of divine revelation can be analyzed objectively in a laboratory. But it means divine revelation cannot be set aside as a mere subjective experience and absolute mystery. Such a construal of knowledge can, in fact, help one to discern between true and false prophecy. We may utilize Lonergan's cognitive theory—i.e., experience, understanding, and judgment—to understand divine revelation. Experience is the beginning of knowledge. The experience of divine revelation may be gained through one's own personal experience or, in the case of someone studying divine revelation, it might be achieved through seeing, reading, dialoguing. The experience of divine revelation will lead to asking the simple question, *what is it?*

By asking this question one begins to analyze the experience of divine revelation. Perhaps, one could further engage in questions such as: when did this happen? where? and how? Asking these questions will enable the researcher to garner ideas, insight, and knowledge of divine revelation. Finally, this acquired knowledge of divine revelation should be brought under critique by asking: Is it? Is it so? Is it this or that? Through such questions, one can

---

[112] *Ibid.*, 89.

compare and contrast different experiences of divine revelation within a given worldview or tradition; analyzing the impact of this experience on individual and community lives; and scrutinizing whether the ethical praxis of the one who experienced divine revelation substantiates the divine percepts.

Thus, when studying divine revelation one must investigate its relationship with sociology (e.g., the deposit of faith), as well as the ethics of the alleged human agent of God. Such critical analysis, without being skeptical initially, has the potential to reach an understanding of divine revelation as authentic and objective.[113]

This exercise is similar to Wright's process of attaining authentic knowledge—a process of question, framing hypothesis, and verification. Wright's process of articulating knowledge emphasizes the importance of the context within which divine revelation was experienced. Wright understands that questions directed to the hypothesis are contextual. In other words, the questions are not asked in a vacuum, but within a community and a tradition. So for instance, in adjudicating a person's claim of receiving divine revelation, one should first analyze the content of the revelation by raising appropriate questions in relation to the worldview and stories of the given particular community. Such questions will give rise to a hypothesis. This hypothesis in turn will consist of data such as whether the content of the revelation is in line with and enhances the deposit of faith of the community, and whether the morality of the alleged receiver of the divine revelation coheres with the stipulations of the deposit of faith. The success of the process of verifying the hypothesis will hinge on how the data are utilized. In all this, the context of the community

---

[113] Notice this whole process is akin to the arguments of Wright, Meyer, and McEvenue (as discussed above) concerning reading and locating the intended meaning of the text.

and its worldview and stories become crucial as it is imperative to ask relevant and contextual questions.

This sort of analysis appears to be an obvious and mundane activity and it is. However, to reiterate Denton's assertion, there is a danger: more often than not common sense can be short circuited and lead one to think that knowledge stems directly from mere sense experiences. It is worth mentioning again Lonergan's view that the template upon which critical realism operates is identical with that of any scientific analysis. However, the Enlightenment thinking has left a deep mark by emphasizing the dichotomy of subjective and objective knowledge. Meyer contends, "Moreover, the unparalleled prestige of scientific knowledge can mislead (and has misled) scientists and others into supposing that the limits of science and the limits of knowledge simply are coterminous; such for example, is the logical positivist view that non-empirical statements are meaningless."[114] In the end, in order to implement a hermeneutics of critical realism one has to be converted to critical realism and its construal of knowledge.

2.3.3. *Tradition as a Means of Preserving and Transmitting Revelation*

If divine revelation is intelligible and studied as objective, concrete knowledge, then divine revelation is also not random or haphazard. As noted above, Wright has shown that every community should be the source of knowledge, and that every experience and knowledge should be evaluated within that given community. This is the only way to know whether a person or community's experience is true and historical in nature. In other words, every community has its own specific tradition that shapes and directs a community. Thus, the knowledge of divine revelation is intrinsically sociological in nature. Alasdair MacIntyre, a moral

---

[114] Meyer, *Reality and Illusion*, 86.

philosopher, has consistently argued that any rationality is mediated by tradition.[115] MacIntyre's work is in contradistinction to the Enlightenment's conception of anti-authority, tradition, and universalism of knowledge, as well as postmodernity's conception of relativism. Instead, MacIntyre argues that moral reasoning is actually embedded within a social context. In other words, rationality is tradition-bound.[116]

So what is tradition? MacIntyre states: "A living tradition then is an historically extended, socially embodied argument, and an argument precisely in part about the goods which constitute that tradition."[117] MacIntyre's understanding of tradition is shaped by his attempt to reclaim Aristotle's understanding of *telos* or good. In doing that, MacIntyre postulates that tradition is open-ended, constantly engaged in arguments to reach a *telos*. This is in contrast to the Enlightenment understanding that the *telos* (or first principle) is already accomplished and utilized as the basis for subsequent arguments. However, MacIntyre in subsequent writings reduces his emphasis on tradition as open-ended (albeit, not jettisoned) and stresses instead that tradition is referential in itself.[118] Thus, he implies that tradition is both authoritative and in process. In other words, tradition provides the framework

---

[115] Alasdair MacIntyre, *After Virtue* (Notre Dame: University of Notre Dame Press, 1981); idem, *Whose Justice? Which Rationality?* (Notre Dame: University of Notre Dame Press, 1988); idem, *Three Rival Versions of Moral Enquiry: Encylopaedia, Genealogy, and Tradition* (Notre Dame: University of Notre Dame Press, 1990). It should be pointed out that McIntyre's works have influenced Wright which is vividly shown in the latter's articulation of critical realism.

[116] J.R. Weinstein, *On MacIntyre* (Belmont: Wadsworth, 2003), 60–80.

[117] MacInytre, *After Virtue*, 222.

[118] This point is suggested by Jean Porter in his analysis of MacIntyre's understanding of tradition-bound rationality. See Jean Porter, "Tradition in the Recent Work of Alasdair MacIntyre," in *Alasdair MacIntyre* (Cambridge: Cambridge University Press, 2003), 38–69.

(authority) for its further evolution (process). Alister McGrath calls this authoritative (or referential) aspect of tradition the transmitted reality.[119] If we translate this understanding of tradition to OT phenomena, this would mean tradition includes institutions, practices, systems of symbols, values and beliefs which stemmed from Yahweh's revelation to ancient Israel.

The evolution of tradition does not necessarily mean fashioning a completely new tradition detached from the existing tradition. It means, instead, re-contextualizing of the tradition to fit into a new social matrix. For instance, a mango seed (tradition) is not a mango (the outcome of the process) just as a mango is not a mango seed. However, the fact of the matter is that, a mango cannot exist without its seed, and only a mango seed can produce mangoes. In terms of Israel's prophecy, it means Yahweh sheds more light on the deposit of faith. Tradition is, indeed, a socially embedded concept. In fact, the OT clearly exemplifies this process of tradition (Exod 10:1–2; 12:26; 13:8, 14; Deut 6:4–9; 11:13–21; Josh 4:21; and Ps 78:5–8). Israel's children were born into their tradition, and they look to their tradition to justify their participation in the culture's practice.

In sum, for Israel this tradition constituted the received divine revelation or deposit of faith. Thus, the revelation that the prophets received had a basis and certain trajectory. The revelation of the prophet did not express a new message, but the revelation was meant to perpetuate the salvation Yahweh had for his people, Israel. Of course, this does not mean that the message of the prophet did not have any significance for the people. First, it was to remind Israel of God's law. Second, through divine revelation Israel could illuminate the received tradition. In this manner, MacIntyre is right to say that tradition is historically extended and socially embodied.

---

[119] See McGrath, *The Science of God*, 220.

The above discussion that tradition is socially embedded also confirms what the critical realists have articulated. McEvenue's argument that ancient Israel should be read with a "compact mentality," instead, of in an anachronistic manner is sound. Moreover, tradition is a process, yet it also acts as a referential point. By reminding ourselves of this fact we will realize that the prophets were not randomly prophesying.

2.4. Revelation and Inspiration

At this point, I will briefly comment on divine revelation and inspiration in conjunction with the prophetic experience. This comment on divine revelation and inspiration is necessitated by the tendency to reduce prophecy to mere inspired-hermeneutical enterprise (*á la* Sanders). There is no doubt that Israel's prophets were involved in inner-biblical interpretation; however, this enterprise was not exclusive to the prophets.[120] In fact, the work of inner-biblical interpretation was chiefly carried out by Israel's scribal community.[121] The point I want to make is that there cannot be any prophecy without revelation. In other words, a scribe can be inspired by Yahweh but that does not make him a prophet. This is not to discount, by any means, the work of the scribes, but divine revelation was what set the prophets apart. With that said, divine revelation and inspiration are correlative terms when it comes to OT prophetic ministry. A prophet such as Jeremiah was, no doubt, inspired by the deposit of faith or earlier received revelation, and yet he also received fresh revelation based on the deposit of faith.

---

[120] See John Day, "Inner-biblical Interpretation in the Prophets," in *"The Place is Too Small for Us": The Israelite Prophets in Recent Scholarship* (ed. Robert P. Gordon; vol. 5; Winona: Eisenbraums, 1995), 230–46.

[121] See Michael Fishbane, *Biblical Interpretation in Ancient Israel* (Oxford: Oxford University Press, 1985).

Two obvious points need to be emphasized here: first, a prophet was an inspired person and second, he received divine revelation. Bloesch comments: "Inspiration depends on revelation and serves revelation."[122] There is, indeed, the spiral dynamic of inspiration and revelation at play when it comes to the prophets and their prophecies. This point is accentuated by Oswalt's suggestion that the prophets were not merely mouthpieces of God, but dialogue partners.[123] In other words, the prophets were so inspired by God and his revelations that they became a dialogue partner with God. This dynamic relationship, in turn, enabled the prophets to receive God's revelation.

The meanings of revelation and inspiration have become almost interchangeable in the post-Reformation period.[124] One of the reasons for this is the discussion of the idea that Scripture is inerrant. For instance, plenary or verbal inspiration postulates that the Scripture does not only contain revelation but it is a revelation in itself because it is inspired or breathed by God (2 Tim 3:16); and subsequently it is completely without error. In this view, revelation and inspiration are collapsed into one phenomenon. Although these concepts are interconnected, there is a fine line of distinction between them which has to be acknowledged in order to understand the life and ministry of Yahweh's prophet.

Revelation as discussed above means God reveals himself to his people through certain events or prophets. Inspiration, on the other hand, can be divided into everyday language of inspiration and biblical inspiration. Inspiration in everyday language would mean being motivated, persuaded, and even willing to do something according to God's will. H. Wheeler Robinson and

---

[122] Bloesch, *Holy Scripture*, 126.

[123] Oswalt, "God," 282.

[124] See Abraham, *The Divine Inspiration*, 1–13; also Sandra M. Schneiders, "Inspiration and Revelation," *NIB* 3:57–63

James Barr, in a more subtle manner, have independently argued that this everyday language understanding of inspiration is akin to the inspiration of the biblical writers.[125] However, the Christian doctrine of inspiration has a deeper meaning. The inspired writers of the Scriptures were chosen and directed by God to preserve as well as to interpret the revelation of God. In this process, however, the scriptural writers were not mechanistic recorders, but God had endowed them with the freedom to use their creative ability to expound the meaning of the revelation.

Thus, both inspiration and revelation have their origins in God. Moreover, inspiration and revelation are correlative terms that together gave birth to the Scripture. However, being inspired by God is not the same as receiving divine revelation; at the same time, being inspired by God is more than just intuitive and aesthetic. This understanding of revelation and inspiration is crucial when it comes to Yahweh's prophets and their prophecies. The prophets had both received divine revelation, and were inspired and creative authors. Thus, it is unfair to reduce prophecy to either an inspired-hermeneutical enterprise or divine revelation. Prophecy is always both.

2.5. Conclusion

In this chapter I have endeavored to articulate critical realism as an epistemological point of view helpful for addressing the issue of true and false prophecy. This approach provides a platform to acknowledge divine revelation—i.e., the kernel of prophecy—as an authentic, subjective knowledge. It also provides the necessary tool in human cognitive theory—i.e., experience, understanding, and judgment—to navigate the discernment of true and false

---

[125] See H. Wheeler Robinson, *Inspiration and Revelation in the Old Testament* (Oxford: Clarendon, 1946), 196; James Barr, *Fundamentalism* (London: SCM, 1977), 131–32.

prophecy. We have seen above in our discussion on revelation and tradition that prophecy at its core is sociological in nature. We will approach these questions on two fronts: (1) what traditions shaped Israel's thinking, and (2) how did Israelite society shape Israel's thinking? It is to that topic we will turn in the next chapter. Specifically, we will be looking to answer the question: what kind of tradition did Israel's prophets embrace?

Chapter 3
YAHWISTIC TRADITION AND ITS DEVELOPMENTS:
A CRITICAL REALIST VIEW

*"Moses received Torah from Sinai and delivered it to Joshua;
Joshua [delivered it] to the elders, the elders to the prophets,
and the prophets delivered it to the men of the Great Assembly."*[1]

3.1. Introduction

The purpose of this chapter is to outline the origin and features of the ancient Israel's Yahwistic tradition from the perspective of critical realism as discussed in chapter two. In doing this, we will be able to locate the matrix of the message of Israel's prophets.

By Yahwistic tradition, I am referring to the religion of ancient Israel, wherein Yahweh as the sole God is emphasized and maintained. There are many evidences in the Bible as well as extra-biblical sources which suggest that the various people and groups in the ancient Israelite society worshipped Yahweh with broader range of beliefs and practices than those that the OT supports. However, this popular religion is not the primary concern of this chapter.

Also by Yahwistic tradition I do not mean the J source whose *siglum* is derived from the German word *Jahweh* (the word for YHWH). In fact, Yahwistic tradition as depicted in the OT is the amalgam of various sources namely J (Yahwist), E (Elohist), P

---

[1] Mishnaic treatise: *pirqê 'abot* chapter 1. Citing it from the Project Gutenberg Ebook produced by Dan Dyckman (2005); cf. Louis Finkelstein, "Introductory Study to Pirke Abot," *JBL* 57 (1938): 13–50.

(priestly material), H (Holiness Code), D (Deuteronomist).[2] These sources have their distinctive traditions and I do not intend to deny or minimize the inner-biblical plurality of views. However, there is no denying the fact that these sources contributed to the notion of Yahwistic tradition. It is within this Yahwistic tradition that the prophetic voices become intelligible and meaningful.

Studying the origin and features of Yahwistic tradition will involve re-orienting our understanding of historiography in light of critical realism. As discussed above, writing history is not just about collecting hard facts and writing without bias.[3] It is, indeed, a combination of hard facts, selective evidences, and narration from one's inclination. For ancient Israel, historiography would then mean writing history from the perspective of their experiences with Yahweh as individuals and a people group.

---

[2] Conventionally, since the work of Julius Wellhausen the Pentateuch has been considered as a book consisting of four sources namely J, E, D, P (i.e., the Documentary Hypothesis). JE sources are considered to be edited and merged sometime after 722 BCE; D material was discovered around 621 BCE; and P material came from the post-exilic time. However, the chronology of the sources is open to discussion and today a sequence of JEP(H)D is favored. See the works of Moshe Weinfeld, *The Place of Law in the Religion of Ancient Israel* (VTSup 100; Leiden: Brill, 2004); and Israel Knohl, *The Santuary of Silence: The Priestly Torah and the Holiness School* (Winona Lake, IN: Eisenbrauns, 2007).

[3] See my discussion above on critical realism, especially Wright's and Abraham's view on history and historiography. It also has to be mentioned here that with the works of Robert Alter, Meir Sternberg and others the literary technique of the Israel's writing has been considerably illumined so much so that ancient Israel's historiography has come to be known as a dovetail of history, art, and theology or ideology. Robert Alter, *The Art of Biblical Narrative* (New York: Basic Books, 1981); Meir Sternberg, *The Poetics of Biblical Narrative: Ideological Literature and the Drama of Reading* (ISBL; Bloomington: Indiana University Press, 1985); Adele Berlin, *Poetics and Interpretation of Biblical Narrative* (BLS 9; Sheffield: Almond, 1983); S. Bar-Efrat, *Narrative Art in the Bible* (BLS 17; Sheffield: Almond, 1989).

Another aspect that has to be clarified while dealing with Yahwistic tradition is the understanding of the role of ancient redactors. In line with the discussion of tradition in chapter two, the writings of ancient Israel, which we have in the OT are an amalgamation of traditions by the scribes.[4] John Van Seters has rigorously argued that sources and traditions of ancient Israel that are believed to be early are actually fictive reconstructions from the Persian period.[5] In a similar way, though with slight differences, David Carr, in his recent work has argued that Israelite texts evolved from one generation to another by means of memory.[6] Carr asserts that the Hebrew Bible is not so much "written in stone" as it is "written in the shifting sand of memory."[7] Moreover, the scribes, while writing, "rarely appropriated earlier compositions in their entirety."[8] As such, the Hebrew texts are not historically reliable.

---

[4] See my discussion above on tradition (77–80).

[5] See John van Seters, *Abraham in History and Tradition* (New Haven: Yale University Press, 1975); idem, *In Search of History: Historiography in the Ancient World and the Origins of Biblical History* (New Haven: Yale University Press, 1983); idem, *Prologue to History: The Yahwist as Historian in Genesis* (Louisville: John Knox, 1992), idem, *The Life of Moses: The Yahwist as Historian in Exodus-Numbers* (Louisville: John Knox, 1994). Other scholars who generally agree with Van Seters conclusion are: Hans Heinrich Schmid, *Der sogenannte Jahwist: Beobachtungen und Fragen zur Pentateuchforschung* (Zürich: Theologischer Verlag, 1976); H. Vorländer, *Die Entstehungszeit des jehowistischen Geschichtswerkes* (Frankfurt am Main: Peter Lang, 1978); M. Rose, *Deuteronomist und Jahwist: Untersuchungen zu den Berührungspunkten beider Literaturwerke*, (ATANT 67; Zürich: Theologischer Verlag, 1981); R.N. Whybray, *The Making of the Pentateuch: A Methodological Study* (Sheffield: Sheffield Academic, 1994).

[6] David M. Carr, *The Formation of the Hebrew Bible: A New Reconstruction* (Oxford: Oxford University Press, 2011), 35.

[7] *Ibid.*, 36.

[8] *Ibid.*, 99.

William M. Schniedewind has cogently outlined the oral culture of Israel in his discussion of when the Bible became a book. He argues that there is a continuum between oral tradition and written tradition. In fact, biblical literature depended on the oral culture of ancient Israelite society before textualization began in the eight century BCE, during the time of King Hezekiah.[9] The oral culture mentality is found in the early writings of the OT, such as Exod 19–20 (the Ten Commandments), where the expression of "writing" down the commandments is not mentioned even once, unlike in the later articulation of the commandments in the book of Deuteronomy (cf. Deut 5:22).[10] Apart from the continuum from oral mentality to the written traditions, one should also give due consideration to what A. Leo Oppenheim calls "the stream of tradition."[11] By this Oppenheim meant that the traditions were studied and transmitted in the scribal school. This argument is similar to what I have argued in chapter two about the deposits of faith. The stream of tradition or the deposits of faith, whether in the oral or writing cultures, were not any one person's property but they firmly belonged to the community. As such, more often than

---

[9] W.M. Schniedewind, *How the Bible Became a Book* (Cambridge: Cambridge University Press, 2004), 1–22, 64–90.

[10] *Ibid.*, 19; See also Susan Niditch, *Oral World and Written Word: Ancient Israelite Literature* (Louisville: Westminster, 1996), 78–88. One can still raise the question concerning the stone tablets as written by the finger of God (Exod 31:18). Schniedewind cogently proposes that the "original contents of the stone tablets written by God seem to have been the divine plans for the tabernacle and Temple. This type of [divine] writing is consistent with the role of writing in early, mostly non-literate societies" (*How the Bible*, 134). It is only after the tabernacle is built that God came to dwell in it, and from here that God spoke the *torah* to Moses. He further contends that Exodus 19–31 reflects Israel's early notion of writing and that the description of the writing of the revelation in Exod 24 is, in fact, inserted by later editor of the text. *Ibid.*, 128–34.

[11] A. Leo Oppenheim, *Ancient Mesopotamia: Portrait of a Dead Civilization* (ed. Erica Reiner; Chicago: Chicago University Press, 1977), 13.

not, the elders in the community acted as guardians to ensure that these traditions were transmitted constructively.

There is no doubt that these traditions have undergone the processes of transcription, compilation, integration, adaptation, expansion and even invention.[12] However, these activities were not done to distort or manipulate the substance of the traditions but to better understand the content as well as to adapt it to a given context. For instance, Karel van der Toorn argues that the present book of Deuteronomy has been subjected to four editions and, yet, the process of edition is very conservative.[13] He postulates that a book such as Deuteronomy was considered Holy Writ and so the occasion for revision, correction, expansion, or supplementation did not come easy.[14] Even when it happened, it was done under strict supervision and the auspices of the priestly leadership.[15] The point is that Yahwistic tradition has its origin in the profound experiences of ancient Israel with Yahweh—i.e., the Patriarchal experiences and the exodus event.[16] It is not a naïve assertion to trace back the origin of Yahwistic tradition to those experiences and event.

The OT is a collection of ancient literature pertaining to faith allegedly as experienced by the Israelites in history. It is, therefore, necessary and significant to respect this truth claim of

---

[12] See the work of Karel van der Toorn, *Scribal Culture and the Making of the Hebrew Bible* (Cambridge: Harvard University Press, 2007), 109–41.

[13] Here the emphasis is on the latter point—conservative editing.

[14] Van der Toorn, *Scribal Culture*, 145.

[15] *Ibid.*, 147–48.

[16] In line with what I have argued, I contend that the final form of the Pentateuch is an outcome of a very long traditioning process that includes both oral and written traditions. Yet, this traditioning processes is not done randomly, rather with care and understanding that it is the revealed word of God. The crucial point here is not necessarily the debate of the early or late dating of the Pentateuch, but the role of the redactors in the traditioning process.

the text before one's predilection takes over its own voice. In other words, and to sum up the above discussion, understanding Yahwistic tradition from the perspective of critical realism would mean first, acknowledgment that there is meaning in the text; second, it would require realigning one's understanding of history—history as dovetail of literature, theology and historical event; and finally, acknowledging the role of divine revelation in the unfolding of Yahwistic tradition just as expressed in the pages of the Scripture.

3.2. Yahwistic Tradition: Its Origin and Features

The debate of the origin of Yahwism has been broadly divided into the American archaeological school (Albright and his students) and the German tradition-historical school (Noth and his students). The former seeks to relate the origin of Yahwism to the Canaanite religion as depicted in the Ugaritic materials (from Ras Shamra), whereas the latter finds the genesis of Yahwism in the awe-inspiring experience of the exodus.

Frank Moore Cross, a student of Albright, was greatly involved in comparative studies to show that Yahweh is none other than the evolution of Canaanite high god El. Cross argues that the traits and features of El are reflected in the earliest tradition of Yahweh and, thus, Yahweh was originally the cultic name of El. The spilt of Yahwism from El came to fruition in the radical differentiation of the cult of early Israel.[17] Moreover, Cross contends that Yahwism absorbed and transformed many mythic features of Baal into its cultic worship up until the ninth century BCE. However, this eventually bloomed into a full-fledged syncretism which, as we find it in the OT, was vehemently opposed by the prophets.[18]

---

[17] F.M. Cross, *Canaanite Myth and Hebrew Epic: Essays in the History of the Religion of Israel* (Cambridge: Harvard University Press, 1973), 71.

[18] *Ibid.*, 190–91.

Cross' notion of Yahweh as the deity evolved out of the Canaanite gods, El and Baal, is chiefly informed by his understanding of ancient Israelite literature as epic cycle.[19] The genre of epic cycle, according to Cross, is different from the Canaanite cosmogonic myth. Israel's epic cycle was shaped by the historical experiences (i.e., Exodus-Sinai-Conquest experiences) as well as the mythic language and worldview of Canaan. Cross states, "In Israel, myth and history always stood in strong tension, myth serving primarily to give a cosmic dimension and transcendent meaning to the historical, rarely functioning to dissolve history."[20]

In this manner, Cross depicts the continuity of ancient Israel and Canaanite religions. By doing this, Cross synthesized two differing genres, namely myth and history which ultimately are bases of two different worldviews (see below). It is one thing to argue that the Israelites used a form of Canaanite religion to express their unique understanding of God; it is quite another to assert that the Israelites fully assimilated the content of her neighbors to express their religion.[21] If Cross is correct, then in essence Israel's worldview is one and the same with that of the Canaanite's worldview. To be fair, Cross' works have provided a frame of reference for the patriarchal period. However, his attempt

---

[19] *Ibid.*, viii–ix.

[20] *Ibid.*, 90.

[21] It has to be noted that one can be rightfully critical about how form and content of a worldview or story or religious ritual can be fully separated—is it not that the content and form are inextricably tied to one another? I think the answer is yes, especially, if we answer that question from our present religious context where almost every religion is fully developed. However, I still think the distinction of form and content can be achieved and utilized in certain circumstances. For instance, a writer can rhetorically utilize this distinction in order to accentuate his point. Also a missionary pioneer can utilize the form of the native non-Christian religion to drive home his/her Christian message simply because the indigenous populations have not developed the cognitive-vocabulary of the new religion.

to explain away the religion of Israel purely from a human perspective without giving a proper place for the role of divine revelation has led him to a conclusion that neglects the text's own claims about itself.

Mark Smith in recent times has done an impressive comparative study of Israelite and Canaanite religions.[22] He argues that the consensus that the Israelite religion fell into syncretism is not founded.[23] Rather, he points out that Israel's culture was akin to that of the Canaan's culture and so was polytheistic in its outlook.[24] One implication of this understanding is that Israel actually worshipped Baal, and that the goddess Asherah was the consort of Yahweh.[25] His contention is that the emergence of Israelite's monolatry (i.e., worshiping Yahweh alone but not ignoring the existence of other gods) was, in fact, Israel's breaking away from its Canaanite past.[26] Smith argues that his conclusion is the result of new archaeological and epigraphic discoveries. However, it has to be noted that archaeological and epigraphic discoveries are meaningless unless aided by interpretation, and interpretation

---

[22] See Mark S. Smith, *The Early History of God: Yahweh and the Other Deities in Ancient Israel* (San Francisco: Harper & Row, 1990); idem, "Yahweh and Other Deities in Ancient Israel: Observations on Old Problems and Recent Trends," in *Ein Gott allein? JHWH-Verehrung und biblischer Monotheismus im Kontext der israelitischen und altorientalischen Religionsgeschichte* (ed. W. Dietrich and M.A. Klopfenstein; OBO 139; Göttingen: Vanderhoeck & Ruprecht, 1994), 197–234; idem, *The Origins of Biblical Monotheism: Israel's Polytheistic Background and the Ugaritic Texts* (Oxford: Oxford University Press, 2001); idem, *The Memoirs of God: History, Memory, and the Experience of the Divine in Ancient Israel* (Minneapolis: Augsburg Fortress, 2004).

[23] Smith, *The Early History of God*, xix–xx.

[24] *Ibid.*, xxiii.

[25] See also the work of William Dever, *Did God have a Wife? Archaeological and Folk Religion in Ancient Israel* (Grand Rapids: Eerdmans, 2005).

[26] Smith, *The Early History of God*, xxiii.

sometimes can be solely directed by one's own subjective imagination.[27] Oswalt argues that no new discoveries or data have been excavated since 1950s, but that it is "prior theological and philosophical convictions that account for the change."[28] Another problem with Smith's work is his lack of acknowledgment of Israel's worldview. It is this worldview that, in fact, provides the deeper sense of any society, culture, and religion.

Worldview is the grid through which humans perceive and interpret reality. It is among the "ultimate concerns" of human beings that one finds worldview.[29] According to Christopher J.H. Wright, "a worldview is a comprehensive set of assumptions that a person or culture makes in answer to several fundamental

---

[27] Archaeology in the field of biblical studies has evolved in time. Biblical archaeology in the early twentieth century functioned in the traditional cultural-historical archaeological mode wherein emphasis was placed on reconstructing history. In the early 1960s a mode of archaeological study developed which is termed as "processual archaeology" or new archaeology. It was an attempt to make archaeological studies more scientific emphasizing anthropological and statistical and systems analyses. As a reaction to this, in the late 1980s and early 1990s interpretive archaeology took shape. Some of its main tenets are: a contextual concern that emphasizes the natural and socio-cultural environment; the role of the archaeologist in terms of interpreting meaning is explicitly recognized; archaeological study is provisional and so contingent on further discoveries. See Lester L. Grabbe, *Ancient Israel: What Do We Know and How Do We Know It?* (London: T&T Clark, 2007), 6–10.

[28] John N. Oswalt, *The Bible Among the Myths: Unique Revelation or Just Ancient Literature?* (Grand Rapids: Zondervan, 2009), 12. In the same vein Bill T. Arnold argues that Smith's contention is not necessarily discoveries of new epigraphic evidences but rather it is the changed scholarly perspective—see "Religion in Ancient Israel," in *The Faces of Old Testament Studies: A Survey of Contemporary Approaches* (ed. David W. Baker and Bill T. Arnold; Grand Rapids: Baker, 1999), 391–420.

[29] Wright, *New Testament and the People of God*, 122.

questions that face humans everywhere."[30] These fundamental questions are: Where are we? Who are we? What's gone wrong? Where's the solution? The answers to these concerns can be profoundly theological in nature as they touch the issues of our very human existence, questions of whether god exists or not, and if god exists how does one relate to this world, and what is the purpose of human existence? In short, worldview is the lens through which a society perceives and interprets its very existence.

Yehezkel Kaufmann and, later, Oswalt have cogently argued that the Canaanite religion was based on the mythical worldview, whereas the Israelite's worldview was based on the transcendence of God and history.[31] According to Oswalt, the mythical worldview is not about primitive thinking, rather it is simply a way of thinking.[32] Mythical worldview is characterized by "continuity" thinking where god, nature, and human beings are continuous with each other.[33] In other words, "the divine is materially as well as spiritually identical with the psycho-socio-physical universe that we know."[34] One of the marks of this thinking is polytheism and since divine, nature, and humans are coterminous, humans can manipulate the gods. Another element of this thinking is that there are no ethical boundaries because what one god might like another might hate. In contrast to this, Israel's worldview was marked by the belief in a creator God who is utterly other than his creation. However, this transcendent God, although distinct from his creation, intervenes in history to redeem his creatures.[35] This God

---

[30] Christopher J.H. Wright, *Old Testament for the People of God* (Downers Grove: InterVarsity, 2004), 17.

[31] Y. Kaufmann, *The Religion of Israel* (trans. M. Greenberg; Chicago: University of Chicago Press, 1960); Oswalt, *The Bible*.

[32] Oswalt, *The Bible*, 47.

[33] *Ibid.*, 43. See also Kaufmann, *The Religion of Israel*, 1–150.

[34] Oswalt, *The Bible*, 43.

[35] *Ibid.*, 63–84.

cannot be manipulated, rather, he is a covenantal God who provides specific ethical norms in order to maintain that covenantal relationship with his people.

Of course, this understanding of Israel's worldview does not mean that ancient Israel was insulated from her milieu. Instead, the Israelite ancestors assumed "continuity" thinking until the transcendent God broke into their lives and revealed himself to them (see Gen 12). However, for Israel, as a people group, the "exodus" made an undeniable impression upon their lives. In fact, Israel consolidated its worldview in the exodus experience. The Israelite worldview began to take shape in the experiences of the patriarchs; however, it was the exodus event that enabled the Israelites to have a deeper experience of Yahweh which reaffirmed their forefathers' experiences as well as laid the foundation for their future. Exod 6:2–8 highlights this point.

In this passage, Yahweh tells Moses that he appeared to his forefathers as God Almighty (אל שדי) and that he did not make himself known to them with the name Yahweh (v. 2).[36] However, interestingly, the name Yahweh does appear in Genesis (see 4:26; 15:2). Moreover, the opening statement, "I am Yahweh," appears three times in this passage which can be understood as saying, "remember I am Yahweh." Nahum M. Sarna states that such identification would lack meaning if no one has heard the name before. He points out that this opening address was common in Northwest Semitic royal inscriptions such as, "I am Mesha," "I am

---

[36] This passage especially v. 3, has created endless discussion, explains the revealing of the name Yahweh. According to source criticism this passage belongs to P source. The critical theory of the nineteenth century argues revealing of the name YHWH in terms of the evolution of Israel's religion. Thus, the patriarch God revealed himself as *El Shaddai*, whereas to Moses and Israel he revealed himself as YHWH. For more discussion on this see Brevard S. Child, *The Book of Exodus: A Critical, Theological Commentary* (OTL; Philadelphia: Westminster, 1974), 111–14.

Shalmaneser," "I am Esarhaddon."[37] Therefore, what does this mean? In Hebrew, names are more than a label; they function as features of person's character.[38] Thus, when Yahweh declares that he is going to make himself known to them by the name Yahweh, he means that he will reveal himself to Israel as he had never before (cf. Ezek 20:5). This is in anticipation to Yahweh's mighty act of Exodus (Exod 6:7). Moreover, note that this passage has ten first-person verbs that relate to the past, present and future. They depict how Yahweh made covenant with Israel's ancestors (v. 4), how he has heard Israel's groan (v. 5), and how he will redeem them and fulfill the promise made with their ancestors (vv. 6–8). Thus, the exodus event consolidated Yahweh's relationship with Israel as well as shaped the way forward.

3.2.1. Israelites' Response to Yahweh's Saving Grace

The theme of Exodus—i.e, Yahweh delivering Israel from slavery in Egypt—is the most prominent theme in the OT. This event is reflected in the hymns, historical narratives, and legal documents of the OT. Noth claims that this theme is the "primary confession (*Urbekenntnis*) of Israel" and the "kernel of the whole subsequent Pentateuchal tradition."[39] Exod 15, which is a hymn (the so-called "Song of the sea"), captures the awe-exalted experience of the Exodus event in the lives of the Israelites. This

---

[37] Nahum M. Sarna, *Exodus: The JPS Torah Commentary* (Philadelphia: The Jewish Publication Society, 1991), 31.

[38] Some other aspects of God revealing his name are: To set him apart from other gods; to identify himself with a community and within history; to enter into an intimate relationship and, thus, make himself exposed to vulnerability. See Terence E. Fretheim, "Yahweh," *NIDOTTE* 4:1297.

[39] Martin Noth, *A History of Pentateuchal Traditions* (ed. and trans. B.W. Anderson; Englewood Cliffs: Prentice-Hall, 1972), 49.

song is one of the earliest materials found in the OT.[40] This song is conventionally divided into two sections: verses 1–12 form the first section which in content looks backward, while verses 13–18 look forward. Oswalt points out that the first twelve verses can be further divided into two sections, according to the usage of the personal pronouns.[41] First, verses 1–5 dwell on the first-person pronoun portraying the affirmation of personal faith in God. Second, in verses 6–12, Yahweh is addressed in the second person pronoun with a continuing contrast between him and his enemies.

The first five verses affirm the personal faith of the Israelite. Prior to this event, each Israelite had encountered God personally and knew him as the God of the ancestors. But now, he is "my God" (15:2). He is the God of Israel. This affirmation of Yahweh as their personal God continues in the verses 6–12, although in the second person pronoun. Here Yahweh is exalted as the one and only God in contrast to the Pharaoh and his army. It is in this experience of exodus that Israel, as a nation, became deeply impressed that there was no other god like Yahweh. Thus, they could sing: "Who is like you, O LORD, among the gods?" (v. 11).[42]

Verses 13–18 look forward to the future where Yahweh will carry the Israelites to the promised land. The word חסד in v. 13 has a special meaning in Hebrew and provides a good expression for the whole story of Israel in relationship with Yahweh.[43] This word has no direct cognate in other Semitic languages. It is generally

---

[40] Cross dates this to the late twelfth century or early eleventh century BCE. Cross, *Canaanite Myth and Hebrew Bible*, 124.

[41] Allen Ross and John N. Oswalt, *Genesis, Exodus* (Carol Stream: Tyndale, 2005), 395.

[42] Sarna, *Exodus*, 79.

[43] Gordon R. Clark asserts, "חֶסֶד is peculiarly and distinctively a Hebrew word." Clark, *The Word Hesed in the Hebrew Bible* (JSOTSup 157; Sheffield: Sheffield Academic, 1993), 267.

translated as faithfulness, steadfast love, or kindness. However, its semantic field cannot be connoted or represented by a single English word. To fully understand it, it must be translated in a sentence. In that regard it means a superior showing undeserving love to his or her inferior subject.⁴⁴ This whole poem is about an undeserving love that Yahweh showed to Israel. Just as Yahweh delivered Israel from Egypt, so also because of his חסד, will he eventually lead them to Canaan. None of the neighboring people such as Edomites, Philistines, Moabites, and Canaanites will be able to challenge Israel. Instead they will melt away by the gracious power of Yahweh displayed through Israel (vv. 14–15).

This song, therefore, embodies Israel's theological expression of Yahweh and their hopeful aspirations in Yahweh. Moreover, this song signifies how the exodus event became the cornerstone for Israel. It is indicated by the echo of v. 2 of the song, "The Lord is my strength and my might, and he has become my salvation" in books like Psalms (18:1–2; 118:14), Isaiah (12:2), and Habakkuk (3:18–19).

---

⁴⁴ See K.D. Sakenfeld, *The Meaning of Hesed in the Hebrew Bible: A New Enquiry* (HSM 17; Missoula: Scholars Press, 1978), 234. Sakenfeld's work contradicts the work of her predecessor, N. Glueck who defines חסד within the context of covenant but having a reciprocal and mutual relationship between the two parties of the covenant treaty—see N. Glueck, *Ḥesed in the Bible* (trans. A. Gottschalk; Cincinnati: Hebrew Union College, 1967)]. In the OT, חסד is chiefly portrayed as the character of Yahweh, although the act of חסד also takes place in the human plane—see D.A. Baer and R.P. Gordon, "חֶסֶד," *NIDOTTE* 2:211–18; Zobel, "חֶסֶד," *TDOT* 5:44–64; H.J. Stoebe, "חֶסֶד," *TLOT* 2:449–64). Yahweh's persistence with the Israelites, in spite of their countless rebellions, demonstrates that חסד is an enduring character of Yahweh. This quality of Yahweh also makes him punish the Israelites so as to bring them to himself. Furthermore, Yahweh expects his people to imitate this character quality of his, even though, as Morris rightly contends, "In men it is the ideal; in God it is the actual" (L.L. Morris, *Testament of Love* [Grand Rapids: Eerdmans, 1981], 81).

3.2.2. Yahweh's Further Revelation

In the exodus event, Yahweh revealed his providential care to Israel and entered into covenantal relationship (also known as Sinaitic covenant) with the Israelites as a people group. However, in order to enter into covenant relationship with his people and to nurture them, he had to reveal more. The Decalogue (20:1–17) and the Book of the Covenant (21:18–23:33) fulfill this further revelation of Yahweh, which reveals chiefly his character. This revelation of Yahweh contains the principles upon which the Yahwistic tradition was established. The exodus event provided the basis for Yahweh to enter into covenant with Israel as a people group (19:5–6).

In relation to this, Oswalt argues that the purpose of the exodus was not merely to release the Israelites from the Egyptian slavery but that "God might bring the Israelites to himself" (see Exod 19:4).[45] Chapter 19 narrates the account of how Yahweh prepares the Israelites in order to receive the terms of the covenant, as recorded in Exod 20:1–23:33.[46] The form of this covenant closely

---

[45] Ross and Oswalt, *Genesis, Exodus*, 432.

[46] According to conventional source analysis, Exodus 19–24 consists of J, E, and P sources. So, for instance, because of the combination Moses appeared to have commuted up and down Sinai on numerous occasions, P's account is considered rather scanty (19:1; 24:15b–18a)—see William H.C. Propp, *Exodus 19–40: A New Translation with Introduction and Commentary* (AB; New York: Doubleday, 2006), 150–54. Otto Eissfeldt also argues that the Decalogue and the Book of the Covenant disrupt the flow of the narrative and therefore, are secondary additions to the narrative that once existed without it—see *The Old Testament: An Introduction* (trans. P.R. Ackroyd; New York: Harper & Row, 1965), 213-19. Furthermore Martin Noth contends that the Decalogue is secondary to the Book of Covenant—see *Exodus: A Commentary* (OTL; Philadelphia: Westminster, 1962), 154. However, Joe M. Sprinkle shows from a synchronic-literary perspective that the awkwardness of the flow of the whole section (Exod 19–24) is the result of a literary technique called

reflects the Hittite suzerainty covenants of the late-second millennium BCE.[47] Thus, Exod 20:1 begins with the introduction

---

synoptic/resumptive-repitition. Thus, he argues that this section is in a chiastic structure:
    A Narrative, the Covenant offered (ch. 19)
      B General regulations, the Decalogue (20:1–17)
        C Narrative, People's fear of God (20:18–21)
      B' Specific regulations (20:22–23: 33)
    A' Narrative, the Covenant consummated (ch. 24)
(see Sprinkle, *'The Book of the Covenant': A literary Approach* [JSOTSup 174; Sheffield: JSOT, 1994], 19–27). It has to be noted that the content of the Exodus 20–24 reflects ancient Near Eastern case laws prior to the monarchical period—see Ross-Oswalt, *Genesis, Exodus*, 471; Paul D. Hanson, *The People Called: The Growth of Community in the Bible* (New York: Harper & Row, 1987), 43.

[47] George E. Mendenhall first brought this to our attention—see "Covenant Forms in Israelite Tradition," *BA* 17 (1954): 50–76. However, this was rigorously contested in the works of Lothar Perlitt and Ernst Kutsch—see L. Perlitt, *Bundestheologie im Alten Testament* (WMANT 36; Neukirchen-Vluyn: Neukirchener Verlag, 1969); Ernst Kutsch, *Verheißung und Gesetz: Untersuchungen zum Sogenannten "Bund" im Alten Testament* (BZAW 131; Berlin: de Gruyter, 1973). They independently argued that Israel's covenant between Israel and Yahweh was a theologoumenon constructed in the late pre-exilic period. Besides these works, Dennis J. McCarthy, later supported by Moshe Weinfeld, argued that the Israelite covenant reflects rather the neo-Assyrian *adê* (vassal treaty)—see D.J. McCarthy, *Treaty and Covenant* (AnBib 21; Rome: Pontifical Biblical Institute, 1963); M. Weinfeld, *Deuteronomy and the Deuteronomic School* (Oxford: Oxford University Press, 1972). However, the vassal treaty, *adê*, of the Neo-Assyrian is actually a "loyalty oath" imposed on (as opposed to committing) to her vassal—see Hayim Tadmor, "Treaty and Oath in Ancient Near East: A Historian's Approach," in *Humanizing America's Iconic Book: Society of Biblical Literature Centennial Addresses 1980* (ed. Gene M. Tucker and Douglas A. Knight; Chico, CA: Scholars Press, 1980), 127–52. Thus, the Neo-Assyrian *adê* is a harsh treaty wherein the sovereign does not bind himself to the subject, rather the sovereign demands an unconditional commitment on the part of the vassal. This harshness of the treaty does reflect the curse list found in Deut 28. However, it has to be noted that Deut 28 also records blessings to those who maintain the covenant. Moreover, Tadmor has convincingly argued that the Neo-Assyrian *adê* is, in fact, borrowed from the

identifying the speaker. Exod 20:2 is the historical prologue that provides the basis for the making of the covenant, while Exod 20:3–23:33 deals with the stipulations. One of the reasons for this form of covenant is to provide a historical context to the covenant between Yahweh and Israel. This is in direct contrast to that of mythical genre where history is not significant.[48] This form also suggests that Yahweh is the suzerain head of Israel.[49] Yet, even though Yahweh is the suzerain of this covenant, he is interestingly not the conqueror or the oppressor; rather he is the deliverer of Israel from slavery as the expression of חסד.

It is this aspect that makes this covenant profoundly different from the other ANE vassal treaties. Sarna calls this covenant unique because nowhere else can one find such a relationship of commitment between a god and his people.[50] The stipulations in the covenant were not merely ethical requirements, but they were designed to maintain the relationship between Yahweh and Israel, and to transform Israel in the light of Yahweh's own image.[51] As

---

Arameans when Tiglath Pileser III defeated them in 732 BCE, and thus was converted into an effective, often brutal instrument of domination. Tadmor asserts, "by the way of the Aramaic intermediaries, the Neo-Assyrian *adê* documents continued the highly developed Syro-Anatolian and possibly also North Mesopotamian second millennium traditions" (Tadmor, *Treaty and Oath*, 145). Thus, the Neo-Assyrian's vassal treaty is but a modified version of the form of the Hittite's vassal treaty. For more information about the relationship between Israelites' covenant and Hittite's vassal treaty—see K.A. Kitchen, *On the Reliability of the Old Testament* (Grand Rapids: Eerdmans, 2003), 283–94.

[48] Ross-Oswalt, *Genesis, Exodus*, 439.

[49] *Ibid.*

[50] Sarna, *Exodus*, 102–3.

[51] The stipulations are not mere ethical requirements but should be understood as a response to YHWH's gracious act, namely, the deliverance of Israel from Egypt. In other words, there is no distinction between grace (or gospel) and law *contra* Gerhard von Rad who is of the view that the connection between Exodus and law-giving themes in the Pentateuch is to be considered secondary—see von Rad, "The Form-Critical Problem of the Hexateuch," in *The*

such this covenant touches every aspect of Israel's life: social, religious, politic, economic, and personal.

The covenant stipulations are divided into two parts: the Decalogue (20:3–17), and the examples that explain the principles in real life situations (20:22–23:33). The first four stipulations of the Decalogue (20:3–8) underline the Israelites' worldview. This worldview is diametrically opposed to the existing mythological worldview, namely that Yahweh is wholly distinct from this world. Thus, Yahweh declares that Israel cannot have any other gods besides him (v. 3). Hanson asserts, "Even as the Decalogue was the crown on the entire corpus of *tôrâ* in the Pentateuch, the first commandment was the jewel in that crown."[52] Furthermore verses 4 and 7–8 oppose the mythical-polytheistic worldview. Yahweh says he cannot be carved into an idol (v. 4), his name cannot be misused—i.e., he cannot be manipulated according to one's own wish and desire outside the covenant relationship (v. 7). The former indicates that Yahweh transcends the world, whereas the latter suggest that Yahweh is not a projection of human anxieties. Moreover, verse 8 affirms the transcendental nature of Yahweh. By instructing Israel to rest on the seventh/Sabbath day, Yahweh is declaring that he is in control of nature and he is the originator of the cosmos.[53]

The remaining six stipulations (20:8–17) deal with how the Israelites should live with one another. Yahweh is a relational God and his people must imbibe this aspect of his nature. Thus, the love for one's family (20:12) as well as for neighbors (20:13–17) should

---

Problem of the Hexateuch and Other Essays (trans. E.W. Trueman Dicken; New York: McGraw-Hill, 1966), 1–78. Paul Hanson asserts, "Deliverance originating in divine grace and obedience based on the human response of gratitude were indivisible aspects of Israel's primal experience as a people" (Hanson, *The People Called*, 57).

[52] *Ibid.*
[53] Sarna, *Exodus*, 111.

spring out from the personal and corporate relationships the Israelites had with Yahweh.

The application of the Decalogue in practice is found in Exod 20:22–23:33. These are called the מִשְׁפָּטִים, which is often translated as the statutes, ordinances, rules, law or judgment.[54] These מִשְׁפָּטִים provide for Israel a basis for practicing מִשְׁפָּט (righteousness) which embodies Yahweh's will.[55] Thus, when Israel reflects these מִשְׁפָּטִים in their praxis they dwell in Yahweh's מִשְׁפָּט; however, when מִשְׁפָּט is distorted, it is most certainly because Israel has not kept the מִשְׁפָּטִים. This results in breaking the covenant relationship between Israel and Yahweh. In relation to this, Hemchand Gossai writes: "They are not a detached set of norms…. They must be seen within the context of the covenant relationship, as claims and expectations of that relationship."[56] Thus, מִשְׁפָּטִים are not mere legal rules or ordinances but they flow out of covenantal obligations. They are

---

[54] מִשְׁפָּטִים is the plural form of מִשְׁפָּט meaning civil laws—see Peter Enns, "מִשְׁפָּט," *NIDOTTE* 2:1142–44.

[55] The word מִשְׁפָּט is also found in other ANE contexts such as in Ugarit and Phoenicia, with the meaning government or authority. In OT this word occurs 422 times, occurring most frequently in the prophetic writings (144 times). The noun מִשְׁפָּט is derived from the verb שָׁפַט (to judge). Thus, the meaning of this noun certainly lies in the area of justice, judgment, and law (see B. Johnson, "מִשְׁפָּט," *TDOT* 9:86–98). However, מִשְׁפָּט encompasses a variety of meanings. For instance, in Num 27:21, it means "decision," in the book of Exodus it means "law, commandment," and in 2 Kgs 17:26, it means custom (*ibid.*, 9:87, 94). Moreover, when someone keeps the מִשְׁפָּטִים, מִשְׁפָּט shall flow—in this case מִשְׁפָּט carries the meaning of "what is right and proper, and righteousness" (*ibid.*, 96). Thus, the noun also means righteousness. This discussion shows that the meaning of מִשְׁפָּט has no standard meaning but has to be considered according to the context of the text. Enns contends that in the prophetic literature מִשְׁפָּט is mostly used to express the "topic of the breach of justice" by the corrupt leaders of Israel (Isa 1:7, 21; 5:7; 10:2; 59:8–9; Hab 1:4) as well as by the people (Jer 5:1; 7:5)—see Enns, *NIDOTTE* 2:1142–44.

[56] Hemchand Gossai, *Justice, Righteousness and the Social Critique of the Eighth–Century Prophets* (New York: Peter Lang, 1993), 177.

the customs of the Yahwistic tradition and from משפטים flow משפט and צדק (justice).⁵⁷

The משפטים in Exod 20:22–23:33 are casuistic or case law in character. However, these casuistic laws are by no means exhaustive; they are a sample of how to apply the Decalogue in action. Many of these case laws are similar to other ANE laws indicating that Israel was indeed existing within her historical milieu. However, these laws corrected, modified, or affirmed the existing laws. The casuistic laws begin with law about worshiping Yahweh (20:23–26). The second theme of the casuistic laws relates to treatment of slaves (21:1–11). In other ANE contexts there are laws that addressed the slave treatment, but certainly not at the beginning of an important treaty.⁵⁸ The reason that Israel's slavery laws are toward the beginning of the covenant stipulations is probably to remind that they themselves were slaves not long ago and that it was imperative that they treat slaves humanely.

---

⁵⁷ Although rare in Akkadian literature, this word is found in other ANE literature such as Ugaritic, and Phoenician inscription. Another comparable word to צדק is Egypt's *maat*. The term does not merely mean truth but it invokes questions such as: What is right? What is correct? See B. Johnson, "sdq," *TDOT* 12:243–64; also David J. Reimer "sdq," *NIDOTTE* 3:744–69. In the OT, the root צדק occurs 525 times and it is regularly connected to human behavior in relation to an assumed standard. It can be simply translated as justice. It is also frequently juxtapose with the word משפט. However, semantically משפט is attached to words such as decision, judgment, and law, whereas צדק alludes to the principle of what is correct and right (B. Johnson, "sdq," *TDOT* 12:248). In fact, the pair of צדק/ צדקה (the feminine form) and משפט often form a hendiadys designating God's order in Israelite society. The kings of Israel in particular and the people in general are to observe God's order in the land by living according to that order (*ibid.*, 260). It is no surprise that the usage of צדק among the writing prophets in the OT revolves around the maintenance of relationship between God and people (see David J. Reimer "sdq," *NIDOTTE* 3:754).

⁵⁸ Ross-Oswalt, *Genesis, Exodus*, 453–54.

Thus, these מׁשפטים portray the compassionate character of Yahweh. They deal with how the Israelites should treat the foreigners (22:21), widows, orphans (22:22–24), and poor (22:25–27). These groups of people are by nature weak, vulnerable, and easy prey for exploitation and extortion. The form of the law concerning this group of people is apodictic, indicating the utmost importance of taking care of them. Again the basis of this law is grounded in the fact that Israel herself was in slavery in Egypt. As Hanson points out: "The moral quality that was to be the hallmark of the Yahwistic community was derived from memory of a specific event in the past, the condition of homelessness in Egypt."[59] Such laws pertaining to the weak in the community are not exclusive to Israel. In fact, it can be found in the prologue of the Code of Hammurabi, too.[60] However, in the Code of Hammurabi the law is loosely directed to the king whereas, in the Book of the Covenant this law is specifically directed to the whole worshipping community.

3.2.3. The Land as Israel's נחלה *(Inheritance)*

These מׁשפטים were not just revealed and given to Israel for the sake of keeping merely as a theoretical concept. Rather, this was necessary in order to maintain the covenantal relationship between Israel and Yahweh, but also because Yahweh was about to provide in the near future the Promised Land to the Israelites—the promise that Yahweh gave to the Israelites' ancestors. The economy of the Promised Land was such that, although the land was given to the Israelites, the land still belongs to Yahweh. It has to be mentioned that the motif of deities owning lands is quite popular in the

---

[59] Hanson, *People Called*, 46.

[60] Bill T. Arnold and Bryan E. Beyer, *Reading from the Ancient Near East: Primary Sources for Old Testament Study* (Grand Rapids: Baker Academic, 2002), 111–14.

context of ancient Near East. The Ugaritic tablets of the Late Bronze age indicate this.[61] Ancient Near Easterners believed that deities possessed lands and demanded devotion from the people living in the land. Israel's understanding was different, however. For the Israelites, it was Yahweh who elected them from outside the Promised Land and brought them there to enjoy the covenantal relationship.

Two factors need to be pointed out concerning the land as Israel's נחלה. First, the land belongs to Yahweh alone. It is in this land that the Israelites were to worship Yahweh and observe Yahweh's משפטים. Second, in reflection to Yahweh's משפטים, the land was to be equally divided among the tribes of Israel (Josh 11:23), which was to be divided further equally among the clans and families (Josh 13:23; 15:20; 14:13–14; 17:3–4; 19:49–50). The land was not a property to be sold or bought. It was Yahweh's property given to Israel as נחלה. This was in contradistinction to other ANE contexts where land was considered as property purely in an economic sense.[62]

In such contexts the result was the amassing of real estate by the rich and powerful which, consequently, led to the further impoverishment of the weak and poor. This understanding of land as נחלה provided the people with the economic provision for each Israelite family. Thus, every family guarded its land inheritance as God's endowment which nobody could snatch away from them. In Num 27, the rights of family land are elaborated. If a father dies without a son then the inheritance of his land would go to his daughters, and if he had no daughter, then the inheritance will pass

---

[61] See CTA 1.III.1; 3.F.16; 4.VIII.14; 5.II.16; also see KTU 1.1.III; 1.3; 1.4.VIII; 1.5.II.

[62] Some biblical passages reflect this purely economic sense. For instance, King David purchased the hill of Samaria from the Jebusite Araunah (2 Sam 24:25) and King Omri purchased from the Canaanite noble, Shemen (1 Kgs 16:24).

to his father's brothers.⁶³ Snatching or forcing someone to sell the family inherited land meant distorting Yahweh's מִשְׁפָּטִים. This dynamic of land as נחלה is played out in the story of Naboth and King Ahab (1 Kgs 21) wherein the king, influenced by his foreign wife, Jezebel, killed Naboth and forcefully stole the latter's land. This invoked Yahweh's judgment, foretold by Elijah and later enacted by Jehu.

3.2.4. Summary of Observations

Yahweh is a transcendent God wholly other from this world. Yet he chose to intervene in history, first to the Israelites' ancestors and later by delivering the Israelites from the Egyptian slavery. In this, Yahweh declared to the Israelites that he is the one and only true God, and thereby laid the foundation to enter into covenantal relationship with the Israelites as a nation. The profound aspect of this covenantal relationship is that, although Yahweh is the suzerain head who established the covenant treaty, he is totally committed to developing Israel as a nation. Yet this does not mean that Yahweh has compromised his sovereignty. He remains the ultimate authority of Israel and the Israelites have to keep the covenant treaty in order to flourish as a nation. This understanding is intrinsic to the Yahwistic tradition.

---

⁶³ Archaeological evidence of an inscribed potshard, called the "widow's plea" ostracon from the period of eight and seventh century BCE demonstrates the biblical view of the importance of preserving the family land. This evidence actually uses the term "נחלה." The shard is a letter of petition from a widow to a royal official. The widow writes that part of her family's land has passed on to her brother-in-law. Although in the letter she requests the official to consider her situation by providing part of her husband's inherited land, this letter clearly shows that the land of the family is preserved. See Pierre Bordreuil, F. Israel, and D. Pardee, "King's Command and Widow's Plea: Two New Hebrew Ostraca of the Biblical Period," *NEA* 61 (1998): 2–13.

In the stipulations of the covenant treaty, it becomes clear that the Israelites were to imitate Yahweh's compassion by treating the foreigner, widow, orphan, and poor compassionately. In doing this, the Israelites could establish righteousness and justice in the land. These demands of Yahweh were not mere ethical requirements constructed by the Israelites. Rather these demands stem from the story of the exodus. The Israelites have learned first-hand the providential care of Yahweh in the exodus event and this act of Yahweh has become their salvation. These ethical stipulations are sign of worship in response to the great act of Yahweh. The moment the Israelites reduce these stipulations to mere ethical requirements devoid of relationship with Yahweh, their worship would go astray. These understandings provided the impetus to nurture the Yahwistic tradition.

Another important factor of the Yahwistic tradition is the concept of נחלה. Although the land was given to Israel as נחלה, its ultimate ownership belongs to Yahweh. This indicates for the Israelites that there is only one God and that the land is not mere commodity that can be bought and sold. Moreover, the dynamic of land reflects the just and compassionate characteristics of Yahweh. Every Israelite's tribe was allotted a plot of land where they could work for their living. In this way, the social structure of the Yahwistic society was ordered in an egalitarian manner.

3.3. Yahwism, Monarchy, and Prophecy

Once Israel occupied the Promised Land, the model of governance was signified by a mixture of *amphictyony* (sacral league) and *symmachies* (military league) models.[64] The tribes of

---

[64] N.P. Lemche points out that there were three primary types of leagues in Greek classical material: *amphictyony* (sacral league), *sympoliteia* (political league) and *symmachies* (military league)—see "The Greek Amphictyony:

Israel dwelled in their own allotted territories, and their social system was characterized by a segmented system.⁶⁵ This segmented tribal system of Israel had no centralized government. Rather, people lived in an agricultural society within an extended family/בית אב setting. A בית אב usually consisted of three or four generations of extended family headed by the father of the household, and it was a primary and self-sufficient social and economic unit. In spite of this loosely connected and self-sufficient existence, the tribes of Israel were united by the worship of Yahweh that stemmed from the exodus experience as well as by the military need to protect one another from their neighboring enemies. In this way, Israel's segmented society had qualities like that of the Greek's *amphictyonic* and *symmachies* societies.⁶⁶

These qualities are reflected in the Song of Deborah (Judg 5). This song is considered one of the earliest traditions that preserved the *modus operandi* of the early Yahwistic community.⁶⁷ It

---

Could it be a Prototype for the Israelite Society in the Period of the Judges?" *JSOT* 4 (1977): 48–59.

⁶⁵ In a segmented social system, a tribe is further divided into clans, and families. An individual in such social system can intersect between families and clans. So for instance, Israelite society during the period of Iron Age I was divided into מטה/שבט (tribe) which was further divided into משפחה (clan) and בית אב (extended family). See Paula McNutt, *Reconstructing the Society of Ancient Israel* (London: SPCK, 1999), 75–94; see also S. Bendor, *The Social Structure of Ancient Israel* (Jerusalem: Simor, 1996).

⁶⁶ However, I agree with Kenton L. Sparks (*contra* Noth) that it is not appropriate to argue that Israel's society was modeled after the Greek amphictyonies. Kenton L. Sparks, *Ethnicity and Identity in Ancient Israel: Prolegomena to the Study of Ethnic Sentiments and Their Expression in the Hebrew Bible* (Winona Lake, IN: Eisenbrauns, 1998), 120.

⁶⁷ Sparks argues that even if the song were composed late, the tradition of this song probably dates back to the twelfth century BCE, the premonarchical period—see *Ethnicity and Identity*, 113; cf. also Jo Ann Hackett, "'There was no King in Israel:' The Era of the Judges," in *The Oxford History of the Biblical*

portrays, first, the coming together of ten tribes, under the leadership of the charismatic judges Deborah and Barack, in order to fight against the "kings of Canaan;" second, they fought in the name of Yahweh.

The book of Judges, which recounts the early Yahwistic community of ancient Israel, however, vividly depicts Israel's increasing difficulty in keeping the covenant's משפטים of Yahweh. As such, there is this recurring breakdown of the covenantal relationship between Yahweh and his people. The book of Judges ends with the narrative of a Levite and his concubine (19–21), which depicts one of the lowest spiritual climates of Israel's historiography. The writer of Judges vividly points out that the oppression of Israel's tribes by foreigners was their punishment for breaking their covenantal relationship with Yahweh.

However, some Israelites thought that the oppression by the foreigners and the lawlessness among themselves was because they did not have a king.[68] Therefore, they demanded a king "like the other nations" (1 Sam 8:5) who could rule over them and protect them from their enemies. To be fair, during this time, it was becoming exceedingly difficult for Israel to continue to exist and function politically, militarily, and socio-economically given their governance model of a decentralized tribal league.[69] It is quite right to say that Israel's theocratic rule as a system—a prescription of the covenant made at Sinai—was becoming an idealistic system.[70] However, there is always the tendency among humans to exclude

---

World (ed. Michael D. Coogan; Oxford: Oxford University Press, 1998), 132–64.

[68] Cf. Sandra L. Richter, *The Epic of Eden: A Christian Entry into the Old Testament* (Downers Grove: IVP Academic, 2008), 194.

[69] See Israel Finkelstein, "The Emergence of the Monarchy in Israel: The Environmental and Socio-Economic Aspects," *JSOT* 44 (1989): 43–74.

[70] Cook, *Social Roots*, 41.

God and his divine revelation in our rationalistic and realistic opinions.

The problem with the Israelites was not really about whether they should have a king or not; rather it was the motive behind their request as it was revealed to Samuel, the last judge and a prophet of Israel (1 Sam 8:7). By demanding a king like that of the other nations, Israel was moving away from the covenant they made with Yahweh at Sinai. At Sinai, Yahweh chose Israel and set them apart from all nations to be his people, but Israel's "motive" in asking for a king was in essence a breach of the Sinaitic covenant.

The institution of monarchy was not something that the early Yahwistic tradition completely rejected it. Already in Exod 18:13–27, which many consider to be a strand of E, there is a glimpse of a centralized model of governance, albeit with some strict regulations (vv. 19–23). This understanding of centralized (or monarchical) governance continued to be supported in the later work in Deut 17:14–20.[71] In this passage, it is clearly pointed out that the king of Israel should be: chosen by Yahweh; a native Israelite; one who is not driven to multiply horses, wives, and gold and silver; but someone who writes for himself on a scroll a copy of the law in the presence of the Levitical priest and reads it every day of his life, so that he may learn to fear the Lord his God. This indicates that the king should be a representative of Yahweh—one who acts on behalf of Yahweh. In other words, Israel's monarchy should be a limited monarchy.[72]

---

[71] *Ibid.*, 42; see also Richter, *Epic of Eden*, 195.

[72] The nature of limited monarchy as the chief characteristic of Israel's Yahwistic understanding of monarchy is discussed by Albrecht Alt, "Die Staatenbildung der Israeliten in Palästina," *KS* II (1930): 1–65; and Cross, *Canaanite Myth*, 219–64.

It is within this concept of limited monarchy that Israel's prophets and prophecies have to be located and analyzed. Prophecy in ancient Israel is as old as prophecy in other ANE contexts.[73] However, it is probably right to argue that Israel's Yahwistic prophets increased with the rise of her monarchy.[74] In the scheme of limited monarchy the king was the representative of Yahweh. Consequently, the king was to be completely faithful to the Yahwistic covenant. It is here that the prophets of Yahweh played a pivotal role in Israel's society. Yahweh's prophets acted as the moral compass of Israel's kings. Because of the system of limited monarchy, the prophets afforded the courage to confront the incumbent king if and when he betrayed the covenant relationship. The OT records numerous such incidents, for instance: Nathan confronted David after he committed adultery with Bathsheba (2 Sam 12:1–14); Elijah pronounced judgment on King Ahab after he forcefully confiscated Naboth's land (1 Kgs 18:16–18; 21:20–24). Some prophets (Nathan, Isaiah) were closely aligned with their monarchy, and some (Elijah, Elisha) were not. But, in general, most of the Israelite prophets acted as loyal opposition of the monarch.[75]

Another feature of the limited monarchy was that Yahweh took charge of Israel's warfare.[76] In other words, Yahweh was the

---

[73] Herbert B. Huffmon, "A Company of Prophets: Mari, Assyria, Israel," in *Prophecy in its Ancient Near Eastern Context: Mesopotamian, Biblical, and Arabian Perspectives* (ed. Martti Nissinen; SBL 13; Atlanta: SBL, 2000), 47–70; see also Moshe Weinfeld, "Ancient Near Eastern Patterns in Prophetic Literature," in *"The Place is Too Small for Us": The Israelite Prophets in Recent Scholarship* (ed., Robert P. Gordon; SBTS 5; Winona Lake, IN: Eisenbrauns, 1995), 32-49.

[74] Hanson, *The People Called*, 97; see also Klaus Koch, *The Prophets: The Assyrian Period* (vol. 1; Philadelphia: Fortress, 1983), 19.

[75] Victor H. Matthews and Don C. Benjamin, *Social World of Ancient Israel 1250–587 BCE* (Peabody, Mass.: Hendrickson, 1993), 214.

[76] See Koch, *Prophets*, 27–28.

supreme commander. In fact, the Israelite king was supposed to go to war without having a prophet beside him (cf. 1 Kgs 20; 22:6–7; 2 Kgs 3:11). Breaking this rule meant breaking the covenant relationship with Yahweh (cf. 1 Sam 13). Thus, the kings of Israel/Judah had to seek Yahweh before they entered into any war, and the prophet of Yahweh acted as the intermediary between Yahweh and the king. Besides this, the prophets were also involved in anointing and deposing kings, especially in the northern kingdom (cf. 1 Kgs 14:7–11; 2 Kings 10). It is only later when the monarchial system was completely corrupted that the prophets began to proclaim messages of repentance and forgiveness to the common people as prominently seen in the latter prophetic books.

There is no doubt that from a phenomenological perspective the role of ancient Israel's prophets and prophecies is akin to that of her neighboring ANE contexts such as Mari and Neo-Assyria. However, in essence there is a fundamental difference. This difference is signified when we locate Israel's prophets and prophecies from the perspective of biblical Yahwism and its understanding of limited monarchy.[77] For instance, prophetic judgment oracles, which are a crucial feature of Israelite prophecies, were almost nonexistent in other ANE contexts. In Israel the judgment oracles were pronounced by the prophets either in relation to the king or the people when the מִשְׁפָּטִים of Yahweh was broken or distorted, whereas, in other ANE contexts, the prophets always assured the support of the gods to the king.

---

[77] This is in contradistinction to the view of Matthijs J. de Jong who argues that ancient Israel's prophets and their roles were completely synonymous to that of her neighboring contexts. De Jong argues that it was the later post-exilic editors who revamped the ancient Israelite prophecies into a unique collection of canonical literature—see "Biblical Prophecy—A Scribal Enterprise: The Old Testament Prophecy of Unconditional Judgement considered as a Literary Phenomenon," *VT* 61 (2011): 39–70.

Another aspect through which Israel's Yahwistic prophets differentiated from other prophets was the content of the declaration of indictment to their kings. The prophets indicted the kings in accordance to the covenant relationship, whereas in the other ANE contexts the indictment against kings from the prophets was because of cultic and ritual accountabilities.[78] Thus, the message of Israel's Yahwistic prophets becomes meaningful and relevant when located and analyzed within the tradition of biblical Yahwism and its understanding of covenant, especially in respect to limited monarchy.

3.3.1. Davidic Covenant

Before concluding this chapter one crucial issue has to be addressed concerning Israel's monarchy, namely the Davidic covenant. It is unfortunate that Saul, the first monarch (or chief of Israel) utterly failed to function within this limited monarchical system (1 Sam 13:5–14; 15:1–35). However, David with all his human failures, tried to live within this system of limited monarchy. Subsequently, Yahweh made a royal covenant with David. The text of 2 Sam 7:1-29 recounts the covenant that Yahweh made with David through his prophet Nathan.[79] This

---

[78] John H. Walton, *Ancient Near Eastern Thought and the Old Testament: Introducing the Conceptual World of the Hebrew Bible* (Grand Rapids: Baker Academic, 2009), 252; see also Herbert B. Huffmon, "A Company of Prophets: Mari, Assyria, Israel," in *Prophecy in its Ancient Near Eastern Context: Mesopotamian, Biblical, and Arabian Perspectives* (ed. Marti Nissinen; Atlanta: Society of Biblical Literature, 2000), 47–70.

[79] This passage falls within the biblical corpus of Deuteronomistic History (Deut–2 Kgs). As against one exilic redactor of this corpus (Noth), or two redactors—a pre-exilic and an exilic (Cross), or three exilic redactors—DtrH, DtrP, and DtrN (Smend, Dietrich, and Veijola), I agree closely with André Lemaire's understanding of "rolling corpus" when it comes to the redactional process of Deuteronomistic History. Lemaire in his discussion of the redactional history of the book of Kings suggests that this book has undergone seven likely

passage consists almost entirely of speeches: David inquiring of Nathan whether to build a house for Yahweh (vv. 1–3), followed by a lengthy oracle of Yahweh to Nathan (vv. 4–11a), then the transmission of an oracle from Nathan to David (vv. 11b–17), which ends with a response of David in prayer (vv. 18–29). One of the themes in this passage that has long been under scrutiny among OT scholars is the *unconditional covenant* Yahweh made with David (vv. 13, 15, 16).[80] This theme of unconditional covenant has generally led some scholars to assert that the Davidic covenant is nothing but royal ideology and, therefore, does not relate to the Sinaitic covenant and its view of monarchy as limited monarchy.

Cross argues that 2 Sam 7:1–7, which contains an oracle denying David's request to make a temple for Yahweh and his ark

---

redactional processes starting from David's time through the exilic period. Thus, he concludes that the book of Kings is an amalgamation of a rolling corpus—see "Toward a Redactional History of the Book of Kings," in *Reconsidering Israel and Judah: Recent Studies on the Deuteronomistic History* (ed. Gary N. Knoppers and J. Gordon McConville; SBTS 8; Winona Lake, IN: Eisenbrauns, 2000), 446–61. For fuller treatments of the views just mentioned, see Martin Noth, *Überlieferungsgeschichtliche Studien, Teil 1: Die sammelnden und bearbeitenden Geschichtswerke im Alten Testament* (Schriften der Königsberger Gelehrten Gesellschaft, Geisteswissenschaftliche Klasse 18/2; Halle: Niemeyer, 1943); Cross, *Canaanite Myth*, 274–89; R. Smend, *Die Enstehung des Alten Testaments* (Stuttgart: Kohlhammer, 1989); W. Dietrich, *Prophetie und Geschichte* (FRLANT 108; Göttingen: Vanderhoeck & Ruprecht, 1972); T. Veijola, *Das Königtum in der Beuteilung der deuteronomistischen Historiographie* (AASF 198; Helsinki: Suomalainen Tiedeakatemia, 1977).

[80] Arnold contends that even if this passage does not explicitly mention the word covenant, the language used here (such as חסד) suggests that it is a covenant; moreover, he also points out that this covenant is confirmed through inner-biblical interpretation. Psalm 89, which is considered a later reflection on 2 Sam 7, explicitly uses the word covenant—see Bill T. Arnold, *1 & 2 Samuel: The NIV Application Commentary* (Grand Rapids: Zondervan, 2003), 479–80.

suggests two crucial points:[81] (1) David was not allowed to follow the Canaanite tradition of kings building temples for their gods; and (2) David was instructed to maintain the tradition of the tribal league.[82] Thus, Cross argues that David was restrained to rule Israel within the system of limited monarchy. This view is supported by Ps 132, which is one of the earliest witnesses to the Davidic covenant.[83]

Cross contends that this Psalm does not reflect the Canaanite ideological motive of the father-son relationship between god and king, and also that the unconditional aspect of the covenant is missing. In this way, Cross suggests that the original Davidic covenant was a conditional and ideologically non-Canaanite covenant. However, it was Solomon and his royal court that interpolated the covenant into an unconditional and ideologically Canaanite covenant and thus, ushered in a full-fledged monarchy in the model of the Canaanite neighbors.[84] Yet it has to be noted that in 2 Sam 7:14, it is clearly pointed out that even David's son will be punished if he commits iniquity. One has to be careful, on the one hand, not to completely disentangle the Davidic covenant from the Yahwistic tradition, thereby, making the Scripture a manipulated royal ideology;[85] or, on the other hand, not to

---

[81] Cross, *Canaanite Myth*, 241. Most believe that David's materials in the books of Samuel come from two sources: "The history of David's Rise" (1 Sam 16:1–2 Sam 5:10) and "The Courts History" (2 Sam 9–1 Kgs 2). If this general consensus is true, then Arnold believes that 2 Sam 6–8 are independent materials collected to characterize David's kingship: "The force of these materials is to illustrate the concluding statement of 'the History of David's Rise' (2 Sam 5:10): 'And [David] became more and more powerful, because the Lord God Almighty was with him'" (Arnold, *1 & 2 Samuel*, 471–72).

[82] Cross, *Canaanite Myth*, 243.

[83] *Ibid.*, 232–34.

[84] *Ibid.*, 260–62.

[85] Cross' distinction of Judean royal ideology and the traditional Yahwistic model of limited monarchy is utilized by Robert Wilson in defining the roles of

seamlessly identify Davidic covenant as superseding the early Yahwistic tradition.[86]

Jon D. Levenson in his deliberations on Zion and Sinai has cogently summarized the issue into two camps: the integrationist and the segregationist. By integrationist, Levenson means those who argue that Davidic covenant and Sinaitic covenant are one and

---

Northern/Ephraimite and Judean prophets. Wilson argues that the Ephraimite prophets sought to salvage the model of limited monarchy based on decentralized government as well as charismatic leadership; as opposed to the Judean policy of centralized and dynastic kingdom (Wilson, *Prophecy and Society*, 135–296). However, it should be noted that some of his construction of the role of Judean prophets is rather forced (*ibid.*, 253). Moreover, Wilson's strict geographical divisions of Ephraimite and Judean theologies have been regarded as untenable. For instance, the message of the prophet Micah who prophesied in Judah is comprised of both Sinaitic as well as Zion theologies. Many scholars have argued that the Sinaitic theology was accidentally transplanted into Micah's text by late editors. In response to this, scholars such as S.L. Cook, Levenson, and Walter Beyerlin have independently argued that Micah, a Judean prophet, was also a proponent of Sinaitic theology—see Cook, *The Social Roots*, 67–120; Jon D. Levenson, *Sinai and Zion: An Entry into the Jewish Bible* (Minneapolis: Winston, 1985), 195–200; Walter Beyerlin, *Die Kultraditionen Israels in der Verkündigung des Propheten Micah* (FRLANT 62; Göttingen: Vandenhoeck & Ruprecht, 1959), 35. Such a distinction of Northern and Southern theologies has led scholars like Daniel E. Fleming to postulate that the OT was written from the Judean ideology using the Northern Kingdom's records—see Fleming, *The Legacy of Israel in Judah's Bible: History, Politics, and the Reinscribing of Tradition* (Cambridge: Cambridge University Press, 2012), xii. Such conclusion is an outcome of the understanding that the Davidic covenant was a manipulative royal document formulated to propagate and maneuver the royal agenda—see also Erhard S. Gerstenberger, *Theologies in the Old Testament* (trans. John Bowden; Minneapolis: Fortress, 2002), 1.

[86] On the discussion of covenant theology from the biblical theology perspective see Peter J. Gentry and Stephen J. Wellum, *Kingdom through Covenant: A Biblical-Theological Understanding of the Covenants* (Wheaton: Crossway, 2012). Gentry and Wellum provide the opposing views of covenant theology by mapping the dispensationalist and continuity perspectives. They, then, articulate a *via media* approach in understanding covenant theology.

the same; whereas by segregationist, he means those who argue that these two covenants are complete different entities.[87] He argues that the integrationist tends to view the Davidic covenant as superseding the Sinaitic covenant.[88] As such, the conditional stipulations pervasive in the Sinaitic covenant are nullified by the unconditional aspect of the Davidic covenant. In objection to this, Levenson cites Moshe Weinfeld who has argued that the Sinaitic and the Davidic covenants are formulated in line with two different types of ANE covenants namely, treaty and grant. The former is conditional whereas, the latter is unconditional. In the former, the vassal is subjected to the king whereas, in the latter, the king is subjected to take care of the vassal. In this manner, the Sinaitic covenant is a "treaty" and the Davidic covenant is a "grant."[89]

However, Gary N. Knoppers has refuted Weinfeld by arguing that all the covenants, whether it be treaty or grant, have to be understood in bilateral terms.[90] The only difference is that some are symmetrical and others are asymmetrical. In other words, in some covenants responsibilities are shared equally between the parties;

---

[87] Jon D. Levenson, "The Davidic Covenant and its Modern Interpreters," *CBQ* 41 (1979): 205–20; see also his discussion on the relationships between Sinai and Zion in *Sinai and Zion*, 187–218.

[88] For Levenson the integrationist includes scholars such as R. de Vaux, "Le roi d'Israel vassel de YHWH," in *Mélanges Eugene Tisserant* (Vatican City: Biblioteca Apostolica Vaticana, 1964), 119–33; K. Seybold, *Das davidischen Konigtum im Zeugnis der Propheten* (FRLANT 107; Gottingen: Vanderhoeck & Ruprecht, 1972); A.H.J. Gunneweg, "Sinaibund und Davidsbund," *VT* 10 (1960): 335–41.

[89] For Weinfeld's work see "The Covenant of Grant in the Old Testament and in the Ancient Near East," *JAOS* 90 (1970): 184–203. Weinfeld examines this grant form covenant in Assyrian and Hittite literatures, as well as documents from Ugarit, Susa, and Elephantine (*ibid.*, 185, 187, 192).

[90] Gary N. Knoppers, "Ancient Near Eastern Royal Grants and the Davidic Covenant: A Parallel?," *JAOS* 116 (1996): 670–97.

whereas, in others the greater responsibility is taken by the powerful party, as in the Davidic covenant.

Levenson contends that the segregationist tends to argue that there is no meeting point between the Sinaitic and the Davidic covenants. As such, there is a strong tendency to label the Davidic covenant as pure royal ideology devoid of any revelation from above. Levenson observes another problem with the segregationist understanding: if the Davidic covenant was so radically un-prophetic, why did it retain the loyalties of so many Yahweh's prophets?[91] Despite these valuable and probing critiques, Levenson's alternate answer is not appealing. He concludes that these two covenants were two different entities composed during two different historical contexts. Thus, he reduces the importance and the degree of influence of the Davidic covenant in comparison to the Sinaitic covenant.[92] He accuses later Judaism and Christian theological expositors for connecting the Davidic covenant with a messianic theme and accentuating its significance.[93] Levenson, in the final analysis, does not see the need to provide a meaningful synthesis of the relationship between the Sinaitic and the Davidic covenants.

One crucial problem with the segregationist view is the inability to consider divine revelation as a significant aspect in understanding history. Of course, this does not mean the integrationist view must be correct. To understand the Davidic covenant (2 Sam 7) one should consider three points. First, one should keep in mind McEvenue's assertion that ancient Israel's mentality was signified by a compact mentality. In other words, in the minds of ancient Israelites there was no adequate

---

[91] Levenson, "The Davidic Covenant," 214–15.
[92] *Ibid.*, 216.
[93] *Ibid.*, 217–18.

differentiation between politics, religion, and history.⁹⁴ Attempting to separate neatly these aspects would lead to anachronism. The issue of ideology as a determining factor in making covenant is rather a projection of modern minds into an ancient context. The notion that human values and beliefs are relativistic and determined by social, economic, and political agendas is an offshoot of modernism and urbanism.⁹⁵ Harvey Cox states that in a modern and secularized world it is politics and not religion that brings unity and meaning to human society, which in turn implies that religion remains meaningful only when it is politicized.⁹⁶ Thus, the religious view in this context is always serving an ideological agenda to promote the politics of the state or the elite. Such an assumption rejects any individual's or society's genuine claim to transcendent beliefs.⁹⁷

It is, therefore, imperative while reading any ancient text that one should be sensitive not to project modern sensibilities into the text lest the text is distorted. Besides this, one should understand that ideology is not always manipulative and negative as it has come to be realized, especially, in biblical study.⁹⁸ Ideology can be constructed by a government of a society not necessarily to exploit

---

[94] McEvenue, "The Rise of David Story," 114. McEvenue's understanding of compact mentality is somewhat related to von Rad's understanding of Israel's knowledge as depicted by pan-sacralism—see Gerhard von Rad, *Wisdom in Israel* (trans. James D. Martin; Nashville: Abingdon, 1972).

[95] Gary A. Herion, "The Impact of Modern and Social Science Assumptions on the Reconstruction of Israelite History," in *Social-Scientific Old Testament Criticism* (ed. David J. Chalcraft; Sheffield: Sheffield Academic, 1997), 78–108. See also the argument on ideology by Meyer in *Reality and Illusion*, 114–43.

[96] Harvey Cox, *The Secular City: Secularization and Urbanization in Theological Perspective* (New York: Macmillan, 1965), 254.

[97] Herion, "The Impact of Modern'," 85.

[98] See James Barr, *History and Ideology in the Old Testament: Biblical Studies at the End of a Millennium* (Oxford: Oxford University Press, 2000), 102–41.

its citizen but as an imperative measure to insure stability and process. Of course, it has to be noted that the ideology constructed with good intention has always the chance of being abused and manipulated by the powers-that-be.[99]

Second, time and again Yahweh reveals himself in history according to the needs and circumstances of his people. As discussed above, Yahweh revealed himself to Moses by revealing his name in anticipation of the exodus event. Later, Yahweh appeared to Moses and the Israelites at Sinai in a shaking mountain, fire, and smoke (Exod 19–20). Just as the exodus event was a defining moment in ancient Israel's history, the reign of David was also a watershed period because David truly took Israel from a loosely connected confederation to a more structured monarchy. Every tradition evolves and adapts according to the change in need and context. Such change, as wrought by the reign of David, did not demand a wholesale transformation in Israel's ancient Yahwistic tradition, but it definitely required some adaptation. This need of adaptation was fulfilled by the Davidic covenant.

Third, in order to understand that the Davidic covenant was not mere royal ideology, the reign of Saul has to be considered. In other words, the legitimacy of this covenant becomes clear when we analyze the Davidic covenant in juxtaposition to the reign and narrative of Saul. Saul could not function within the system of limited monarchy. In 1 Sam 13:1–22, we see how a limited monarchy should function. The king cannot initiate war except when guided by a higher authority. The king could receive the command only from Yahweh and his prophet. This text demonstrates the uniqueness of the Israelite's monarchy in an ANE

---

[99] For more information on this read Clifford Geertz, "Ideology as a Cultural System," in *The Interpretation of Cultures: Selected Essays* (New York: Basic Books, 1973), 193–233.

context.¹⁰⁰ The text goes on to show how Saul completely broke the outworking of limited monarchy when he offered the burnt offering by himself. Consequently, Samuel the prophet of Yahweh rebuked Saul's act as foolish and pronounced that his kingdom would not endure (vv. 13–14; cf. 1 Sam 15:1–35). Against this, David is portrayed as someone who clearly had the desire to obey Yahweh's voice (2 Sam 7:4–17). Arnold writes: "This chapter [2 Sam 7], more than any other, answers these questions irrevocably: David is not like Saul. He is as much an ideal ruler of God's people as Saul was an inadequate one."¹⁰¹

It is within this setting that Yahweh made the covenant with David. In light of this, the Davidic covenant is closely tied with the Sinaitic covenant. In fact, the credibility of the Davidic covenant depended on the observance of the Sinaitic stipulation by David's house (i.e., 1 Kgs 8:25; 9:4–5 and in fact, the whole of 1–2 Kings).¹⁰² The debate of unconditional and conditional aspects of the covenant will not solve this problem, as Knoppers has indicated that every covenant has to be understood in a bilateral manner.¹⁰³ Therefore, the Davidic covenant neither supersedes nor

---

¹⁰⁰ Arnold, *1 & 2 Samuel*, 198.

¹⁰¹ *Ibid.*, 474.

¹⁰² If the kings of the northern kingdom [such as Baasha (1 Kgs 15:34), Zimri (16:19), Omri (16:26), and Ahaziah (22:53)] were accused, in the regnal formulas of the books of Kings, of walking in all the ways of Jeroboam (son of Nebat) and in his sin which he made Israel to sin; then the Judean kings were also accused of not expelling male shrine prostitution from the kingdom (see 1 Kgs 14:24; 15:3) and for doing evil in the sight of Yahweh (2 Kgs 23:32, 37; 24:9, 19).

¹⁰³ Knoppers, "Ancient Near Eastern Royal Grants," 694–97. Besides this, Knoppers in another article argues that the promises in the Davidic covenant do not simply relate to dynastic succession but that the authors of 2 Sam 7 (the Deuteronomist) and 1 Chr 17:1–15 (the Chronicler) "employ the Davidic promises as a cipher to structure and evaluate the united kingdom, the division, and the Judahite monarchy." Concurrently, he contends that the crux of Davidic

sabotages, but rather complements, the Sinaitic covenant. The Davidic covenant hinges on the Sinaitic covenant in order to accomplish its promise.

Thus, the Davidic covenant does not nullify the system of limited monarchy as espoused by the Yahwistic tradition. However, there is no denying the fact that in the course of the Judean monarchy the Davidic covenant was abused and caused both the rulers as well as the *vox populi* to fall into pseudo spirituality. It has to be noted that Jeroboam, the first king of the northern kingdom, was also given the similar covenant to that of the Davidic covenant by the prophet Ahijah the Shilonite (1 Kgs 11:26–38). However, Jeroboam could not live according to the conditions of the covenant. As a result, the promise of dynasty for all generations was revoked just as Saul's kingdom was taken from him by Samuel.[104] It is, indeed, the inability of the kings of both the northern and the southern kingdoms to rule within the Yahwistic system of limited monarchy that brought downfall to these nations.

3.4. Conclusion

In this chapter, I have argued that the Yahwistic tradition was not necessarily opposed to monarchy. However, it does espouse a radical form of monarchy namely, a monarchy that was limited by

---

covenant is more than the Messianic theme; in fact, it touches the broader themes of Israelite life such as the election of Zion, the ritual procession of the Ark, victory in war, the establishment of the Temple, the survival of the Southern Kingdom and so on—see Knoppers, "David's Relation to Moses: The Contexts, Content and Conditions of the Davidic Promises," in *King and Messiah in Israel and the Ancient Near East: Proceedings of the Oxford Old Testament Seminar* (ed. John Day; JSOTSup 270; Sheffield: Sheffield Academic, 1998), 91–118.

[104] S. Talmon, "Kingship and the Ideology of the State," in *The Age of the Monarchies: Culture and Society* (ed. Abraham Malamat; vol. 5; Jerusalem: Massada, 1979), 3–26.

Yahweh and other divinely-appointed authorities, such as prophets and priests. Limited monarchy simply means that the Israelite king was to be a true representative of Yahweh in leading his chosen and covenant people. In other words, the king was not only to make sure that the covenant relationship was intact between the people and Yahweh, but that he was to be completely subservient to Yahweh. This is vividly indicated by the fact that Israel's wars were to be initiated by Yahweh.

I also argued that the Davidic covenant was a necessary adaptation of Yahwistic tradition as Israel moved away from a decentralized tribal league to a more centralized and structured monarchial system. It is not the Davidic covenant that led to the downfall of Judah. Rather, it was the inability of kings to rule within the scheme of a limited monarchy that led to the downfall. In fact, this is also true for the northern kingdom. It is within this scheme of limited monarchy that we have to understand the role of Israel's prophets and their prophecies.

This articulation of the larger picture of Yahwistic tradition and its developments will enable us to understand better the context in which Israelite prophets received and delivered Yahweh's revelation. This understanding, in turn, will provide a scope in comprehending the conflicts among the prophets. Thus, in the next chapter we will utilize the above construal of Yahwistic tradition in order to study the prophetic conflict.

Chapter 4
THE SOCIO-ECONOMIC AND POLITICAL CONTEXT OF THE ANCIENT ISRAELITE PROPHET IN AN AGRARIAN SOCIETY

> *"[The] biblical texts from monarchic times can only be interpreted with sufficient precision and inter-connectedness when viewed as witnesses to a dynamic social process reverberating through all dimensions of Israel's life."*[1]

4.1. Introduction

The goal of this chapter is to investigate the plausible socio-economic and political background of the ancient Israelite prophet within an agrarian society. This will enable us to understand better the prophetic conflict specifically found in the book of Jeremiah (627–586/7 BCE), and generally in the OT. To achieve this goal, I will investigate the dynamics of an agrarian society in relation to ancient Israel's culture and monarchy. By exploring the socio-economic and political background, this chapter will consider the possible factors that gave rise to false prophecy, and also examine the role of the support group of the prophets in distinguishing true and false prophecy.

This study will also suggest that the contemporaries of the ancient Israelite prophets had a sufficient, but not foolproof, capacity to distinguish a true prophecy from a false one. In other words, prophecy is intelligible and not haphazard, if studied from a critical realist point of view and scrutinized through a synthetic analysis.

---

[1] Marvin L. Chaney, "Systemic Study of the Israelite Monarchy," *Semeia* 37 (1986): 53–76.

4.2. Ancient Israel's Agrarian Society: A Sociological Analysis

Applying a sociological method in OT study does not need justification as it has been a fruitful practice since the nineteenth century, for instance, in the work of W. Robertson Smith.[2] Since then a host of biblical scholars and sociologists have contributed to the social scientific study of the OT (i.e., applying sociology and anthropology to OT studies). The use of social science in the study of OT is broadly divided into two waves.[3] The first wave includes the works of scholars such as Louis Wallis, Johannes Pedersen, Max Weber, Antonin Causse, Gustav Dalman, Roland de Vaux, Albrecht Alt, and Martin Noth. At times, however, these scholars either did not adequately develop their social scientific methodologies, or they did not use sound judgment in applying the same to OT interpretation. Consequently, the first wave declined as comparative, linguistic, literary, and historical approaches took precedence over social science criticism in OT studies. The works of George Mendenhall, and Norman Gottwald ushered in the second wave.[4] Today, many scholars utilize a social scientific

---

[2] W. Robertson Smith, *Lectures on the Religion of the Semites: First Series, The Fundamental Institutions* (New York: Macmillan, 1927 [1889]).

[3] It was Frank S. Frick who first used the expressions "first wave" and "second wave." See Frank S. Frick, "Norman Gottwald's *The Tribes of Yahweh* in the Context of 'Second-Wave' Social-Scientific Biblical Criticism," in *Tracking "The Tribes of Yahweh:" On the Trail of a Classic* (ed. Roland Boer; London: Sheffield Academic, 2002), 17–34.

[4] For further discussion on this, see Charles E. Carter, "A Discipline in Transition: The Contributions of the Social Sciences to the Study of the Hebrew Bible," in *Community, Identity, and Ideology: Social Science Approaches to the Hebrew Bible* (ed. Charles E. Carter and Carol L. Meyers; SBTS 6; Winona Lake, IN: Eisenbrauns, 1996), 3–36; cf. also Ronald Simkins and Stephen L. Cook, "Introduction: Case Studies From the Second Wave of Research in the Social World of the Hebrew Bible," *Semeia* 87 (2001): 1–14; Robert R. Wilson, "Social Theory and the Study of Israelite Religion: A Retrospective on the Past Forty Years of Research," in *Social Theory and the Study of Israelite Religion:*

method in analyzing the OT.[5] The methods and theories applied are at best eclectic; however, without a doubt this second wave of the use of social science criticism has contributed significantly to the study of OT.[6]

In this investigation of the sociological aspects of ancient Israel, I will utilize Gerhard Lenski and Patrick Nolan's model of macrosociology. Their work provides the interpretive framework, or heuristic model from which to evaluate the ancient Israelite agrarian society.[7] Macrosociology in its approach is inductive, cross-cultural, and comparative in nature. It focuses on the historical development of particular cultural patterns and studies societies as a whole, rather than the individual parts of societies.

Lenski and Nolan contend societies are vibrant entities whose changes are greatly initiated by subsistence technological advances.[8] Utilizing a macrosociological perspective that studies a society as a systemic, evolutionary component which responds to its environmental changes, Lenski and Nolan classify societies into nine categories based on their primary mode of subsistence.[9]

Essays in Retrospect and Prospect (ed. Saul M. Olyan; SBLSBS 71; Atlanta: Society of Biblical Literature, 2012), 7–18.

[5] Some scholars in this second wave include Robert Wilson, Thomas Overholt, Victor Matthews, Don C. Benjamin, Lester L. Grabbe, Richard A. Horsley, Stephen L. Cook, Carol Meyer and Phyllis A. Bird.

[6] Scholars of the second wave utilize both sociological as well as anthropological methods. In the sociological analysis, the dominant methods applied in studying the OT are Karl Marx's social theory, Max Weber's structural-functional, and Gerhard Lenski's macrosociology. Besides these, anthropological and comparative methods have also been employed in studying the OT.

[7] Patrick Nolan and Gerhard Lenski, *Human Societies: An Introduction to Macrosociology* (London: Paradigm, 2009).

[8] *Ibid.*, 57.

[9] The categories of societies are: hunting and gathering societies; simple horticultural societies; advanced horticultural societies; simple agrarian

Systemic comparison portrays that within any type of society, broad similarities exist, which when studied a pattern or model of that type emerges. However, Lenski and Nolan insist that subsistence technology, although it is the most powerful factor that influences the dynamic of societies, is not the only factor. That is why they contend that "there are differences among societies within a given societal type just as there are differences among individuals in the same age categories."[10]

The type of society into which ancient Israel generally falls, is that of an agrarian society. The technological transformation which gave rise to an agrarian typology in Eastern Mediterranean generally was the invention of the plow alongside the use of animal energy and the discovery of metallurgy. The new technology greatly enhanced the agricultural products. As a result of the increase in economic surplus the possibility of developments in these societies such as urbanization, literacy, and empire building increased as well. By examining agrarian societies cross-culturally, Lenski and Nolan summarized the common patterns of these societies:

> [E]very advanced agrarian society was much like the rest with respect to its fundamental characteristics. Class structure, social inequality, the division of labor, the distinctive role of urban populations in the larger society, the cleavage between urban and rural subcultures, the disdain of the governing class for both work and workers, the widespread belief in magic and fatalism, the use of the economic surplus for the benefit of the governing class and for the construction of monumental edifices, high birth and

---

societies; advanced agrarian societies; industrial societies; fishing societies; maritime societies; and herding (*ibid.*, 64).

[10] *Ibid.*, 73.

death rates—all these and more were present in all advanced agrarian societies.[11]

Thus, generally in an agrarian society there is class stratification between the working peasant and the elite urban bureaucrats such as the powerful government, military, cultural, and social positions.[12] Also the economy of an agrarian society was controlled by the state monarchy whose motive in most cases was empire building and expansion through warfare which in turn exerted pressure on peasants who had to work harder to produce more food and pay taxes.[13] Lenski summarizes it this way: "in these [agrarian] societies the institutions of government are the primary source of social inequality."[14]

Within this agrarian context, the role of the religious leader such as the priest or the prophet becomes interestingly significant. As a result, the religious leaders, since they perform services which the general masses valued, became rather popular and revered. Furthermore, common people revered them because they derived their authority from an agent higher than the elites and the monarch. This put the religious leaders in a situation where they could even make demands on the economic surplus.[15] Moreover, in many cases the ascension of the king to the throne was ceremoniously confirmed by the religious clergies. However, this act sometimes led to conflict between the monarch and the

---

[11] G. Lenski, P. Nolan and J. Lenski, *Human Societies: An Introduction to Macrosociology* (New York: McGraw-Hill, 1995), 219—quoting from the 7th edition, since the latest edition does not have this passage anymore, although the notion still remains intact.

[12] G. Lenski, *Power and Privilege: A Theory of Social Stratification* (Chapel Hill: University of North Carolina Press, 1984), 210.

[13] *Ibid.*, 219–20.

[14] *Ibid.*, 210.

[15] *Ibid.*, 67.

religious leaders. Very often this conflict could be defused by compromise between the two groups. Because of such a significant role, the religious leaders found themselves at the higher echelon of the class stratification.

There was also a widespread belief in fatalism and magic among the people of the ancient agrarian societies.[16] Given the struggle and the difficult economic plight of the majority of people with limited resources, coupled with their strong belief in fatalism, elements like magic or belief in supernatural forces which promised easy relief and comfort became tantalizingly popular. It is therefore not surprising that many ancient agrarian societies adhere to divination, shamanism, and generally to polytheism.

4.2.1. Ancient Israelite Society and Agrarian System

The introduction of monarchy in ancient Israel, which also signifies a shift from Iron Age I to Iron Age II, is broadly marked by a change in settlement patterns.[17] It was due to necessity that Israel turned from an intermittent rule of judges to a monarchy. However, this systemic shift of governance was feasible because of their practice of agriculture as a subsistence means of living which in turn produced economic surplus. The early monarchical system

---

[16] Nolan and Lenski, *Human Societies*, 166–67.

[17] Scholars generally divide first millennium of ANE history into the following: Iron Age II encompasses the time of the divided kingdom c. 920 BCE, and is further divided into Iron II A (920/930–722 BCE), Iron IIB (722–605 BCE), and Iron IIC (605–539 BCE)—see Arnold, *Introduction to the Old Testament*, 41. However, many Israeli archaeologists presume Iron Age II starts with the period of United Monarchy. The former depends on historical events, whereas the latter on archaeological sense. See William G. Dever, "Social Structure in Palestine in the Iron II Period on the Eve of Destruction," in *The Archaeology of Society in the Holy Land* (ed. Thomas E. Levy; London: Leicester University Press, 1995), 416–31. Since this section of my chapter is more of a macro-analysis aided by archaeological study, I will follow here the latter trend.

of Israel was based on her Yahwistic tradition of patrimonial authority.

Generally, ancient Israel's society was structured in a three-tier form of patrimonial authority, wherein just as every patriarch functioned as the paterfamilias of his בית אב, the king acted like the patriarch in his kingdom and, ultimately, Yahweh was regarded as the supreme patrimonial lord over all of Israel.[18] David's reign was marked by governmental innovations, but not at the expense of the traditional system. David instituted a new complex bureaucracy to administer the state (2 Sam 8:15–18; 20:23–26) and created a new military unit consisting of foreign mercenaries (2 Sam 8:18; 20:23). However, David also kept the traditional leadership (elders and priests) intact, which is reflected in his seeking their support for the confirmation of his rule (2 Sam 2:4; 3:12, 17, 21; 5:1–3). His appointment of two priests, Zadok (a non-Levite) and Abiathar (a Levite), suggests this thinking of applying conservative change to his governmental system. Although David's reign set the pace, it was under Solomon that the monarchic societal system greatly and successfully developed (1 Kgs 4:7–19).[19]

The installation of a monarchical system accelerated the change of settlement patterns in ancient Israel. Urbanization began towards the end of Iron Age I but it was the introduction of a monarchy that led to the rise of real cities.[20] In fact, many rural settlements of Iron Age 1 (e.g., Ai, Shiloh, Mt. Ebal) disappeared, whereas some (e.g., Mizpah [Tell en-Nasbeh], Dan, Hazor, Jerusalem, Gezer, and Lachish) were transformed into cities in Iron

---

[18] Philip J. King and Lawrence E. Stager, *Life in Biblical Israel* (Louisville: Westminster John Knox, 2001), 4–5.

[19] Cook asserts: "David judged correctly that Israel's older societal system would not simply bow out of the picture as a new state system developed" (*The Social Roots*, 148).

[20] Avraham Faust, *The Archaeology of Israelite Society in Iron Age II* (trans. Ruth Ludlum; Winona Lake, IN: Eisenbrauns, 2012), 259.

Age II.[21] The urban centers were the outcome of a complex networking of different factors such as an increase in population, change in political system, growth in military power, an increase in division of labor, and an increase in administrative personnel. H. Reviv argues that the urban populations were the "servants of the king," who were comprised of foreign experts in areas that would benefit royal projects (1 Sam 21:8; 2 Sam 8:16; 20:23; 1 Chr 18:15; 27:25), merchants, and construction experts.[22] As a result, many of these urban populations were also close supporters of the monarch.

Rural villages, as noted, were abandoned initially during the beginning of Iron Age II. This might be due to the threat posed by the Philistines and the settlements forced by the new monarch.[23] Avraham Faust argues that during the initial phase of the Monarchical period there were no rural settlements in the kingdom's heartland; although cultivation of agricultural lands was conducted from the central settlements.[24] However, at some stage after the unveiling of the monarchy, many farmers migrated back to new rural settlements.[25] In fact, Broshi and Finkelstein estimated that seventy percent (a conservative figure) of the population lived

---

[21] *Ibid.*, 256.

[22] H. Reviv, "The Structure of Society," in *The Age of the Monarchies: Culture and Society* (ed. Abraham Malamat; 5 vols. Jerusalem: Massada, 1979), 4:138–39.

[23] Faust, *Archaeology*, 258.

[24] *Ibid.*

[25] *Ibid.*, 259, 262. Interestingly, Faust comments that this process of the abandonment of rural areas and later settlement in new rural areas signifies that a kingdom was established in the central hill country. This is in contradistinction to the view that Israel and Judah were developed as kingdoms only during the ninth and eighth century BCE respectively.

in rural areas. This rural population comprised mostly farmers.[26] It was in this rural settlements that ancient Israel's societal framework was somehow maintain and preserved.[27]

Along with this change of settlement pattern, the monarchy also intensified social stratification in ancient Israel. Although social classes in the modern sense, where social groups opposed ideologically to one another, did not exist, there was certainly class stratification.[28] With the establishment of the monarchy many new classes emerged within the kingdom. These new classes were both organizationally and economically dependent on the monarchy.[29] Many of these groups include merchants, military, administrative staff, artisans, and others who supported the royal activities and, thus, thrived at the cost of the royal economy.

The upper class included the social, economic and political elites such as senior administrative staff, senior officers, the high priesthood, the majordomo, the scribes, and the "king's servants." The middle class included the holders of positions in the royal administration such as one responsible for implementing the royal policy in administration, justice, military, the royal economy, craftsmen, merchants, urban agriculturists, and also rural, wealthy farmers. The lower class included most of the rural agricultural population, foreigners, slaves, unemployed, beggars, and criminals. Note that there were rural, wealthy farmers who were considered middle class, and so one can imagine there existed a mild class division in the rural areas as well. Furthermore, when considering this class stratification during the time of divided monarchy, the

---

[26] M. Broshi and I. Finkelstein, "The Population of Palestine in Iron Age II," *BASOR* 287 (1992): 47–60; cf. also Paula McNutt, *Reconstructing the Society of Ancient Israel* (Louisville: Westminster John Knox, 1999), 152.

[27] See Faust, *Archaeology*, 262.

[28] See R. de Vaux, *Ancient Israel: Its Life and Institutions* (New York: McGraw Hill, 1965), 72–73.

[29] Faust, *Archaeology*, 20

northern kingdom displays all three of the class divisions, whereas in the southern kingdom the division comprises only the upper and the lower classes. This shows that in Judah the class stratification was sharper and greater.[30]

The relationship between the urban and rural settlements is often described as central (urban) and periphery (rural). Although, there is some truth in this assertion, the relationship between them is more complex. It is true that the urban settlers depended on the rural populations' agricultural products and taxes for its existence, and yet it is also true that the rural population needed the aid of the king and his urban administration for security, as well as law and order both internally and externally.[31] Moreover, even in the urban centers there were marginal and poor populations who could be described as the peripheral or the oppressed group. With that said, there is no doubt that the rural peasants were the main engine of economy for the royal activities and its urban settlements, as in any agrarian society. Some of the implications of such settlement patterns and social stratification in ancient Israelite societies will now be considered.

4.2.1.1. Adaptation of the Traditional System

Urbanization led to the loosening of the tribal traditional system of ancient Israel. Many migrated to urban centers because it promised luxury and comfortable living. However, the truth was that material goods were limited, and this made it exceedingly difficult for the majority of the urban population to live within traditional בית אב (extended family) and מִשְׁפָּחָה (clan) settings. The בית אב was replaced by the nuclear family, as it was more practical

---

[30] *Ibid.*, 270.
[31] Lenski and Nolan, *Human Societies*, 155.

to take care of a smaller family than a large, joint family.³² The clan system became weak as the nuclear family and individual became more prominent. This change in kinship structure is reflected when we compare the law regarding the rape of a virgin

---

³² There is a debate as to whether the basic social unit during this period was a בית אב or a nuclear family. For the former argument see S. Bendor, *The Social Structure of Ancient Israel: The Institution of the Family (beit 'ab) from the Settlement to the End of the Monarchy* (Jerusalem: Simor, 1996), 121–23; B. Lang, "The Social Organization of Peasant Poverty in Biblical Israel," in *Anthropological Approaches to the Old Testament* (ed. B. Lang; Philadelphia: Fortress, 1985), 83–99; J.S. Holladay, "The Kingdoms of Israel and Judah: Political and Economic Centralization in the Iron Age II A–B (ca. 1000–750 B.C.E)" in *The Archaeology of Society in the Holy Land* (ed. T.E. Levy; London: Leicester University Press, 1995), 368–98; and for the latter argument see N.P. Lemche, *Early Israel* (Leiden: Brill, 1985), 249–59. However, this debate is, perhaps, generated because of the fluidity of the term בית אב, as members of one בית אב might vary from another. Israel's tribal system of social classification is highlighted in the story about the sin of Achan. In this story, Yahweh instructs Joshua: In the morning you shall come near by your tribes; the tribe (שבט) that Yahweh takes shall come forward by clans; the clan (משפחה) that Yahweh takes shall come forward by households; and the household (בית) which Yahweh takes shall come forward one by one (גבר) (Josh 7:14). Thus Israel's tribal system of social classification was divided into tribe, clan, family/household, and, finally, individuals. The בית אב generally consists of extended families of three or four generations. It might include "several generations of family members, depending on who is claimed as the paterfamilias, along with his wife or wives, sons and their wives, grandsons and their wives, the unmarried sons and daughters, slaves, servants, *gērîm*, aunts, uncles, widows, orphans, and Levites who might be members of the household" (King-Stager, *Life in Biblical Israel*, 40; see also Stager, "The Archaeology of the Family in Ancient Israel," *BASOR* 260 [1985]: 1–35). In line with this definition, it might be that בית אבים existed in rural settlements but also in the urban centers among the wealthy minority elite who had the means to organize and live together as a large, joint family. However, with the general mass in the urban settlements, it might be that the concept of בית אב continued, but because of the lack of resources many did not have the luxury to organize themselves and live as a big family.

girl in the Covenant Code (Exod 22:15–16) and its later modification in Deut 22:28–29. In the Covenant Code, the rapist is charged to pay a dowry, whereas Deuteronomy required the rapist to pay a fine of fifty shekels of silver. The custom of paying a dowry implies two points: (1) the kinship community is large, and (2) the dowry is paid to the bride's father to compensate for the loss of labor. However, such implications are ignored by the law found in the book of Deuteronomy.[33] Thus, this suggests the decline of the status of בית אבות.

Interestingly, this disintegration of the traditional family system empowered the monarchy as "it became easier to establish criteria for a new territorial division according to administrative principles favored by the Monarchy."[34] The creation of an administrative district by the monarchy changed the tribal boundaries and provided the channel for the monarchy to defuse the tribal agenda and enforce its view with greater ease. Such activity of the monarch also impacted another feature of the tribal framework. The tribal elders who played a prominent role in ancient Israel's society became less potent. Although they were incorporated into the royal governmental system, their power was no longer penetrative as it was before the establishment of the monarchy.[35] The disintegration of the tribal framework, in other words, gave rise to centralization where monarchical power became the ultimate authority.

4.2.1.2. An Oppressive Economy

As mentioned above the establishment of monarchy ushered in a sharp class stratification. The upper class comprising of the royal administration and the army in the kingdom depended on the

---

[33] See Faust, *Archaeology*, 264.
[34] Reviv, "Structure of Society," 125–46.
[35] *Ibid.*, 142.

monarch's grants and privileges, who either provided for them by giving away an Israelite's property or by awarding them a non-Israelite's land acquired through conquest. The monarchy found allies in the urban settlers whose tribal link was weak and who depended on the monarch for their survival. Coupled with this, the monarch also was involved in building projects, such as royal palaces and temples. All these extracted the resources of the common people living in the rural villages. The resources extracted were not only taxes and agricultural surplus, but also human resources in the form of corvée (cf. 2 Sam 20:24; 1 Kgs 5:13–18; 11:28; 15:22).[36]

The creation of the monarchy's professional, standing army in Israel (1 Sam 8:11–12) also came at a heavy expense of the general masses. Often the populace of Israel found themselves at the mercy of the military's dictates. As J. David Pleins writes:

> The populace would have to supply goods for the sustenance of the soldiers and military officials. In addition, the peasants would be called on to serve as forced laborers in the construction of military fortifications. The tendency would be for a military elite to develop, and this elite would acquire economic clout in the form of land given by the ruler as payment to military personnel for services rendered to the state (1 Sam 8:14–15).[37]

In line with this, Israel's peasant majority might have suffered a great deal during Israel's Aramean wars and during the Assyrian domination in the eighth and the seventh centuries BCE. No doubt

---

[36] D. Snell, "Taxes and Taxation," *ABD* 6:339; Holladay, "Kingdoms," 382.

[37] J. David Pleins, *Social Visions of the Hebrew Bible: A Theological Introduction* (Louisville: Westminster John Knox, 2001), 255; cf. Holladay, "Kingdoms," 382.

the economics of Israel's new societal system had the most shattering impact on the traditional, village-based mode of life.[38] The traditional practice of permanent land tenure was almost paralyzed with the rise of state-based economics in Israel. *Latifundialization* (derived from the term *latifundia*, meaning large estate) became prevalent, as royal officials and elite urban settlers grabbed enormous amount of land from the poor.[39]

---

[38] In recent times scholars such as Avraham Faust and Walter J. Houston have argued (although, Houston depends on Faust's archaeological findings) that the Israelite rural settlements were peaceful, less stratified, and that the traditional framework was intact throughout the monarchical period. In other words, the agricultural villages were homogenous. As such they contend that the prophetic references (in the books of Amos, Isaiah, Micah, and Jeremiah) to social stratification and economic oppression relate to the urban centers alone and do not suggest the oppression of the rural villages by the urban elites. See Faust, *Archaeology*, 172, 265; Walter J. Houston, "Exit the Oppressed Peasant? Rethinking the Background of Social Criticism in the Prophets," in *Prophecy and Prophets in Ancient Israel: Proceedings of the Oxford Old Testament Seminar* (ed. John Day; New York: T&T Clark, 2010), 101–17. However, Faust's archaeological findings and arguments are not without loopholes. Faust's himself remarks on numerous occasions that "the archaeological knowledge of rural settlement is very limited" (Faust, *Archaeology*, 129, 206, 234, 272). Moreover, he treats rural and urban settlements as two different entities without any relationship between them. Marvin Chaney argues against Faust and Houston that "If a broader spectrum of archaeological evidence is examined, it reveals that urban elites had greater impact upon the political economy of the countryside than Faust and Houston wish to acknowledge." Marvin L. Chaney, "The Bible, the Economy, and the Poor," *Journal of Religion & Society, Supplement Series* 10 (2014): 34–60. Chaney further points Faust's archaeological findings of "strongholds" and "fortress" in the rural areas (for Faust's discussion on strongholds and fortress see Faust, *Archaeology*, 189, 192–93) suggests the presence of the elite power in the rural agricultural villages. For a more detailed critique of Faust's and Houston's works see Chaney, "Bible," 49–53.

[39] D.N. Premnath, *Eighth Century Prophets: A Social Analysis* (St Louis: Chalice, 2003), 20–24.

Moreover, the plight of the peasant majority was exacerbated by the involvement of the monarchy in foreign trade. The principal imports—especially during the eighth century BCE—were luxury goods, military equipment, and building materials for royal projects.[40] These imports were made possible for the urban elites at the expense of the poor peasants. Chaney writes: "The exportable commodities were finite and varied with erratic growing conditions, but the elite's appetite for luxury, military, and monumental imports was virtually limitless."[41] Such an economic gap created by foreign trade between the urban elites and the peasant majority is vividly highlighted in the indictments of the eighth century prophets (Mic 2:1–5; Amos 4:1–3; 6:4–7; Hos 9:1–3; Isa 5:11–13).

This situation, moreover, was worsened by a judiciary system that favored the rich and the powerful (cf. Isa 1:21–23; 5:23; 10:1–2; 32:7), which in turn provided leeway to the rich elite of the society to coerce small village farmers into debt, foreclosure, and ultimately permanent loss of their ancestral land. In this way the forfeited lands were confiscated and added to the growing estates of the wealthy elite. Concurrently, the former owners became either day laborers or slaves on their ancestral lands. The prophet Isaiah addresses this issue in Isa 5:8, "Woe to those who add house to house and join field to field, until there is no more room, so that you have to live alone in the midst of the land!" This dirge is

---

[40] Chaney, "Bible," 37.

[41] *Ibid.* Chaney points out that the peasants were forced by the monarchic state and its urban elites ("command economies") to invest in farming olive and wine instead of their usual mixed subsistence. This is archaeologically supported by the presence of rock-cut oil and grape processing installations in the hill country of the eighth century. See Premnath, *Eighth Century Prophets*, 58–66. Also Faust's findings of "towers" and "fortress" in the rural agricultural area suggest the forced activity of the monarchic state upon the peasant majority. See Faust, *Archaeology*, 178–89.

aimed at those rich, elite land-grabbers, whose exploitative actions were threatening the collapse of one of Israel's core, traditional systems—the נחלה, which ensured a permanent land assignment to one's lineage.

4.2.1.3. The Corrosion of faith in Yahweh

Early Israel struggled to maintain the Yahwistic tradition's belief system as the system evolved over time. This is vividly depicted in the book of Judges—the period just after Israel had entered the Promised Land. As discussed in chapter three, the instituted monarchy was limited, in that the monarch was supposed to rule within the משפטים of Yahwistic beliefs and traditions.[42] Yet, it was the monarchy that aided the corrosion of faith in Yahweh. The appointment of competing priests or non-traditional priests by the monarch provided the platform for slowly eroding the traditional Yahwistic belief system. David appointed Zadok, a non-Levitical priest, and Abiathar, a traditional Levitical priest. However, Zadok interestingly appears to have taken precedence over Abiathar (2 Sam 15:24, 29, 35; 19:12; 20:25). David also appointed his sons as priests (2 Sam 8:18). Later when the kingdom was divided, Jeroboam the king of the northern kingdom built altars in Dan and Bethel and appointed priests from among all the people who were not Levites (1 Kgs 12:31). Not surprisingly these priests supported the royal agenda at the expense of Yahwistic traditional belief. This is exemplified in the stance of Amaziah, the priest of Bethel who staunchly supported his royal patron against the prophet Amos (Amos 7:10–13).

---

[42] See also the discussion of J.J.M. Roberts, "In Defense of the Monarchy: The Contribution of Israelite Kingship to Biblical Theology," in *Ancient Israelite Religion: Essays in Honor of Frank Moore Cross* (ed. Patrick D. Miller, Paul D. Hanson, and S. Dean McBride; Philadelphia: Fortress, 1987), 377–97.

The expansion of the kingdom during the time of David and Solomon also affected the character of the religion of common people (and the popular religion) of Israel. The text of 1 Kgs 9:20–22 describes the assimilation of the Canaanite population into Israel during the time of Solomon. Perhaps, the excavated figurines common among early Israelites and Canaanites reflect this process of cultural assimilation.[43] Moreover, the foreign policies of Israel, such as making alliances with foreign nation states through marriages affected the traditional belief system of Israel. Solomon erected shrines for his wives' gods on the mountain east of Jerusalem (1 Kgs 11:7; 2 Kgs 23:13).[44] King Ahab of the Omride

---

[43] Thousands of terracotta figurines (both anthropomorphic and zoomorphic) have been found at most of the excavated sites of the Canaanite and Israelite periods. Among these figurines are traditional fertility goddesses who are depicted as naked and supporting prominent breasts with their hands. Some scholars think that this fertility goddess is Astarte. Astarte (Ashtaroth in plural form) is a fertility goddess of the Canaanites, the Sidonians and the Philistines (1 Kgs 11:5; 1 Sam 31:10). The Babylonians and the Assyrians called her Ishtar. Astarte/Ashtoreth is the god of storm and the consort of Baal. See Avraham Negev ed., "Astarte; Ashtoreth," in *The Archaeological Encyclopedia of the Holy Land* (Nashville: Thomas Nelson, 1986), 39–40. However, recent scholars think that this goddess is none other than Asherah because of recent discoveries at Kuntillet Ajrud and Kirbet el Qom. However, this debate of Astarte or Asherah remains unclear. See Raz Kletter, "Between Archaeology and Theology: The Pillar Figurines from Judah and the Asherah," in *Studies in the Archaeology of the Iron Age in Israel and Jordan* (ed. Amihai Mazar; JSOTSup 331; Sheffield: Sheffield Academic, 2001), 179–216. See also Erin Darby, *Interpreting Judean Pillar Figurines: Gender and Empire in Judean Apotropaic Ritual* (FAT II 69; Tübingen: Mohr Siebeck, 2014).

[44] Gabriel Barkay points out the foreign influences in other aspects of Israel's kingdom during Solomon's reign. He asserts, "These foreign influences are evident in the general concepts of urban planning, in individual building plans, and in construction techniques. Many details of Solomonic architecture reveal the influence of the neo-Hittite culture of northern Syria, the Canaanite-Phoenician culture of the Lebanese coast, and probably Egyptian culture as

dynasty of the northern kingdom married to Jezebel, the Sidonian princess, which brought Phoenician Baal worship directly to Samaria. A Baal temple was built in Samaria and scores of Baal prophets were inducted (1 Kgs 16:32; 18:19). The marriage of Athaliah, daughter of Ahab and Jezebel, to the Judahite, Joram son of Jehoshaphat, brought the Baal cult into Judah. A Baal temple was built, apparently in Jerusalem, where a Baal priest by the name Mattan was employed (2 Kgs 11:18). This monarchical activity of building altars for foreign gods and partly embracing them was lifted to an unprecedented height by Manasseh (2 Kgs 21).

The international trade in which the monarchy was involved not only imported luxurious items and building materials, but also religious beliefs and practices. This is clearly depicted by the excavated site of Kuntillet 'Ajrud along the "Gaza Road," about fifty kilometers south of Kadesh-Barnea.[45] It was a desert sanctuary and also a caravanserai with interesting murals, religious graffiti, and inscriptions projecting mythological beings and religious symbols and referring to Yahweh, El, Baal, and Asherah. This site does not signify a major Judean sanctuary, but sheds light on the plausible syncretistic nature that might have occurred to people of different places and cultures—such as Israel, Judah, Phoenicia, Philistia, and the South Arabian kingdoms—while meeting for trade and commerce. Thus, these artistic and epigraphic relics bear witness to the religious tensions that might have existed between a Yahwistic belief system and the broader world of Mediterranean multi-culturalism.[46]

---

well" ("The Iron Age II-III," in *The Archaeology of Ancient Israel* [ed. Amnin Ben-Tor; trans. R. Greenberg; New Haven: Yale University Press, 1992], 306.

[45] Amihai Mazar, *Archaeology of the Land of the Bible 10,000–586 B.C.E* (New Haven: Yale University Press, 2009), 446.

[46] J.S. Holladay, "Religion in Israel and Judah under the Monarchy: An Explicitly Archaeological Approach," in *Ancient Israelite Religion* (ed. Patrick

4.2.2. Israel's Prophets in their Agrarian Context

It is insufficient to talk about Israel without mentioning the role of its prophets and prophecies. When one surveys the history of ancient Israel, the prophets played prominent roles at decisive junctures. For instance, Moses, the prophet *par excellence*, aided Israel in establishing a covenant relationship with Yahweh. Samuel, a priest and a prophet, played a vital role in instituting the monarchy in Israel. Later, a host of Yahweh's prophets played creative and innovative roles in sustaining and nurturing the Israelite, Yahwistic tradition. In short, Israel's prophets were intrinsic to her society.

It is no surprise, then, that we find in the OT numerous prophets and prophetesses actively involved in shaping Israelite society. These prophets even had their own guilds (sometimes known as the "sons of the prophets" [cf. 2 Kgs 6:1–7]) and practiced prophecy as profession (cf. 1 Kgs 20:35; 2 Kgs 5:22; 9:1). However, as I have pointed out earlier, it is paramount to understand the role of Israel's prophecy in conjunction with the "limited monarchy." The prominent role of the prophet during the early part of the monarchical period was to monitor the king and his policies, to ensure that they were in line with Yahweh's מִשְׁפָּטִים. This role naturally vested immense power in the prophets in Israel (see discussion in chapter three).

However, in an agrarian context where the resources for survival were limited and where the governing class considered political power and status as means of self-aggrandizement and not to raise the living standard of the common people (also known as the proprietary theory of the state), the dynamics of the prophets

---

D. Miller, Paul D. Hanson, and S. Dean McBride; Philadelphia: Fortress, 1987), 249–302. See also Arnold, "Religion in Ancient Israel," 391–420.

were never straightforward.[47] For the legitimacy of his reign and policies, the monarch needed the confirmation of the prophets. Concurrently, one could imagine that the prophets needed the royal court to sustain their group as well as to maintain their status. In the ANE context, it was not uncommon for prophets to receive gifts and money from the king or higher authority or even the general public.[48] Hence, corruption among the prophets became a distinct possibility.

Apparently, many prophets were employed in Israel's royal court. For example, David had two court prophets in Gad (2 Sam 24:11; cf. 2 Chr 29:25) and Nathan (2 Sam 7:1; 12:1–15), and King Ahab of the Omride dynasty had four hundred prophets directed by Zedekiah ben Chenaanah (1 Kgs 22). This type of environment— limited subsistence resources and craving for power and privileges—is a perfect recipe for power manipulation or compromising one's stance in any context, not least, an ancient agrarian society. It is in this kind of general context that Micah denounced some of his colleagues who prophesied peace when their teeth have something to bite but declare war against the one who puts nothing into their mouths (Mic 3:5; 2:6–11).

Of course, this does not mean that all the kings and prophets of Israel were power mongers and unjust people by the standard of the Yahwistic tradition. However, the want of personal gain,

---

[47] For the proprietary theory of state, see Nolan-Lenski, *Human Societies*, 162–63.

[48] For example, Balaam was offered money and honor by king Balak of Moab to curse Israel (Num 22); Elisha was presented with six thousand shekels of gold and other gifts from Naaman of Syria for curing the latter's leprosy (2 Kgs 5:1–14); the Mari prophets (*āpilum, muḫḫûm, qammātum*) are also recorded as receiving gifts from the king (cf. ARM, 26, 194, 217, 218, 219, 227). See Jean-Marie Durand, *Archives épistolaires de Mari* I/1 (ARM 26; Paris: Editions Recherche sur les Civilizations, 1988), 194, 217–19, 227.

power, and privileges conditioned many of them.⁴⁹ Before moving further one point needs to be noted concerning the prophets of the royal court and prophets independent of the royal administration.⁵⁰ This distinction does not mean that the royally supported prophets were all corrupted whereas, other prophets were true prophets. This is suggested by the fact that prophets such as Nathan and Isaiah although, directly related to the royal administration, prophesied and functioned according to the vision of Yahwistic tradition. As will be discussed below even some Israelites kings and royal officials aspired to live within the framework of Yahweh's משפטים. Thus, it is incorrect to assume *a priori* that a prophet is corrupted and false because of his/her affiliation to the royal court. Rather it is the covenant relationship between Yahweh

---

[49] Cook argues similarly that the Levitical priests, who were supposed to nurture the Yahwistic tradition among the people, in fact, were corrupted by the want of power, material privileges and comfort. Cook further argues that the prophet Jeremiah, a Levite himself, was critical of these compromised Levites—see Stephen L. Cook, "The Levites and Sociocultural Change in Ancient Judah: Insights from Gerhard Lenski's Social Theory," in *Social Theory and the Study of Israelite Religion: Essays in Retrospect and Prospect* (ed. Saul M. Olyan; Atlanta: Society of Biblical Literature, 2012), 41–58.

[50] James K. Mead points out that there are three categories of biblical prophets. The first category includes those associated with the cultic life of Israel such as Samuel. The second category includes the prophets supported by the royal administration such as the large group of prophets at King Ahab's court who were basically the mouthpiece of the king himself. However, in this category we can also include prophets such as Nathan and Isaiah who were guided by the principles of Yahwistic tradition in spite of their dependence on the royal administration. Finally, the third category includes prophets who were independent of the royal support such as Elijah, Elisha and their company of prophets (2 Kgs 6:1). See James K. Mead, "The Biblical Prophets in Historiography," in *Ancient Israel's History: An Introduction to Issues and Sources* (ed. Bill T. Arnold and Richard S. Hess; Grand Rapids: Baker Academic, 2014), 262–85.

and his prophets that become crucial in distinguishing a true from a false prophet.

The vast majority of the kings, beginning with Solomon and, especially, the kings of the northern kingdom were involved in intermarriages with foreign wives to strengthen their foreign relations. However, in the sight of the Yahwistic prophet this relationship formed by intermarriages was not acceptable because it showed the king's lack of trust in Yahweh. Moreover, these intermarriages welcomed foreign religions immediately into the society of the Israelites. There is no doubt, attitudes toward the prophets varied; with some assuming Israel's prophets were narrow-minded people in comparison to the commonality of international alliances. Yet, we must also point out that there was little distinction between sacral and profane entities during this era. In fact, everything was viewed and interpreted from the sacral perspective.[51] Therefore, support of the foreign policies of the monarchs by any prophet sent a suspicious signal about his credibility as Yahweh's prophet.

4.2.2.1. Institutionalizing the Yahwistic Tradition

The prophetic conflict in 1 Kgs 22 provides a glimpse of the religio-politcal climate of the king and the prophetic community. This prophetic conflict needs to be understood within the wider context of King Ahab's marriage to Jezebel (1 Kgs 16:29–34; 18:1–46) and his dealing with Naboth (1 Kgs 21:1–29). Earlier in the narrative, the prophet Elijah condemns King Ahab for building a place of Baal for his wife Jezebel. He is also condemned by Elijah for snatching away the נחלה (ancestral land) of Naboth. Yet,

---

[51] Gerhard von Rad calls this "pan-sacralism" (von Rad, *Wisdom in Israel* [trans. James D. Martin; Harrisburg: Trinity International, 1993], 63; cf. also McEvenue's view of "compact mentality" of ancient Israelite society—see *Interpretation and Bible*, 113–14).

in 1 Kgs 22 King Ahab has no qualms in consulting Yahweh's prophets (although instigated by King Jehoshaphat of Judah) concerning waging war with the Arameans over Ramoth-Gilead. This shows Ahab's contradictory belief system. That is, he acts to please his wife at the cost of his traditional Yahwistic beliefs, but still consults Yahweh's prophets about waging war against the Arameans. This depicts the attitude of a person being consumed by power and status. In other words, Ahab completely lacked integrity.[52] King Ahab had already determined his course of action to attack the Arameans even before he consulted the prophets.

Now the manner in which the four hundred prophets under Zedekiah ben Chenaanah performed their prophecy, especially when he held the iron horn, is very Yahwistic in practice (cf. the horn imagery with Moses' blessing on Joseph [Deut 33:17]; see also Pss 21–22, 61, and 83). As the narrative recounts, Zedekiah and his band of prophets prophesied that Yahweh had given victory to the king. However, up to this point in the drama another prophet named Micaiah ben Imlah was missing. Probably, Micaiah was no different from these court prophets in either position or rank, except that "he never prophesies good concerning me [Ahab], but evil" (1 Kgs 22:8).[53]

Micaiah did not share the optimistic prophecy of these prophets, rather he prophesied Ahab's defeat and the scattering of Israelites on the hills without a leader (v. 17). Interestingly, the prophecy of Micaiah concerns not necessarily the king, but the people of Israel being scattered. Yet, Ahab's focus is on himself and his royal agenda, instead of repenting and returning to

---

[52] Moberly argues that integrity is the key to discernment. In this case, Ahab surely lacked the needed ingredient to be discerning—see *Prophecy and Discernment,* 126.

[53] See also Norman K. Gottwald, *All the Kingdoms of the Earth: Israelite Prophecy and International Relations in the Ancient Near East* (New York: Harper & Row, 1964), 69.

Yahweh.⁵⁴ There are no reasons cited for Micaiah's objection of the popular voice, but his prophecy might have been a response to Ahab's refusal to expel Baalism and his action against Naboth which resulted in breaching the Yahwistic covenant. This prophetic conflict suggests that, unlike Micaiah, those four hundred prophets of Yahweh under Zedekiah had been sold out to their craving of power and privileges.⁵⁵ Moshe Greenberg's opinion about the nature of Israel's prophets is quite accurate: "By the 9th century, the northern prophets had become institutionalized, and the accompanying decay began to show."⁵⁶

The word "institutionalized" connotes negativity. It implies that the Yahwistic tradition was merely reduced to empty rituals

---

⁵⁴ Moberly, *Prophecy and Discernment*, 115.

⁵⁵ Beyond this, however, we should note that this narrative, as the other narratives in OT, is recounted artistically, utilizing intentional rhetorical skills. Two narrative features I want to point out here. The first concerns the setting. The narrator succinctly elaborates the royal setting (1 Kg 22:10) as the kings wait for the prophets to prophesy. The reason the narrator provides this setting is to contrast with Micaiah's vision on heavenly court (vv. 19–23) and to expose the true nature of the earthly court. The second point concerns the rhetorical skills in the narrative. Much has been said about the "lying spirit" from Yahweh's court that enticed King Ahab (vv. 19–23). However, it has to be understood as a deliberate rhetorical ploy utilized by Micaiah in order to drive his message home. Micaiah's prophecy of defeat for the king has been rejected and therefore this was his desperate attempt to let King Ahab realize his ill motive. It has to be noted that the reason for this prophecy was to persuade the king to repent and return to Yahweh, and not just to declare judgment. Moberly commenting on this says: "Micaiah has a communicative strategy similar to that of Nathan in his famous confrontation with David (2 Sam 12:1–7). The golden rule is simple: Don't state the obvious." Thus, Micaiah makes a heightened dramatic scene to persuade King Ahab to heed his prophecy. For more detailed explanation about this "lying spirit" (see Moberly, *Prophecy and Discernment*, 116–20).

⁵⁶ M. Greenberg, "Religion: Stability and Ferment," in *The Age of the Monarchies: Culture and Society* (ed. Abraham Malamat; 5 vols.; Jerusalem: Massada, 1979), 79–124.

without any content. This also means that the so-called prophets were not sensitive to the further revelation of Yahweh. Such institutionalizing of the prophetic office (and Yahweh cultic worship in general) led to the misrepresentation of the traditional Yahwistic beliefs. This is exemplified by distorting the phrase "the day of Yahweh" (cf. Amos 5:18–20) and reducing worship of Yahweh to mere ritual practice (cf. Amos 5:21–27).

The phrase "the day of Yahweh" is connected to a popular eschatology of Israel, perhaps, one that goes back to the earlier Yahwistic tradition of holy war (Judg 7; cf. Isa 9:4) wherein Yahweh intervenes in history on behalf of Israel in vanquishing her enemies.[57] It was a day of victory and celebration for Yahweh's people. However, this understanding was intrinsically connected to the covenant relationship between Yahweh and Israel—blessings for maintaining the covenant and curses for breaking the covenant (cf. Lev 26; Deut 27–28). For Yahweh to intervene and redeem Israel, the people needed to observe the covenant stipulations. Unfortunately, for Israel, they were blind to the covenant relationship. Therefore, prophets such as Amos and Joel declared that judgment will be directed to Israel itself.[58] Institutionalization

---

[57] Gerhard von Rad, "The Origin of the Concept of the Day of Yahweh," *JSS* (1959): 97–108. See also Paul R. House, "The Day of the Lord," in *Central Themes in Biblical Theology: Mapping Unity in Diversity* (ed. Scott J. Hafemann and Paul R. House; Grand Rapids: Baker Academic, 2007), 179–223; John Barton, "The Day of Yahweh in the Minor Prophets," in *The Old Testament: Canon, Literature and Theology: Collected Essays of John Barton* (Hampshire: Ashgate, 2007), 279–88.

[58] Arnold argues that the prophet Amos turned the Israelite's positive expectation of the day of Yahweh into a negative expectation. He further argues that such emphasis on the concept of the day of Yahweh by the eighth century prophets BCE generally gave rise to OT eschatology and apocalypticism—see Arnold, "Old Testament Eschatology and the Rise of Apocalypticism," in *The Oxford Handbook of Eschatology* (ed. Jerry L. Walls; Oxford: Oxford University Press, 2008), 23–39.

of the concept of "the day of Yahweh" reduced Israel's belief in Yahweh into a mere theoretical concept without proper critical reflection. This misconception became popular because of the wrong motives of Israel's cultic leaders, of which the prophets partly belonged.

It is imperative here to clarify a common mistake in the deliberation of true and false prophecies. It has been pointed out that true prophets promised doom, whereas false prophets promised peace.[59] This was generally the case. However, a true prophet could also prophesy peace and victory (cf. Isa 7). The important and crucial point is the covenant relationship. In other words, if the relationship is maintained then blessings, peace, and victory will follow, but if the covenant is broken, judgment is inevitable. The issue of doom and peaceful prophecies cannot be understood dogmatically but only in consideration of the covenant relationship. At the same time, false prophecy is not exclusively about misreading the tradition and the historical context, but it is most importantly about degeneration of morality in relation to the covenant relationship with Yahweh, or, as Moberly has it, integrity.[60]

The institutionalizing of the cult and the prophetic office also reduced Israel's worship into mere ritual, devoid of practical action. Because of this, Israelite religion was in "danger of becoming a pagan religion."[61] Most of Israel's eighth-century prophets critiqued their society for gathering in throngs to worship

---

[59] See Crenshaw, *Prophetic Conflict*, 52–54.

[60] See Moberly, *Prophecy and Discernment*, 126. James A. Sanders is right in pointing out that false prophecy is a result of a dogmatic interpretation of the tradition. But his judgment is not complete when he argues that false prophecy is a consequence of misreading the tradition—see "Hermeneutics in True and False Prophecy," 21–41; see also my discussion on Sanders view in Chapter 1.

[61] John Bright, *A History of Israel* (Louisville: Westminster John Knox, 2000), 262.

lavishly in the major temples without enacting justice for the poor and needy. Thus, the effect of institutionalization had severe consequences on the spirituality of Israelite society. It negated the organic and right relationship between Yahweh and his people and, subsequently, among his people themselves. It made Israelite religion sterile and made their spirituality anemic and ineffective.

4.2.2.2. The Blurred Spirituality of the Vox Populi

If the eighth century BCE is called the golden period of ancient Israel's prophets and prophecies, then both the northern and the southern kingdoms during this period can be called anything but desirable in their socio-economic and religious aspects. In fact, from the perspective of the Yahwistic tradition it was as bad as Sodom and Gomorrah on the verge of Yahweh's judgment (cf. Amos 4:11; Isa 1:9–10). Politically, both the states were relatively stable during the first half of the eighth century.[62] However, as noted above, the royal and wealthy elites economically oppressed the peasant majority.

Interestingly, this corruption was found in every level of the society. In other words, even the poor, if given the chance, oppressed other poor persons. This was the reason why prophets like Amos and Micah, though they sharply criticized the wealthy ruling class, prophesied against the whole nation (cf. Mic 7:1-7; Amos 3:1; 5:1-3).[63] By this time, religious decay was widespread.

---

[62] Both the states were ruled by able leaders: King Jeroboam II (786–746 BCE) of the northern kingdom and king Uzziah (783–742 BCE) of the Southern kingdom. Moreover, the international politics favored their reigns. Damascus the chief tormentor of the region fell to Adad-nirari III (811–784 BCE) of Assyria. However, Assyria had her own internal issues which curtailed her international involvement. This led both the rulers of Israel and Judah to flourish and to stretch their territories. For more detail, see Bright, *History of Israel*, 255–59.

[63] For more on this, see Mark Daniel Carroll R, *Contexts for Amos: Prophetic Poetics in Latin American Perspective* (JSOTSup 132; Sheffield:

Many great shrines of the northern kingdom were full of worshipers who lavishly supported the holy places (Amos 4:4–5; 5:21–24), yet they were far from what Yahweh desired. At the same time, the local shrines (במות) at many places were overtly pagan. Many of them practiced the rites of the fertility cult (Hos 1–3; 4:11–14). It is significant that the Samaria Ostraca depicts that the common suffix of personal names were either "Ba'al" or "Yahweh."[64] Although some of the names using Baal might simply mean "Lord," an appellation of Yahweh, Bright contends that, "The conclusion is inescapable that many Israelites were worshipers of Ba'al."[65]

In the southern kingdom many sorcerers and fortunetellers were popular, and worship of Asherim (groves of trees), and carved images was practiced (Mic 5:12–14). Micah indicates in 6:16 that Judah has imported these forms of worship from the house of Ahab. As mentioned above, archaeologists have discovered pillar-shaped figurines from the eighth and seventh centuries in Jerusalem. Curiously, these figurines were found not in sanctuaries, but in private homes.[66] In relation to this worship of carved images, Isaiah prophesied: "They shall be turned back and

---

Sheffield Academic, 1992), 182–85, 222–24, 273–77; Philip Peter Jenson, *Obadiah, Jonah, Micah: A Theological Commentary* (New York: T&T Clark, 2008), 100.

[64] W.F. Albright, *Archaeology and the Religion of Israel* (Doubleday Anchor Book, 1969), 155. See also Mazar, *Archaeology*, 410.

[65] Bright, *History of Israel*, 261. Also Jeffrey H. Tigay in his work surveys the evidences of divine names in Hebrew epigraphic documents. He concludes that the overwhelming number of divine names represent Yahweh followed by Baal. If anything Tigay's work suggest that the normative religion of Israel during the monarchy period was Yahwism but that there was also the presence of religious syncreticism—see Tigay, *You Shall Have No Other Gods: Israelite Religion in the Light of Hebrew Inscriptions* (HSS 31; Atlanta: Scholars Press, 1986), 37–41.

[66] King-Stager, *Life in Biblical Israel*, 348.

utterly put to shame—those who trust in carved images, who say to cast images, 'you are our gods'" (Isa 42:17; 44:9–17; cf. Jer 44:15–25).

One obvious reason for such allurement to carved images and foreign gods and goddesses among the northern and southern kingdoms during the monarchial period is the institutionalizing of the Yahwistic belief system which jeopardized their commitment. Another reason, although interconnected with the first, could be the belief in magic which was widespread in ancient agrarian societies. In relation to the belief in magic, it has been argued that the countless excavated goddess figurines in Jerusalem might have been used as magical objects. Although this is inconclusive,[67] the agrarian context supports this argument. In addition, the fact that these figurines were disposed as domestic waste in the streets and pits also suggests that they might have served as amulets or "luck charms," and did not represent a major deity.[68] Belief in magic and supernatural forces was common because they provided an easy escape from life's challenging problems and uncertainties.

Perhaps, for many common people a hard economic plight made them susceptible to practices such as divination, sorcery, the horoscope, and prophecy. Put in another way, it was the needs of the people or the fragility of the people's spirituality (partly caused by the institutionalizing of faith) that also encouraged the growth of false prophecy. The slippery part of this dynamic is that as time elapsed the line between the true and false tradition increasingly becomes thin and elusive. Thus, it can be assumed that in such an environment there might have been prophets who genuinely

---

[67] See Kletter, "Between Archaeology," 201, 203–4.

[68] H.J. Franken and M.L. Steiner, *Excavations in Jerusalem 1961–1967: The Iron Age Extramural Quarter on the South-East Hill* (vol. II/V; Oxford: Oxford University Press, 1990), 128; cf. also G.E. Wright, *Biblical Archaeology* (Philadelphia: Westminster, 1962), 118.

thought they were prophesying the right message without realizing where they went wrong. In the end, they fell victim to institutionalized religion and, eventually, false prophecy.

4.2.3. Summary of Observations

The description above of the Israelite monarchy and prophets within an agrarian context indicates the complexity of Israelite societies. In navigating this complexity, it becomes clear that Israelite Yahwistic belief has three variations: official religion, popular religion, and the religion of the true Yahwistic prophets and their adherents. All three variations have the same genesis of belief and have Yahweh as the common denominator; he was the central deity of their religion. However, the official religion propagated by the monarchy and its administration utilized Yahwistic belief as a means of forwarding their agenda, which very often was diluted by the incorporation of foreign deities and selfish motives. The result was the institutionalization of Yahwistic faith. The popular religion considered Yahweh to be the central deity; however, in many cases because of the people's strong inclination towards magic and fatalism, it became easy to slip into syncretism or polytheism. It is in between these two sub-stratums of Yahwistic belief that the true prophets of Yahweh endeavored to sustain and further make relevant the Yahwistic tradition of old. The interactions of these three variations of Yahwistic belief, in the spheres of socio-economics and politics, made the situation more complex and, with time, perplexing. It is within this complex context that the distinction between true and false prophecies may be identified.

Thus, one can argue that a false prophet is someone who supports the institutionalizing of official religion. In other words, a false prophet is someone who remains blind to the agenda of the status quo. However, the reason for such attitude of the so-called false prophet might not be necessarily straightforward. For some the reason might be related to their material and physical gain from the monarchy and its administrative system; whereas for others it might be the inability to understand and read the complexity of their situation. As time elapsed this inability to reflect critically upon their received tradition and the existing circumstances, in turn, empowered the so-called false prophets to unassumingly abuse their prophetic status by exploiting the economic plight of the common people, who could be an easy prey to magic and false comfort. A true prophet, on the other hand, is someone who was rooted in his or her old Yahwistic tradition and yet remained open to Yahweh's further illumination.

It is incorrect, therefore, to argue that a true prophet was an ardent critic of the institution of monarchy.[69] It is clear that Yahwistic tradition did not abhor monarchy *per se*, but it only insisted that Israel's monarchy should be a "limited monarchy." Thus, a true prophet aspired to make sure that Israel's monarchy functioned within the norm of Yahwistic tradition.

---

[69] I agree with Grabbe that it is wrong to depict a true prophet in the OT as someone who criticizes the power that be and a false prophet is an ardent supporter of the monarchy. However, I disagree with Grabbe's argument in reaching that conclusion. He argues utilizing evidence from social anthropology that in some modern societies the so-called false prophets were dead against the existing government. Therefore, a prophet in the OT cannot be deemed true only on the basis of his/her anti-monarchial view. Grabbe's argument is uncritical because as I articulated above the OT Yahwistic prophets were not against monarchy *per se* but only insisted for "limited monarchy." Grabbe failed to consider questions such as why did the so-called true prophets in the OT reject monarchy if they did so? What kind of monarchy was rejected? What was the context of the Israelite society in which the prophets minister? For Grabbe's view, see "Jeremiah among the Social Anthropologist," in *Prophecy in the Book of Jeremiah* (ed. Hans M. Barstad and Reinhard G. Kratz; BZAW 388; Berlin: de Gruyter, 2009), 80–88.

4.3. The Support Group of the Yahwistic Prophets

To reiterate, the true prophets of Israel were the bearers of the old Yahwistic traditions. This does not, of course, mean that they were narrow minded and unprogressive traditionalists. Rather, they tried to keep the covenantal relationship with Yahweh intact without falling into traditionalism.[70] As bearers of certain traditions, one can assume that the prophets had a support group who stood behind them. Sociologically this is true, as Robert Wilson argued: "In societies where prophecy is tolerated or encouraged, a prophet requires social support throughout the entire prophetic experiences."[71] Contrary to Wilson's argument, however, not all the prophets act or prophesy according to the wishes and penchants of their support groups.[72] Rather, in some instances, both the prophet and his support group have a common vision, stemming from one common tradition.

Since the introduction of the monarchy in Israel and the revamping of her society, there existed two competing systems of governance: one gravitated towards the royalty and its urban machination; the other towards the old Yahwistic tradition under

---

[70] Jaroslav Pelikan's distinction between tradition and traditionalism succinctly describes my understanding of Israel's true prophets as the bearers of the Yahwistic tradition. Pelikan contends, "Tradition is the living faith of the dead; traditionalism is the dead faith of the living. Tradition lives in conversation with the past, while remembering where we are and when we are and that it is we who have to decide. Traditionalism supposes that nothing should ever be done for the first time, so all that is needed to solve any problem is to arrive at the supposedly unanimous testimony of this homogenized tradition" (*The Vindication of Tradition: The 1983 Jefferson Lecture in the Humanities* [New Haven: Yale University Press, 1984], 65).

[71] R.R. Wilson, "Interpreting Israel's Religion: An Anthropological Perspective on the Problem of False Prophecy," in *"The Place is Too Small for Us": The Israelite Prophets in Recent Scholarship* (ed. Robert P. Gordon; SBTS 5; Winona Lake, IN: Eisenbrauns, 1995), 332–44.

[72] *Ibid.*, 339.

some elders, Levites, scribes, prophets, and at times, even princes (cf. Jer 1:18; 34:19; 37:2; Ezek 7:27; 22:29). This second group is also popularly known as the עם־הארץ (literally, "people of the land"). In an agrarian society such competition among the ruling class is not unusual. As such there were factions within the ruling class who clashed with one another to enhance their personal gain and agenda. Lenski describes this factional struggle as "struggles between opposing factions of the privileged class, each seeking its own special advantage, or, occasionally, a small segment of the common people seeking political advantage and preferment for themselves."[73] As we shall see below the עם־הארץ did have their political agenda but they also struggled for instituting Yahweh's משפטים in Judah.

It has to be noted, however, that the nomenclature עם־הארץ is not used in the northern kingdom. This does not mean that a similar concept and movement was not present in the northern kingdom, but such a movement did not gain the traction that it did in the southern kingdom. The understanding of this term, "people of the land" is contentious. Mayer Sulzberger argued that this phrase is the *terminus technicus* of a political group in ancient Israel that arose after the death of Joshua and remained active until the Hellenistic period.[74] De Vaux, on the other hand, contended that this phrase is merely a generic term representing all the people of the land.[75] Ernest Nicholson's study of this term suggests that each text relating to this term should be considered contextually.[76] Clearly, Nicholson's conclusion is sound because in some passages

---

[73] Lenski, *Power and Privilege*, 211.

[74] M. Sulzberger, *The AM HA-ARETZ: The Ancient Hebrew Parliament* (Philadelphia: Julius H. Greenstone, 1910), 8–13.

[75] De Vaux, *Ancient Israel*, 71.

[76] E.W. Nicholson, "The Meaning of the Expression 'am ha'arez in the Old Testament," *JSS* 10 (1965): 59–66; see also B. Halpern, *The Constitution of the Monarchy in Israel* (HSM 25; Chicago: Scholars Press, 1981), 196–98.

the phrase relates to fully enfranchised, land-owning citizens (cf. Gen 23:7), whereas in others it relates to the whole Jewish population (cf. 2 Kgs 11:14; 2 Chr 23), still in other passages it refers to a political body probably made up of some leading members of the country population (cf. 2 Kgs 21:24; 23:30; 25:19). Moreover, the expression of this term in the post-exilic period has different meanings in that the returnees considered themselves as the people of the land or the indigenous people with pure blood without any intermarriages (cf. Neh 13:23; Ezra 9:1, 11; 2 Chr 13:9). Thus, it was used in a pejorative sense.[77] However, the suggestion that some of the passages with the phrase, "people of the land," during the pre-exilic period related to a group of people having a similar vision and inclinations should be taken seriously.

Another contentious point relating to this phrase is, if the "people of the land" is a political entity, then who are its members? Some interpret the members of this group as the "proletariat," whose existence is to revolt against the authorities and its noble members somewhat similar to that of a class struggle.[78] However, this might be a modern anachronism of class struggle for it was not common among the ancient agrarian peasants to revolt. Such revolt was more prevalent, rather, among the elite factions.[79]

Further, some argue that the group consists of enfranchised landed gentries. Cook connects these free landed gentries to the

---

[77] In the post exilic period this term is used in its plural form. See Joseph P. Healey, "AM HA'AREZ," *ABD* 1:168–9. For the late development of the usage of this term see A.H.J. Gunneweg, 'AM HA'ARES—A Semantic Revolution," *ZAW* 95 (1983): 437–40.

[78] See specifically, K. Galling, "Die israelitische Staatsverfassung in ihrer vorderorientalischen Umwelt," *AO* 28 (1929): 5–64.

[79] See Cook, *Social Roots*, 46; also P. Dutcher-Walls, "The Social Location of the Deuteronomists: A Sociological Study of Factional Politics in Late Pre-Exilic Judah," *JSOT* 52 (1991): 77–94.

village elders.⁸⁰ He further argues that the rural areas of the monarchic-period had modest but erected boundary walls, suggesting that there existed a local administrative body.⁸¹ This local administrative body likely consisted of the village elders, the patriarchs of the extended family (בית אב).⁸² The archaeological study of Iron II Israel also indicates that the elders (זקנים) were still the decision-making body for the rural communities even during the monarchic times.⁸³ Another view concerning the members of the "people of the land" is provided by J.A. Soggin who contends that the body represented those who were faithful to the Yahwistic tradition and worshipped God in the spirit of the prophets.⁸⁴ Similarly, P. Dutcher-Walls while dealing with texts relating to the "people of the land" (2 Kgs 22–23; Jer 26, 29, and 36) points out that this group is represented by different sub-groups such as the priest, prophets, scribes, and nobles.⁸⁵

The arguments independently put forward by Soggin, Cook, and Dutcher-Walls, when combined together, make more sense in understanding the members, the vision and aspiration of this group. Again it comes back to our discussion of limited monarchy. Israel's monarchy was supposed to be limited in nature which meant that the monarchy had to function within the broader notion of the Yahwistic tradition. Prophets no doubt played a crucial role, but they were well supported by people such as the elders, the

---

⁸⁰ Cook, *Social Roots*, 45–65, 170–73; see also H. Reviv, *The Elders in Ancient Israel: A Study of a Biblical Institution* (Jerusalem: Magnes, 1989), 113–19.

⁸¹ Cook, *Social Roots*, 170.

⁸² *Ibid.*, 170; See De Vaux, *Ancient Israel*, 69.

⁸³ Holladay, "Kingdoms," 389; Faust, "Rural Community in Ancient Israel during the Iron Age II," *BASOR* 317 (2000): 17–39.

⁸⁴ J.A. Soggin, "Der judäische 'am-ha'ares und das Königtum in Juda," *VT* 13 (1963): 187–95.

⁸⁵ See Dutcher-Walls, "Social Location ," 77–94.

Levites, the scribes, and probably people who had a common vision to revitalize Yahwistic tradition and Yahweh's sovereignty in Judah.[86] Many of this group, most notably the elders and the Levites, were marginalized from their traditional roles. Moreover, just as many prophets compromised their message for personal gain, many elders and Levites were also less than exemplary in their motives.[87] However, the members of this group, the "people of the land," have survived the allurement of the monarchy's self-aggrandizing distortion of the Yahwistic משפטים. In this sense, this group can be technically termed the remnant, the faithful ones.

Furthermore, B. Oded asserts that "'the people of the land' was a political-social element which was loyal to the house of David."[88] Oded's stance takes away the broader contention that the "people of the land" stands for the Yahwistic tradition irrespective of the political dynasty. As noted earlier, it is true that this term does not occur even once in the northern kingdom. Moreover, this group betrayed a pro-Davidic position when it played an important role in upstaging Queen Athaliah (2 Kgs 11), a rare non-Davidic ruler, from the throne of Judah. Yet, a closer reading of the other texts (cf. 2 Kgs 22–23; Jer 26, 29, and 36) where the "people of the land" plays an important role, suggests that the main concern of this group moved beyond the royal dynasty to revitalize Yahwistic tradition and to preserve the sovereignty of Yahweh. The non-usage of this term in the northern kingdom does not necessarily mean that a similar movement was not present. In fact, the prophets and the elders collaborated with one another in judging

---

[86] See also Gerhard von Rad, *Studies in Deuteronomy* (trans. D. Stalker; SBT 9: London: SCM, 1953), 63–65.

[87] For an elaborate discussion on this see Cook, *Social Roots*, 170–94; also Cook, "Levites and Sociocultural Change," 41–58.

[88] B. Oded, "Judah and the Exile," in *Israelite and Judaean History* (OTL 39; ed. John H. Hayes and J. Maxwell Miller; Philadelphia: Westminster, 1977), 435–88.

and reprimanding the kings in the northern kingdom as well (cf. 2 Kgs 6:28). We can only speculate why a counterpart group did not gain traction in Israel as it did in Judah. Perhaps the reason is that the elders in the northern kingdom were complicit with the Israelite monarchy, which led to severe factions among the elites, resulting in the frequent and bloody succession of the kings. Whatever, the case might be, the supporters of Yahwistic tradition in northern kingdom could not gather momentum to direct their kings and society.

However, in Judah the Yahwistic movement gained support and played a prominent role in the society to sustain their vision. Dutcher-Walls argues that this group gave shape to the so-called Deuteronomistic History.[89] It is this group, "the people of the land," that identified and supported true Yahwistic prophets, but called out and rejected false prophets.

4.4. Conclusion

In this chapter, I explored the socio-economic, religious and political background of the ancient agrarian Israelite society by utilizing the macrosociology of Lenski and Nolan. This analysis has enabled us to investigate some features of the complex societal dynamics which gave rise to false prophets and prophecies. The inability of the monarchy to function within the system of limited monarchy clashed directly with the aspiration and vision of the true Yahwistic prophets and their supporters. A monarchy driven by its fixation on power and privileges in a society with minimum goods could only generate corruption and oppression. Unfortunately, many prophets fell into the trap laid down by the monarchy and its

---

[89] Dutcher-Walls, "Social Location," 92–93. In a similar vein, Cook contends that Yahwistic belief "became the official religion of Israel with the triumph of the Hebrew Bible as Israel's written Scripture and with the rise of Judaism" (*Social Roots*, 45).

machinations which led to the degeneration of some prophets' from their earlier conviction and commitment.

The inability of the monarchy to function within the limited monarchy was indicative of their failure to lead the people of the society according to the Yahwistic tradition. Consequently, the spirituality of the *vox populi* was compromised and became ineffective. This provided another platform, not just for false prophets to arise, but to thrive. However, not all was lost as there was still a vestige of the people who remained faithful to their old Yahwistic tradition, perhaps because the awe-inspiring experience of Yahweh that their ancestors encountered was still alive in them. One of the terms applied to this group on occasion was the עם־הארץ. It is this group that played a vital role in delineating true prophecies from false ones.

Chapter 5
PROPHETIC CONFLICT IN JEREMIAH 26–29

> *"One will not deny that the so-called false prophets felt equally inspired and were equally sincere. Yet some prophets were wrong and others were right."*[1]

5.1. Introduction

The last four chapters have established a platform for this present chapter whose task is to analyze the text of Jer 26–29 on the theme of true and false prophecy. The analysis of the text will be informed by the development of Yahwistic tradition within an ancient agrarian Israelite society. In chapter four I mapped the general socio-economic and religious scenario of an ancient agrarian Israelite society. The dynamics that I pointed out remain in general the context of the prophet Jeremiah. However, as every historical period has its unique developments, I will provide pertinent background information that shaped the time and message of the prophet Jeremiah before analyzing the text.

The intention here is to argue that it is the core of the Yahwistic tradition that enabled the ancient Israelites to adjudicate the competing prophecies. The core of the Yahwistic tradition is embodied in the concept of משפטים which functioned as the *regula fidei* even as the tradition developed in order to make sense of different challenges made necessary by the change of milieu. This chapter will also deal briefly, in an excursus, on the criteria of distinguishing true and false prophecy as found in Deut 13:2–6

---

[1] Simon J. De Vries, *Prophet Against Prophet: The Role of the Micah Narrative (1 Kings 22) in the Development of Early Prophetic Tradition* (Grand Rapids: Eerdmans, 1978), viii.

(13:1–5 [Eng.]) and 18:21–22. Thus, this chapter will first deal with the text to show how Jeremiah the prophet ministered within the core framework of the Yahwistic tradition; and then briefly contextualize Deut 13:2–6 (13:1–5 [Eng.]) and 18:21–22 in the light of the discussion of the prophetic conflict in Jer 26–29.

5.2. Mapping the Context of the Prophet Jeremiah

In this section, I will not rehearse Judah's history of seventh and the early sixth centuries BCE *per se*, as it is dealt with in many books on the history of ancient Israel. My task in this section is to examine the results of the subjugation of Judah by Neo-Assyria and its impact on Judah's internal socio-economic and political affairs. This examination will have implications for understanding the prophetic conflict in the book of Jeremiah.

According to Jer 1:2, Jeremiah began his ministry on the thirteenth year of the reign of King Josiah (627 BCE) and lasted a few years after 587 BCE, spanning approximately forty-five years.[2]

---

[2] The date concerning the beginning of Jeremiah's ministry is debated. One of the crucial factors for this debate is that the book of Jeremiah does not record much about King Josiah's famous reform except for a few instances (3:6; 25:3; 36:2) where the King is positively remarked. As such William L. Holladay has argued that the thirteenth year of the reign of King Josiah was the date of the birth of Jeremiah—see *Jeremiah 2* (2 vols; Hermeneia; Mineapolis: Fortress, 1989), 25. In this way, Holladay could argue that Jeremiah's active ministry began only towards the end of Josiah's reign and, therefore, did not have much occasion for Jeremiah to comment on the reforms made by King Josiah. However, it has to be noted that the primary aim of the book of Jeremiah is to account for the fall of Judah in the hands of Babylon and, therefore, the book primarily recounts the events after 609 BCE (the year King Josiah was assassinated), and so the book concentrates on the last three kings of Judah—i.e., Jehoiakim, Jehoiachin, and Zedekiah. This does not rule out Jeremiah's ministry during King Josiah's reign. Perhaps, his ministry was sporadic and largely supportive of the King's policy. By asserting the beginning of Jeremiah's ministry in Josiah's thirteenth year as recorded in the Jer 1:2, one can also suppose the undated oracles in chapters 2–20 to have come from the period of

Jeremiah's ministry was specifically directed to address the covenantal disobedience of the people of Judah and to identify the rise of Babylon as the imminent coming of Yahweh's punishment. This message of Jeremiah was not innovative, rather it hinged on the understanding of Yahwistic tradition, that is, breaking the Yahwistic covenant leads to punishment.

Moreover, prior to Jeremiah's birth, the northern kingdom of Israel collapsed in 721 BCE under the yoke of Assyria, and the reason for this catastrophe was Israel's failure to live within Yahweh's מִשְׁפָּטִים. Again in 701 BCE, despite the destruction of Judah's surrounding towns and cities, Jerusalem was allegedly protected by Yahweh from Sennacherib's hand because Hezekiah gave in to the counsel of prophet Isaiah (2 Kgs 19:6–7, 32–34). These incidents might have informed Jeremiah's acute understanding of his social, economic, and religious environments, and yet he was called by Yahweh to communicate Yahweh's own will to the Judeans.

Jeremiah's prophetic ministry began to dawn just when the control of Assyria over the region of Syria-Palestine was declining. However, in order to understand Jeremiah's context, it is imperative to examine the impact left by imperial Assyria on Judah. From the late eighth century BCE to the mid-seventh century BCE, the region of Mesopotamia, Syria-Palestine and also for a period of time southern Egypt (c. 674–663 BCE) were under the control of Assyria and thus, Assyrian domination was established in this whole region.[3] This period is also known as the

---

Josiah's reign and before the rise of Babylon to power—see Jack R. Lundbom, *The Early Career of the Prophet Jeremiah* (Lewiston, NY.: Edwin Mellen, 1993), 62–63; also J. Andrew Dearman, *Jeremiah and Lamentation: The NIV Application Commentary* (Grand Rapids: Zondervan, 2002), 26–27.

[3] See Ephraim Stern, *Archaeology of the Land of the Bible: The Assyrian, Babylonian, and the Persian Periods 732–332 BCE* (vol. 2; New York:

epoch of *pax Assyriaca*. It is marked by the growth of international business, especially for maritime trade, with Phoenicia as one of the central seaports.[4] The establishment of such Assyrian control over this region was made possible by subduing the smaller nations—e.g., Syria in 732/1 BCE and the northern kingdom of Israel in 721 BCE.[5] The implication of instituting *pax Assyriaca* was profound for the diminutive nation of Judah. The peak of Assyrian domination occurred during the later reign of King Hezekiah (715–686 BCE), but largely under the reign of King Manasseh (697/6–643/2) who remained for the most part a faithful vassal of the imperial Assyria.[6]

Doubleday, 2001), 3. Oded Lipschits, *The Fall and Rise of Jerusalem: Judah under Babylon Rule* (Winona Lake, IN: Eisenbrauns, 2005), 1.

[4] Avraham Faust and Ehud Weiss, "Judah, Philistia, and the Mediterranean World: Reconstructing the Economic System of the Seventh Century B.C.E," *BASOR* 338 (2005): 71–92; for a broader perspective of the growth of market and economy in ancient Near East and Europe during this time see, Susan and Andrew Sherratt, "The Growth of the Mediterranean Economy in the Early Millennium BC," *WA* 24 (1993): 361–78.

[5] By 734–722 BCE, Assyria had conquered areas such as Golan and the Gilead in the northern part of Transjordan and the territory of the northern kingdom. Then by 721–700 BCE, the conquest of Philistia was consolidated and Judah, except for Jerusalem, was destroyed and conquered. During this period, Assyrian provinces such as Gilead, Megiddo, Dor, and Samaria were established. The period of 674–663 BCE also saw Egypt under constant threat from the Assyrians (see Stern, *Archaeology of the Land*, 3).

[6] The book of Chronicles indicates that Manasseh rebelled once against Assyria (2 Chr 33:11–16) but he was subdued and exiled. Apart from that he is mentioned as a committed vassal, perhaps because he had no other political alternative. Yet, it has to be mentioned that Manasseh enjoyed the support of Assyria in terms of economic development as a vassal. But the internal politics were far from stable (2 Kgs 21:3–4)—see Christopher R. Seitz, *Theology in Conflict: Reactions to the Exile in the Book of Jeremiah* (BZAW 176; Berlin: de Gruyter, 1989), 33–37. Note also the overlapping of dates between Hezekiah's and Manasseh's reign. Edwin Thiele argues that Manasseh began his rule as co-regent with Hezekiah before becoming the full-fledged king. See Edwin R.

The effect of Assyrian domination over Judah was that of seismic social change. The contact and interaction of Judah with imperial Assyria disbanded the socio-economic and political aspects of Judean life. The imperial practice of importation and deportation of conquered citizens led to frequent and serious intermingling of people of different traditions and belief systems, causing the disintegration of the national structure of the conquered vassal. Samaria (or *Sāmerīna*, as it was called by the Assyrians) of the northern kingdom became one of the provinces of Assyria where the imperial power imposed a two-way deportation policy. Interestingly, Judah did not suffer in this way, although the Assyrian annals claim that Sennacherib transported 200,150 people from the spoils of Judah in 701 BCE.[7] Nevertheless, Judah's foreign contact increased markedly due to the influx of foreign groups into their neighboring regions. Alteration in Judean demography—i.e., refugees from Samaria and the rural areas of Judah migrated into Jerusalem, and Judah experienced frequent contact with other foreigners—caused social and internal political tensions.

Thiele, *The Mysterious Numbers of the Hebrew Kings: A Reconstruction of the Chronology of the Kingdoms of Israel and Judah* (3d ed.; Grand Rapids: Eerdmans, 1983), 173–74. See also Tadmor, Hayim, "The Chronology of the First Temple Period: A Presentation and Evaluation of the Sources," in *J. Alberto Soggin, An Introduction to the History of Israel and Judah*, (Valley Forge: Trinity Press International, 1993), 394–417.

[7] *ANET*, 287–88. Although the number of deportation is a little exaggerated, Stephen Stohlmann argues that this number is relatively correct—see "The Judean Exile of 701 B.C.E," in *Scripture in Context II: More Essays on the Comparative Method* (ed. William W. Hallo, James C. Moyers, Leo G. Perdue; Winona Lake, IN: Eisenbrauns, 1983), 147–75; also see the argument of B. Halpern, "Jerusalem and the Lineages in the Seventh Century BCE: Kinship and the Rise of Individual Moral Liability," in *Law and Ideology in Monarchic Israel* (ed. Baruch Halpern and Deborah W. Hobson; JSOTSup 124; Sheffield: Sheffield Academic, 1991), 11–107.

Consequently, one can envisage in Judah during this lengthy imperial period attempts to preserve and redefine their cultural identity according to the change of time and circumstance. Kenton L. Sparks contends that "ethnic identity is created and nurtured when small peripheral social modalities live under the imperial pressures of a powerful core civilization."[8] During the reign of King Hezekiah (post-721 BCE), there were efforts to revive and collect literatures on Yahwistic tradition besides his cultic centralization and political revolt against imperial Assyria. Schniedewind asserts that the intention to collect Yahwistic literatures by Hezekiah was politically motivated—i.e., it set out to restore the Davidic-Solomonic kingdom of the olden days.[9]

Although there is truth in that, such motivation is directly or indirectly hinged on revitalizing ethnic identity and cultural boundaries. Furthermore, it is also highly likely that Hezekiah became a genuine supporter of Yahwistic tradition who listened to Yahwistic prophets such as Micah and Isaiah (cf. Jer 26:17–19; 2 Kgs 19:6–7). In line with this, the prophet Micah, it is argued, was a village elder from Moresheth, and we have argued above that village elders were part of the Yahwistic group known as the "people of the land."[10] It is during this period in history, according to Schniedewind, that traditional stories of the twelve tribes found their way into the books of Genesis and Exodus.[11] It appears that during Hezekiah's reign the Yahwistic movement gained greater momentum and the cultural ethnic identity was given emphasis and redefined in accordance with the need of the time.[12] This

---

[8] Sparks, *Ethnicity and Identity in Ancient Israel*, 219.

[9] See Schniedewind, *How the Bible Became a Book*, 64–90.

[10] Hans Walter Wolff, "Micah the Moreshite—The Prophet and His Background," in *Israelite Wisdom: Theological and Literary Essays in Honor of Samuel Terrien* (ed. J. Gammie et al.; Missoula: Scholars Press, 1978), 77–84.

[11] Schniedewind, *How the Bible Became a Book*, 81–84.

[12] Cf. Sparks, *Ethnicity and Identity*, 222–25.

movement gathered further and aggressive momentum later during the reign of King Josiah, the grandson of Hezekiah.

Again, the incidents of 721 and 701 BCE impacted the demography and the settlement pattern of seventh-century BCE Judah. The influx of refugees from the northern kingdom to Jerusalem resulted in the expansion of Jerusalem and its population.[13] The incident of 701 BCE left most of the cities and towns of Judah, especially in Shephelah, completely destroyed resulting in the unprecedented expansion and the growth of Jerusalem's population. In fact, Jeremiah himself might have been a refugee in Jerusalem from the province of Anathoth. It is argued that Jerusalem's status and the number of its residents were probably equal to the size of the rest of Judah during the seventh century BCE.[14] Margreet Steiner calls Jerusalem of the seventh century "a primate city, a city very much larger than other settlements, where all economic, political and social power is centralized.... It must have had complete economic control over the countryside."[15]

---

[13] Mordechai Cogan writes, "[E]xcavations in Jerusalem have shown that the capital's developed area tripled or even quadrupled at the same time. Two of the city's new neighborhoods are known by name, the Mishneh ("Second" Quarter) and the Maktesh ("Mortar" or "Valley" Quarter)" ("Into Exile: From the Assyrian Conquest of Israel to the Fall of Babylon," in *The Oxford History of the Biblical World* [ed. Michael D. Coogan; Oxford: Oxford University Press, 1998], 242–75).

[14] The size and population of Jerusalem in the ninth century BCE were approximately thirty-two acres and eight thousand, respectively; it grew to one hundred and thirty acres and thirty thousand in population in the eight century BCE. In the seventh century, Jerusalem's size and population were around one hundred fifty acres and forty thousand, respectively. Schniedewind, *How the Bible*, 68; also Stern, *Archaeology of the Land,* 164.

[15] Margreet Steiner, "Jerusalem in the Tenth and Seventh Centuries BCE: From Administrative Town to Commercial City," in *Studies in the Archaeology*

Another notable impact was the change of settlement areas. The once populated Shephelah was mostly destroyed; but areas such as the Negev and the Judean desert began to be inhabited by many Judeans.[16] The shift of settlement could be mainly for practical reasons, namely the need to grow grains.[17] Assyria established a military post in the Shephelah, and most of Judah's rural areas were reassigned to the loyalist kings of Ekron and Ashkelon and so Judeans were left to find conducive land to produce grain.[18] There is also the possibility that the change in settlement pattern was to participate in the Arabian trade.[19] Faust and Weiss have argued that Judah during this time not only flourished in her population but even economically prospered because of the peace wrought by the institution of *pax Assyriaca*.[20]

However, Israel Finkelstein and Neil A. Silberman believe that the settlement of Judah and its economic growth were mostly state-

---

of the Iron Age in Israel and Jordan (ed. Amihai Mazar; JSOTSup 331; Sheffield: Sheffield Academic, 2001), 280–88.

[16] Avraham Faust, "Settlement and Demography in Seventh Century Judah and the Extent and Intensity of Sennacherib's Campaign," *PEQ* 140.3 (2008): 168–94.

[17] Israel Finkelstein and Neil Asher Silberman, *The Bible Unearthed: Archaeology's New Vision of Ancient Israel and the Origin of its Sacred Text* (New York: Free, 2001), 266.

[18] See H. Spieckermann's work on the deployment of a military post in the Shephelah. Spieckermann, *Juda unter Assur in der Sargonidenzeit* (FRLANT 129; Göttingen: Vandenhoeck & Ruprecht, 1982), 141; for further details about the reassignment of Judean rural areas by Assyria post-701 BCE, see Halpern, "Jerusalem and the Lineages," 41–49.

[19] Israel Finkelstein, "The Archaeology of the Days of Manasseh," in *Scripture and Other Artifacts: Essays on the Bible and Archaeology in Honor of Philip J. King* (ed. M.D. Coogan, J.C. Exum, and L.E. Staeger; Louisville: Westminster John Knox, 1994), 169–87.

[20] Faust-Weiss, "Judah, Philistia, and the Mediterranean World," 75.

managed.²¹ Judah was a vassal of imperial Assyria, and the former had to pay heavy taxes and also transport building materials for Assyrian imperial building projects (*dullu ša šarri*).²² For instance, Esarhaddon (680–669 BCE) recounts in the Assyrian annals that Manasseh transported timber to Nineveh along with other loyal vassals.²³ Judah also had to aid Assyria with soldiers during the latter's engagement in war.²⁴ Again Assurbanipal (669–627 BCE) mentions Manasseh, following him for his first military campaign against Egypt/Nubia.²⁵

All these phenomena meant that the common people were under constant and considerable pressure to produce more resources not just for their nation's elites, but also to meet their imperial power's demands. In fact, the practical economic condition of the common people of Judah was no different from that of the former eighth century BCE, and if anything the burden was heavier. Consequently, one encounters the prophet Jeremiah criticizing the existing oppression of the poor by the elites (Jer 5:27–28; 22:13–19).

Furthermore, Judah as a vassal state of Assyria began to import some of the latter's religious customs. It has been argued by many scholars that Assyria did not impose her deities on her vassal simply because Assyria did not have any such foreign policy.²⁶

---

²¹ Finkelstein-Silberman, *Bible Unearthed*, 269; cf. Halpern, "Jerusalem and the Lineages," 61, 64.

²² The vassals were obligated to pay annual tribute (*maddatu, pirru*, and *biltu*) accompanied by special gifts (*nūmurtu*) and levies (*bitqu*) to the Assyrian king—see J.N. Postgate, *Taxation and Conscription in the Assyrian Empire* (Rome: Pontifical Biblical Institute, 1974), 18, 57–62, 111–30, 146–66; also Spieckermann, *Juda unter Assur*, 312.

²³ *ANET*, 265–317.

²⁴ Postgate, *Taxation*, 218.

²⁵ *ANET*, 294.

²⁶ J.W. McKay, *Religion in Judah under the Assyrians, 732–609 BC* (SBT 2/26; London: SCM, 1973), 69–72; Morton Cogan, *Imperialism and Religion:*

Yet, it is also agreed that the existence of Assyrian gods and goddesses in Judah (2 Kgs 21; 23:4–14) were either their own choice or assimilation by the process of diffusion.[27] Such an act of syncretism was not new to ancient Judah, nor in the northern kingdom. However, it suggests that the religious decay continued and deepened during this time and that the voices of Yahweh's prophets went unattended.

5.2.1. Judah's Internal Politics in Relation to Egypt and Babylon

Such massive shifts in Judah's social life led to instability of her internal politics. As noted in chapter four it is typical in an agrarian society to find factional struggles among the ruling class.

Assyria, Judah, and Israel in the Eight and Seventh Centuries B.C.E (SBLMS 19; Missoula: Scholars Press, 1974), 88–96.

[27] Even McKay and Cogan agree with this view. See also Daniel R. Miller, "The Shadow of the Overlord: Revisiting the Question of Neo-Assyrian Imposition on the Judean Cult during the Eighth-Seventh Centuries BCE," in *From Babel to Babylon: Essays on Biblical History and Literature in Honour of Brian Peckham* (ed. Joyce R. Wood, John E Harvey, and Mark Leuchter; LHB/OTS 455; New York: Clark, 2006), 146–68. These scholars are in disagreement as to whether the astral cult (rooftop altar) is an Assyrian import or indigenous to the Northwest Semitic region. The fact that the rooftop altar is mentioned in an Ugaritic text (Kirta myth) indicates that it might have originated among the West Semitic people: see McKay, *Religion*, 23–59; for Kirta text see Krt 1, text 125 in C.H. Gordon, *Ugaritic Textbook* (Rome: Pontifical Biblical Institute Press, 1965), 192–93; also M.D. Coogan, *Stories from Ancient Canaan* (Philadelphia: Westminster Press, 1978), 58–74. Nevertheless, R.H. Lowery points out that the rooftop altar mentioned in 2 Kgs 23:12 is in relation to King Ahaz who submitted Judah to the yoke of imperial Assyria. For him, this suggests that Judah actually imported some astral cult practices from Assyria. Historically, Assyria was heavily inclined toward astronomical divination, and so when Ahaz submitted Judah to Assyrian vassalage, it is possible that he also introduced Assyrian astral cult practices either by obligation or by imitation. See R. Lowery, *The Reforming Kings: Cults and Society in First Temple Judah* (JSOTsup 120; Sheffield: Sheffield Academic, 1991), 203–6.

Such factional struggles were primarily motivated by gaining economic and ideological privileges. The factional fight appears to have reached its peak in Judah during her last years of existence as a kingdom. This is quite vividly depicted in the succession drama which unfolded after the death of King Manasseh. The power of Neo-Assyria waned slowly by the mid-seventh century BCE, mainly because of the rise of Median and Neo-Babylonian forces. The death of Ashurbanipal in 627 BCE accelerated the end of the Assyrian empire. By 612 BCE Nineveh, the capital of Assyria, was conquered and completely razed by the Neo-Babylonian and Median forces, and in 609 BCE the last king of Assyria, Aššur-uballiṭ II was defeated and its last territory, Haran, was captured by the same force.[28]

The gradual downfall of Assyria, however, played a vital role in the political sphere both inside and outside Judah. Outside Judah, Egypt and Babylon began to vie for domination over the territories once belonging to imperial Assyria. Both Egypt and Babylon had common motives to extend their domination and control the Syria-Palestine region, particularly for economic gain and as defense strategy.[29] This tussle for domination between Egypt and Neo-Babylon had internal political consequences in Judah.

There is truth in the argument that political inclinations in Judah, such as pro-Assyrian or pro-Babylonian or pro-Egyptian, were not necessarily the outcome of any political ideology, rather they were political *de facto* and sometimes political opportunism.[30] However, political opportunism most often reflects a fundamental

---

[28] See Lipschits, *Fall and Rise of Jerusalem*, 19.

[29] *Ibid.*, 25–31.

[30] Richard Nelson, "Realpolitik in Judah (687–609 B.C.E)," in *Scripture in Context II: More Essays on the Comparative Method* (ed. William W. Hallo, James C. Moyer, and Leo G. Perdue; Winona Lake, IN: Eisenbrauns, 1983), 177–90.

political proclivity. For Judah, the steady demise of Assyria indeed gave rise to such political factions among its ruling class.[31] Perhaps, even by Manasseh's time, such internal political differences were brewing as reflected in 2 Kgs 21:16: "Moreover, Manasseh shed much innocent blood, till he filled Jerusalem from one end to another." By the time Manasseh was succeeded by his son Amon, there is clear evidence that there were factions within Judah's royal administration.

The Deuteronomistic historians point out that Amon followed in the religious footsteps of his father (2 Kgs 21:20–21); however, within two years time he was killed by "his servants" (2 Kgs 21:23).[32] We do not know the reason why he was killed, but Seitz argues that given the situation—i.e., the decline of Assyria and the ascendency of Egypt under Psammetichus I—"it is most likely that these factions disputed Judah's stance vis-à-vis Egypt and Assyria."[33] If that is the case, then it is very likely that the assassins of Amon were pro-Egyptian who wanted to gain autonomy from Assyria.[34] However, Amon's assassins were subdued by the "people of the land" who instead installed an eight-year-old Josiah as their ruler. These "people of the land" were neither pro-Assyrian nor pro-Egyptian, but as I have discussed in the last chapter, they

---

[31] See Seitz, *Theology in Conflict*, 38.

[32] Tomo Ishida points out that Amon was 22 years old when his father Manasseh died at the age of 67. In other words, Amon was born when Manasseh was 45 years old. This implies that Amon was not the first born but most probably had elder siblings. On this ground Ishida argues that the royal court might have had factions giving rise to court intrigues similar, perhaps, to the succession narrative of Solomon. Tomo Ishida, "'The People of the land' and the Political Crisis in Judah," *Annual of the Japanese Biblical Institute* 1 (1975): 23–38; see also T. Ishida, *The Royal Dynasties in Ancient Israel* (BZAW 104; Berlin: de Gruyter, 1977), 153–55.

[33] Seitz, *Theology in Conflict*, 39.

[34] See Abraham Malamat, "The Historical Background of the Assassination of Amon, King of Judah," *IEJ* 3 (1953): 26–29; Ishida, "Political Crisis," 36.

appear to be ardent supporters of Yahwistic tradition who wanted to have a political will of their own.[35] Thus, Josiah, when installed as the king, ruled under the direct supervision of the "people of the land." It is only logical and reasonable, therefore, that King Josiah (641/640–609 BCE) ushered in one of the most radical and aggressive Yahwistic reforms in Judah's history (2 Kgs 22–23 and 2 Chr 34–35).[36]

Josiah's cultic reform was not only aggressive but also extensive in the sense that his reforms extended into the north in Bethel and even Samaria.[37] One of the reasons that such cultic reforms were even possible was the waning of Assyrian control over Syria-Palestine and the tussle between Egypt and Babylon for control of this region.[38] However, Josiah's reform act was short

---

[35] See also Seitz, *Theology in Conflict*, 67.

[36] Second Kgs 22–23 states that Josiah's reform took place during his eighteenth year (623/22), whereas 2 Chr 34–35 assumes the reform to have taken place in several stages: eighth year, twelfth year and culminating in the eighteenth year of Josiah's reign. For a good overview of historical and archaeological discussion on Josiah's reform see Brad E. Kelle, "Judah in the Seventh Century: From the Aftermath of Sennacherib's Invasion to the Beginning of Jehoiakim's Rebellion," in *Ancient Israel's History: An Introduction to Issues and Sources* (ed. Bill T. Arnold and Richard S. Hess; Grand Rapids: Baker Academic, 2014), 350–82.

[37] Philip Davies questions the historicity of Josiah's reform—see *In Search of 'Ancient Israel'* (JSOTSup 148; Sheffield: Sheffield Academic, 1992), 41–42. Rainer Albertz, in response to Davies contention, argues for the historicity of Josiah's reform in the seventh century BCE—see "Why a Reform Like Josiah's Must Have Happened," in *Good Kings and Bad Kings* (ed. Lester L. Grabbe; LHB/OTS 393; London: T&T Clark, 2005), 27–46.

[38] The Assyrian royal annals are dated to 639 BCE, whereas the Egyptian texts discuss their own internal affairs; for more information about the Egyptian texts see Anthony J. Spalinger, "History of Egypt (3d Intermediate-Saite Period [Dyn. 21–26])," *ABD* 2:353–64; Kenneth A. Kitchen, *The Third Intermediate Period in Egypt, 1100–650 B.C.* (Warminster: Aris & Phillips, 1986). The Babylonian chronicles have the most data about this period. For more

lived as he was killed at Megiddo in 609 BCE by Pharaoh Neco II (of the 26th [Saite] dynasty) on his way to support Assyria's fight against Babylon.[39] Josiah was succeeded by Jehoahaz (609 BCE), who was anointed to be the king by the "people of the land" (2 Kgs 23:30). It has to be noted that the act of anointing only took place when there is conflict for the throne in the process of succession.[40]

Jehoahaz (a.k.a., Shallum) ruled for only three months before the Egyptian Pharaoh replaced him with his elder half-brother, Jehoiakim (609–597 BCE). Jehoahaz was incarcerated in Riblah and later exiled to Egypt where he died (Jer 22:11). With the installation of Jehoiakim (a.k.a., Eliakim) as the king, Yahwistic

---

information about the nature and content of the Babylonian Chronicle, see Bill T. Arnold, "The Neo-Babylonian Chronicle Series," in *The Ancient Near East: Historical Sources in Translation* (ed. Mark W. Chavalas; Malden: Blackwell, 2006), 407–26. However, even here the relevant portion for our period is covered only from 626–623 BCE, and then after a period of nine years it resumes from 616–594 BCE. The Babylonian chronicle recounts that Assyria maintained relative stability until 627 BCE, but from 626 BCE Babylon under Nabopolassar is depicted as no longer under the control of Assyria. Later when the chronicle resumes in 616 BCE, it alludes to the presence of the Egyptian army in support of Assyria. It might be that Josiah's reform took place sometime during the period which the Babylonian chronicles are missing, that is, when Assyria was losing its power to Babylon and when Egypt was not able to penetrate and control the Syria-Palestine region. See Kelle, "Judah in the Seventh Century," 372–78.

[39] Assyria was reduced to a mere nominal state in Haran because of the expansion of Babylon. Egypt, on the other hand, was trying to gain a stake in the Syria-Palestine region. Egypt made Riblah its center and it is possible that the motive of Josiah's killing was to convert Judah into yet another Egyptian center in Syria-Palestine. Concurrently, Egypt went on to assist Assyria against Babylon in 609 BCE because Egypt knew that Assyria could still be used as a buffer state to defend its occupation in Syria-Palestine. However, both the Egyptian and Assyrian forces were defeated; in fact, Assyria existed no longer as nation after 609 BCE. See Lipschits, *Fall and Rise of Jerusalem*, 20.

[40] A. Malamat, "The Years of the Kingdom of Judah," in *The World History of the Jewish People* (vol IV/I; Jerusalem: Massada, 1979), 205–21.

tradition and its supporters suffered a setback. In fact, the "people of the land" were imposed with heavy taxes (2 Kgs 23:35). The swift installation of Jehoiakim and the heavy taxation of the "people of the land" indicate Jehoiakim's political proclivity towards Egypt. These also suggest that Jehoiakim had a pro-Egyptian support group, a faction possibly dating back to the time of Amon's assassination.[41]

Perhaps it is appropriate to ask, why was Jehoiakim pro-Egyptian? One should remember that during this time (609–606 BCE) the rise of Babylon was not certain yet and therefore, by aligning with Egypt, Jehoiakim and his supporters were perhaps betting that Egypt would retain hegemony in the area. Besides this, allegiance to Egypt was less burdensome than being a vassal to Assyria had been. The only tribute Jehoiakim had to pay Egypt was during his succession, and in return Jehoiakim expected Egypt to help him with military aid.[42] Again the manner of Egypt's interest in Syria-Palestine was different than Assyria's and Babylon's. The latter's interest was purely military domination, whereas Egypt's was more economically motivated and militarily cautious.[43] Egypt was more lenient towards her vassals, and thus the vassals afforded more space for their local interest.

It was also during the reign of Jehoiakim that Jeremiah's prophetic ministry began to accelerate. Jeremiah's message was in direct contrast with Jehoiakim's foreign policy. Rather than Egypt, Jeremiah urged Judah to submit to Babylon (Jer 13:20; 25:1–9); he even prophesied against Egypt (Jer 46:1–12). Jeremiah also did not shrink away from criticizing Jehoiakim for his interest in maintaining his state and indulging in building a royal palace at the

---

[41] See Seitz, *Theology in Conflict*, 80–81.

[42] *Ibid.*, 91.

[43] Anthony Spalinger, "Egypt and Babylonia: A Survey (c. 620 B.C.–550 B.C.)," *Studien zur Altägyptischen Kultur* 5 (1977): 221–44.

expense of the general populous in spite of the tenuous political environment (Jer 22:13–23; 25:1–9; 36:30–31).[44] Jeremiah, with the help of Baruch, also composed a scroll during this period (36:1–8), which was read (vv. 11–19), destroyed (vv. 20–26) and rewritten (v. 32). Jeremiah went ahead with all this even when he knew that his life was in danger. For instance, the prophet Uriah ben Shemaiah was put to death by Jehoiakim for delivering a similar message to that of Jeremiah (Jer 26:20–23). Yet, he was not alone in this endeavor. We can infer that the "people of the land" who based their ideology on Yahwistic tradition were behind him.

Coming back to the bigger political picture, although Egyptian and Assyrian forces were defeated in Haran in 609 BCE by Babylon, this was just the beginning of the tussle between Babylon and Egypt for the control of Syria-Palestine. The beginning of this tussle signified the downward spiraling of the Judean kingdom. Lipschits rightfully opines that, "this decline was the result of the small kingdom's location in the struggle between great empires. But it was also the outcome of the reckless and improvident policy of the last kings of Judah and of political and religious turmoil among various sectors of the Jerusalem elite."[45]

The fight for supremacy over Syria-Palestine between Egypt and Babylon reached a relative conclusion when Babylon soundly defeated Egypt in 605 BCE in the Battle of Carchemish. However, it has to be noted that this was by no means the end of Egypt's interest in the region of Syria-Palestine. Nonetheless, after Egypt's defeat, Judah and Jehoiakim became a vassal of Babylon. Babylon did not replace or depose Jehoiakim from the throne, but heavy

---

[44] It is argued that the building project was carried on in imitation of Egyptian architecture. Yohanan Aharoni argues that this project was probably situated at Ramat Raḥel (probably biblical Beth-Haccherem; Jer 6:1). He also contends that this citadel was Jehoiakim's summer residence and an important military outpost—see "Excavations at Ramat Raḥel," *BA* 24 (1961): 98–118.

[45] Lipschits, *Fall and Rise of Jerusalem*, 42–43.

taxes were levied on Judah. By this time Nebuchadnezzar (604–562 BCE) of Babylon had succeeded his father (Nabopolassar) and he knew quite well that Egypt was the main factor that might cause problems for the young Babylonian empire and its control over Syria-Palestine. Thus, in 601 BCE, Nebuchadnezzar launched an attack against Egypt, and the battle ended in a deadlock. Both sides suffered losses, but apparently Nebuchadnezzar endured the greater loss, as he had to return to Babylon to regroup before staging another attack.[46]

The Babylonian retreat gave the impression to Judah and other small kingdoms in Syria-Palestine that Babylon was not as strong as it appeared. In fact, Jehoiakim revolted against Babylon during this time and once again became a vassal to Egypt. It is only in the winter of the sixth year of Nebuchadnezzar's reign that he began to reestablish his control over Syria-Palestine.[47] Thus, in 597 BCE Nebuchadnezzar drove out the Egyptians and took control of Judah. Jehoiakim died during this period, and his son Jehoiachin (597 BCE) succeeded him, eventually submitting himself to the Babylonians. Consequently, Jehoiachin along with his family, administrators, and able citizens were taken into exile to Babylon (2 Kgs 24:13–16). Jehoiakim's short reign of eleven years began as a vassal of Egypt, and then circumstances forced him to side with Babylon, and finally in poor judgment he rebelled against Babylon which led to his end. It has to be noted that in spite of Jeremiah's active ministry during Jehoiakim's reign, the prophet went silent during the latter's submission to Babylon.

---

[46] A.K. Grayson, *Assyrian and Babylonian Chronicles* (Winona Lake, IN: Eisenbrauns, 2000), 20, 101.

[47] Lipschits contends, "This evidence supports the idea that there was a break in the continuity of Babylonian rule over Palestine and a period when the area was subject to Egyptian influence, perhaps even actual Egyptian rule" (*Fall and Rise of Jerusalem*, 51).

Nebuchadnezzar installed Zedekiah (also called, Mattaniah, 597–587 BCE), the uncle of Jehoiachin, as the ruler of Judah, the third of Josiah's sons to sit on the Judean throne. However, Nebuchadnezzar still had problems in Babylon and one such problem happened on the tenth year of his reign (595/594 BCE). There was a revolt in Babylon which required attention from Nebuchadnezzar himself, and although he could subdue this revolt once again it sent signs of weakness to his vassals. It is most likely that during this time instability began to surface in Syria-Palestine. Even in Egypt during this period Psammetichus II (595–589 BCE) and later Hophra (589–570 BCE) began to show great interest in expanding Egypt's territory and control.[48] As a result, diminutive kingdoms such as Edom, Moab, Ammon, Tyre, Sidon, and Judah conspired to revolt against Babylon. The book of Jeremiah reports the meeting of these nations in Jerusalem (Jer 27). It is almost certain that this anti-Babylonian coalition could not have developed without Egypt's support.[49]

From the above discussion, we can assume that Zedekiah's decision to rebel against Babylon was based on his assessment that Babylon's rule in Syria-Palestine was weakening, and on his belief that Egypt was powerful enough to support and assist the anti-Babylon coalition. This opposed Jeremiah's prophecy, which was rooted in the Yahwistic tradition. For Jeremiah, Judah had broken the covenant relationship with Yahweh by oppressing poor and twisting the truth. Therefore, Judah was to submit to Babylon as an acceptance of judgment from Yahweh. Rebelling against Babylon for Jeremiah was rebelling against Yahweh.

But Zedekiah went ahead with his assessment only to realize that his calculation about Egypt was inaccurate. Egypt retreated in the face of the Babylonian army, and Zedekiah was captured and

---

[48] *Ibid.*, 63.
[49] *Ibid.*, 64.

oppressed (his son's were killed before his eyes, then he was blinded), Jerusalem and its temple were burnt down and destroyed.[50] In line with this, Lipschits argues that, "The decision reached by the nation's leaders in Jerusalem to pursue the revolt even after the retreat by Egypt and the renewal of the Babylonian siege on Jerusalem is proof that additional, stronger factors were at work in their decision to rebel. It is likely that Zedekiah was also influenced by the activists in Jerusalem and the prophets who promoted rebellion against Babylon."[51] Apparently, Jeremiah and the "people of the land" could not regain their power as when Josiah was the king. However, they continued to aspire to re-institute the Yahwistic tradition in Judah as well as to persuade the later kings, especially through the prophet Jeremiah. In other words, the fracture in royal administration continued to persist.

5.2.2. *Summary of Observations*

The situation in the seventh and early sixth centuries of Judah's history was intense and complex. International politics were unstable, with Assyria waning in power, and Babylon and Egypt vying to fill the vacuum created by the demise of imperial Assyria. Within Judah, the internal political dispute between the factions of the administrative ruling class was growing. The Yahwistic tradition flourished during the time of Hezekiah and Josiah, but toward the final days of the Judean kingdom the pro-Egyptian faction became dominant especially during Jehoiakim and Zedekiah. As noted above, the politics of the Yahwistic tradition was neither pro-Assyrian nor pro-Babylonian, but they were more inclined towards religious and social independence whereby Judah could exercise the rights of limited-monarchy. Jeremiah's message of submission to Babylon was not necessarily a message of pro-

---

[50] *Ibid.*, 70.
[51] *Ibid.*, 72.

Babylon, rather it was a message of judgment from Yahweh for violating the covenant relationship. This is verified by Jeremiah's later oracles concerning the nations where Babylon is also specifically mentioned as incurring Yahweh's judgment (Jer 50). In contrast to this, the pro-Egyptian faction, according to this Yahwistic tradition, was seeking political space to continue to oppress the poor and twist justice for their personal profit. It is within this environment that Jeremiah's ministry flourished and his confrontation with the so-called false prophets occurred.

5.3. *Locating the Text*

First, a brief comment on the redaction of the book of Jeremiah is necessary.[52] The book by no means is redacted chronologically or with literary coherence in its final form. However, after the works of Duhm and Mowinckel, there was a general consensus in the historical-critical study of the book of Jeremiah and its literary sources.[53] The final form was argued to be the outcome of a redactional process, consisting of three sources: the poetic oracles of the historical Jeremiah, the prose redaction of Baruch (the scribe of Jeremiah), and finally the interpretive reflection of the Deuteronomistic historians.

---

[52] Here I will be dealing with the text as presented in the Masoretic Text (MT) which is also the standard version translated in our English Bible. However, there is also the Septuagint (LXX) version of the text of Jeremiah. The LXX version is shorter, about one-eighth, than the MT; the section of the "oracles against the nations" is located in the middle, and the order of the oracles against the nations varies. Holladay sums up the problem and debate of the relationship between MT and LXX in this manner: "In the main, is the LXX a shortened form of the MT, or is the MT an expanded form of the LXX? Or is the question unanswerable? Is the ideal of a 'more original' text form unattainable?" (W.L. Holladay, *Jeremiah: A Commentary on the Book of the Prophet Jeremiah* [Hermeneia; 2 vols; Minneapolis: Fortress, 1986–1989], 2:3).

[53] Cf. S. Mowinckel, *Zur Komposition des Buches Jeremia* (Kristiania: J. Dybwad, 1914); Duhm, *Buch Jeremia*.

The poetic sections were considered to be authentic to Jeremiah, whereas the prose sections were deemed a secondary addition. However, today, such a consensus no longer exists. Three commentaries on Jeremiah are noteworthy, those of Carroll, Holladay, and McKane.[54] These three take different approaches in understanding the redactional process of the book. Carroll's and Holladay's construal of the process of redaction stands in sharp contrast to each other: the former argues that the final form of the book is merely a literary construct of the exilic community, in fact he is skeptical about the existence of the person Jeremiah;[55] whereas the latter attempts to locate the whole book within the historical person and event of the prophet Jeremiah. In conjunction with this, McKane argues that the book is an outcome of a "rolling corpus." There is no doubt that Carroll and Holladay have contributed to our understanding of the formation of the book; however, there is a more fruitful avenue to take with the concept of McKane's rolling corpus. McKane contends:

> What is meant by rolling corpus is that small pieces of pre-existing text trigger exegesis or commentary. MT is to be understood as a commentary or commentaries built on pre-existing elements of the Jeremianic corpus.... In general, the theory is bound up with the persuasion that rolling corpus 'rolled' over a period of time and was still rolling in the post-exilic period."[56]

---

[54] R.P. Carroll, *Jeremiah: A Commentary* (OTL; London, 1986); Holladay, *Jeremiah*; William McKane, *A Critical and Exegetical Commentary on Jeremiah* (ICC; 2 vol; Edinburgh, 1986–1996).

[55] Carroll, *Jeremiah*, 55–65.

[56] McKane, *Commentary* 1, xv.

McKane's construal of rolling corpus, though helpful, also suggests that the book of Jeremiah is an arbitrary and error-filled work.[57]

As I argued in chapter three, we must give attention to the *how* of the redaction process. In other words, how cautious were the redactors in interpreting the received tradition? There is no doubt that interpretation and reinterpretation will take place within a tradition as time and space changes because tradition is not a dogma. However, this does not mean that interpretation is a mindless enterprise. The fact that there is a tradition means there is a guardian of the tradition which might be the community itself or the elders of the community. In the case of the prophet Jeremiah, he was supported by the "people of the land" who shared a common vision in the Yahwistic tradition. This "people of the land" might have played a vital role in the redactional process. Such a construal of the redactional process would indicate a place for the prophet Jeremiah in history and that his prophecy was relevant in a particular moment during a specific period in Israel's history.

A plethora of literature has been written on the connection of the book of Jeremiah and the Deuteronomistic history (Deut–2 Kgs). There is no doubt that Jeremiah's final form has the impression of the theological concepts of the Deuteronomistic (Dtr) historian.[58] Some scholars argue that this is because the final redactor of Jeremiah is the Dtr historian; while others argue that

---

[57] Cf. Osuji, *Where is the Truth?*, 45.

[58] Both Jeremiah and the Deuteronomistic history are pro-Sinaitic in inclination. They share common social views, demanding Israel to treat her neighbor in a brotherly manner (see Deut 5:20; Jer 9:4–9), from judges to deliver justice (Deut 16:18–20; Jer 7:5–6, 9; 8:8), from kings not to shed innocent blood (Deut 19:10; 21:8; Jer 2:34; 7:6; 22:3). They also share common phraseology and diction. Besides these, the emphasis on covenant is crucial in both the corpuses.

the similarity is the result of the common cultural milieu in which both Jeremiah and the Dtr redactor lived.[59] As a way of bridging these two views, Holladay avers, "[Jeremiah] drew on Proto-Deuteronomy, and exilic redactors of Deuteronomy sometimes drew on Jrm's words."[60] No doubt the process was complex, but whatever the case might be, there is a deep theological interconnectedness between the book of Jeremiah and the Dtr history. Patricia Dutcher-Walls has argued that the provenance of the Dtr historian is related to the "people of the land."[61] This "people of the land" consists of likeminded people from different walks of life such as landed gentries, community elders, Levites, prophets, royal officials, and priests. If this group is the bearer of Yahwistic tradition and the support network of the prophet Jeremiah, then it is not surprising at all that the theological conceptualities of Jeremiah and of the Dtr historian are in harmony with each other. It is from this perspective that I will approach the text for the current project.

5.3.1. *Jer 26–29*

Despite the lack of surface-level structure of the book of Jeremiah, it has been argued that the book can be broadly divided into two thematic sections. The first section comprises chapters 1–25, which deal with the theme of "uprooting and overthrowing."

---

[59] For the former view see W. Thiel, *Die deuteronomistische Redaktion von Jere 1–25* (WMANT 41; Neukirchener-Vluyn: Neukirchener Verlag, 1973); also see E. W. Nicholson, *Preaching to the Exiles: A Study of the Prose Tradition in the Book of Jeremiah* (Oxford: Blackwell, 1970). For the latter view, see H. Weippert, *Die Prosareden des Jeremiabuches* (BZAW 132; Berlin: de Gruyter, 1973); also see Ehud Ben Zvi, "A Deuteronomistic Redaction in/among "The Twelve?" A Contribution from the Standpoint of the Books of Micah, Zephaniah and Obadiah," in *Those Elusive Deuteronomists: The Phenomenon of Pan Deuteronomism* (ed. S.L. McKenzie; JSOTSup 269; Sheffield: Sheffield Academic, 1999), 232–61.

[60] Holladay, *Jeremiah*, 2:53.

[61] Dutcher-Walls, "Social Location of the Deuteronomists," 77–94.

The second section consists of chapters 26–52, and they address "building and planting" a new Israelite community.[62] Within this broad division, Jer 26–29 falls in the second section of the book and it explicitly deals with the issue of true and false prophecy. Brueggemann puts these chapters in perspective:

> These four chapters can be grouped together, both for reasons of convenience and because of a common theme. The grouping is in part a matter of convenience, for it is clear that the four chapters do not form an obvious and natural literary corpus. They do, nonetheless, form an in-between group of chapters. On the one hand, ch. 30 begins a quite new grouping with its accent on promise and hope, and its poetic casting. On the other hand, ch. 25 stands by itself, so that most scholars understand it to be a climactic statement at the end of the first half of the book of Jeremiah. In any case, it is not likely that ch. 26 has any integral connection to ch. 25. Between chs. 25 and 30, then, are chs. 26–29, which may be grouped together by default.[63]

Chapter 26 initiates a series of prose narratives in chronological order concerning the prophet Jeremiah and his public ministry.[64] Also, chapter 26 comprises a message delivered

---

[62] Louis Stulman, *Jeremiah* (AOTC; Nashville: Abingdon, 2005), 14–15.

[63] Walter Brueggemann, *A Commentary on Jeremiah: Exile and Homecoming* (Grand Rapids: Eerdmans, 1998), 229.

[64] Jeremiah 27:1, according to a majority of the manuscripts, including the MT, has this incident occurring at the beginning of Jehoiakim's reign, whereas 27:12 has it during Zedekiah's reign. There is also an apparent discrepancy in 28:1 when it says the event happened in the beginning of Zedekiah' reign in the fourth year. J. Andrew Dearman avers, "The more likely explanation is that the chronological headings for chapters 26–28 have become mixed during the

by Jeremiah at the temple and the reaction of the audiences during the reign of Jehoiakim. Chapters 27–28 recount the event during Zedekiah's reign perhaps around 595/4 BCE when Judah was conspiring against Babylon. Finally, chapter 29 deals with the issue of false prophecy in an address to those who were exiled in 597 BCE. My main task here is to analyze the text from the perspective of true and false prophecy, utilizing sociological and political insights gained in the previous chapters of this study.

5.4. Interpreting The Text
5.4.1. Jer 26: Prophet versus Prophet

Chapter 26 sets out the broad setting of prophetic conflict that will take place in chapters 27–29. Jer 26 can be structured accordingly: vv. 1–16 serve as the main body of the narrative; vv. 17–19 and 20–24 function as two separate sub-narratives that supplement the main body.[65] Verses 1–16 are described as a court case: arrest and accusation (vv. 8–9); the trail process (vv. 10–15), including a speech from the prosecution (v. 11), and the defense (vv. 12–15); and finally the legal verdict (v. 16).[66] The event of this passage took place as a consequence of Jeremiah's Temple sermon in the beginning of the reign (בראשית ממלכות) of Jehoiakim (v. 1), probably during one of the annual festivals, perhaps the feast of Booths.[67] As discussed above, Jehoiakim reigned approximately

---

process of transmitting the material to final written form" (*Jeremiah and Lamentation*, 247).

[65] Leslie C. Allen, *Jeremiah: A Commentary* (OTL; Louisville: John Knox, 2008), 295–96.

[66] See Holladay, *Jeremiah*, 2:102.

[67] See Holladay, *Jeremiah*, 2:103. Holladay also argues that the phrase בראשית ממלכות is a technical term meaning the "accession year." Holladay's conclusion is based on the understanding that this phrase corresponds to the Akkadian term *rēš šarrūti* which has a technical meaning. Mesopotamia used an accession year system. The accession year was the time between a king's

for eleven years (609–598/7 BCE). He was installed by the Egyptian Pharaoh, Necho II, after Jehoahaz, who reigned for only three months and was deposed from the throne. Jehoahaz was anointed by the "people of the land" to succeed Josiah. But when Jehoiakim was installed by Necho II, not only was Jehoahaz exiled to Egypt, but the "people of the land" were also heavily taxed. The reign of Jehoiakim saw the transitioning period of Judah from the ascendency of Yahwistic tradition under Josiah and his supporters, the "people of the land," to the politically inclined pro-Egyptian faction.

The pro-Egyptian faction was, of course, not a regime with a new ideology, but they were the faction that envisaged the monarchy and its administration as functioning outside the concept of a "limited monarchy."[68] They consisted of royal administrators who wanted to take advantage of their status and exploit the poor for their own material gain and luxurious living. Within this context they were the opportunists who wanted support from Egypt to carry out their ambitions. Egypt provided the perfect ally for this faction to execute its motives; Egypt's foreign policy appeared to have been that of minimum intervention on her vassals. As in the eighth century BCE, the political objective of the pro-Egyptian faction was made possible by factors like the institutionalization of religion. As previously discussed, the institutionalization of religion gave them false security in Yahweh, namely, that Yahweh would protect Jerusalem and its temple irrespective of Judah's

---

accession and the following New Year and not the first year of his reign. However, Cogan has shown that Akk *rēš šarrūti* is Heb בשנת מלכו (2 Kgs 25:27)—see "A Technical Term for Exposure," *JNES* 27 (1968): 133–35. In line with this, Lundbom argues that the event reported here in ch. 26 need not necessarily be that of Jehoiakim's accession year—see *Jeremiah 21–36: A New Translation with Introduction and Commentary* (AB 21B; New York: Doubleday, 2004), 286.

[68] See my discussion above in section 5.2.1, "Judah's Internal Politics."

response.⁶⁹ Institutionalized Yahwism was a change in the understanding of Yahwistic tradition. It was based on a dogmatic construal of Yahweh's faithfulness toward Jerusalem and its temple. This ideology also syncretized other cultic gods and practices.

Jeremiah was instructed by Yahweh to stand at his house's courtyard and speak to all the cities of Judah (people of Judah) that came to worship (v. 2). Jeremiah was specifically commanded not to גרע (withdraw or hold back), a word of what Yahweh has revealed him to speak. This expression is a formula found generally in ANE legal and wisdom texts (e.g., Prov 30:6; Eccl 3:14). This expression is also found in Deut 4:2 and 13:1 (12:32 [Eng.]), where Moses instructs the Israelites not to withdraw anything from what he commands them. However, in this passage it is Yahweh who commands Jeremiah not to subtract anything from his word no matter how unwelcome they might be for the people. This further indicates, that a prophet sent by Yahweh was not to speak only what people wanted to hear but to declare boldly Yahweh's message. In other words, courage and commitment were needed for Jeremiah to speak the whole word of Yahweh—a message that would particularly hurt the people of Judah.

Jer 26:3 indicates the love Yahweh had towards his people in spite of their stubbornness: אולי ישמעו וישבו איש מדרכו הרעה ונחמתי אל־הרעה אשר אנכי חשב לעשות להם מפני רע מעלליהם ("Perhaps, they will listen, and each of them will turn from his evil way so that I may relent of the disaster which I plan to do to them because of their evil deeds").⁷⁰ Verse 3 also reveals Yahweh's hope that Judah

---

⁶⁹ See my discussion on "institutionalized religion" in ch. 4.

⁷⁰ Three verbs are noteworthy here: שמע (listen), שוב (turn), and נחם (relent). In the OT, the verb שמע "to hear" is used 1159 times and in the book of Jeremiah 158 times. It may simply mean the physical capacity to listen (cf. 2 Sam 19:36), but in many instances this word carries a heavy theological meaning. Especially in the book of Jeremiah, this word means listening to Yahweh in relation to

might "שמע" and "שוב." This is signified by the particle "אולי." The hope of Yahweh is that the people will turn from their evil ways so that he might change his mind concerning the calamity he had devised for Judah. Yahweh hopes that his people might turn away from their evil ways and listen to him. It is because of this hope that Yahweh continued to persist and show steadfast love (חסד) to a recalcitrant Israel.[71]

---

covenantal law. Furthermore, it also connotes not only passive listening, but an active response. In this case, it resembles Ugaritic usage of this word which means to hear and obey—see Rütersworden, "שָׁמַע," *TDOT* 15:253–79; H. Schult, "שמע," *TLOT* 3:1375–80; K.T. Aitken, "שמע," *NIDOTTE* 4:175–81). The next verb שוב means "to turn" or "to return." It occurs 1050 times in the OT, of which it is found 111 times in the book of Jeremiah. Again this word can be used basically to refer to physical movement (cf. Gen 15:16) or theologically, שוב means to repent or "turn from your evil ways" (2 Kgs 17:13). This word is closely connected with שמע theologically; that is, if one listens and obeys Yahweh's precepts, then he or she is turning away from evil ways. In relation to this, Graupner asserts that retuning to God is not a human accomplishment; rather it is God's work. Again within the context of Jeremiah, this word has to be understood in relation to the covenantal relationship between Israel and Yahweh—see Graupner, "שוב," *TDOT* 14:484–511; J.A. Soggin, "שוב," *TLOT* 3:1312–17; J.A. Thompson and Elmer A. Martens, "שוב," *NIDOTTE* 4:55–59). Finally, the root meaning of the word נחם means "to restore to life." This word in the OT is found mostly in the *piel* verbal form (51 times), which can be understood as "to comfort" (cf. Gen 37:35). However, in Jer 26:3, the verb occurs in the *niphal*. It occurs 48 times in this form in the OT, of which 37 times it is translated as "to feel pain" or "to regret" or "to repent" (the other 11 are translated as "to take comfort" or "to take revenge"). This word in the form of *niphal* is closely related to another word namely, חסד meaning steadfast love. Again חסד is a covenantal language describing Yahweh's character—see H.J. Stoebe, "נחם," *TLOT* 2:734–39; Mike Butterworth, "נחם," *NIDOTTE* 3:81–83; see also Osuji, *Where is the Truth?*, 128 n.32. Thus, within the context of Jeremiah all three verbs are interconnected through a common theme; namely, the covenantal relationship between Israel and Yahweh.

[71] See my discussion of חסד in ch. 3 n.44.

It is here that the role of the Yahweh's prophets becomes crucial and, to a certain extent, defined. The prophets were sent in order to guide the Israelites in the right path (cf. Jer 7:25–26). In other words, if the people were on the right path there was no need for the existence of the prophet. However, since Israel did not turn away from its evil ways, Yahweh continued to send prophets.[72] Thus, Yahweh's act of sending prophets is the manifestation of his חסד. Yet, it has to be noted that Yahweh's חסד has limits, for his judgment will come when his persistent love is continuously ignored. This shows that Yahweh is slow to anger but also a jealous and wrathful God (Joel 2:13). Such an understanding of Yahweh puts Jeremiah's prophetic ministry in perspective.

Verses 4–6 contain the oracle Jeremiah received from Yahweh. The formula אם־לא in v. 4 begins the protasis of Jeremiah's message which extends to v. 5: "if you do not listen to me, to walk in my law that I have set before you, and to listen to the words of my servants the prophets." Verse 6 forms the apodosis: "Then I will make this house like Shiloh, and I will make this city a curse for all the nations of the earth."[73] However, v. 5 does not perfectly complete the protasis. Jeremiah does not simply say, "Listen to the words of my servants the prophet," but rather he continues saying, "(those) whom I send to you urgently, although you have not listened." Holladay argues that the latter statement disrupts the flow of the protasis.[74]

Holladay's concern for the technicality of the protasis is understandable here as the conditional aspect of protasis is blunted.

---

[72] This also suggests that Jeremiah comes from a rich and long tradition of Yahwistic prophets (cf. Jer 7:25–26). See also H. Lalleman-de Winkel, *Jeremiah in Prophetic Tradition: An Examination of the Book of Jeremiah in the Light of Israel's Prophetic Tradition* (Leuven: Peeters, 2000).

[73] Shiloh was the ancestral sanctuary of Israel destroyed by the Philistines (Ps 78:60; 1 Sam 4:11). Shiloh is situated some 20 miles north of Jerusalem.

[74] Holladay, *Jeremiah*, 2:104.

However, the statement does not necessarily interrupt the meaning of the protasis; rather, it provides a fuller meaning within the context of Jeremiah. Yahweh's prophets were just not about the past but they have repeatedly been sent (note the present participial construction of אנכי שלח) to guide and shape Judah's life and yet Judah has not listened to them.[75] In other words, in spite of the recalcitrance of the Judeans, if they were to turn back by observing the משפטים and by listening to the words of the prophets, there would be hope for Judah. The Judeans, however, had created an illusion that Jerusalem, as God's chosen place, was secure and that it would not meet the fate of Shiloh.

Verse 7 describes the audience of Jeremiah: the priests, the prophets,[76] and כל־העם ("all the people"). As discussed in chapter four, within an agrarian society both the priests and the prophets were significant personnel in the royal system. They could not only anoint a king to the throne and approve or disapprove the king's agenda; they could also manipulate the will of the people. However, we do not know the exact constituency of "all the people." Perhaps, "all the people" refers to those common people present in the temple (cf. v. 2), but concurrently they might even include the elders who supported Jeremiah and play a vital role later in this chapter (see v. 17).[77]

---

[75] See the note of Lundbom on this verse, *Jeremiah 21–36*, 288.

[76] Note that these prophets (v. 7 and also vv. 8, 11, and 16) are identified as "false prophets" in the LXX.

[77] I disagree with Allen who argues that these "people" were in fact the elders responsible for judicial administration in the city—see *Jeremiah*, 299. My understanding of "all the people" as the crowd present in the temple that might even include some elders is shared *mutatis mutandis* by Holladay—see *Jeremiah*, 2:104–05.

In verse 8, the prophet Jeremiah is arrested (תפש) and accused stating מות תמות ("you shall surely die").[78] The reason for the accusation is made clear in v. 9 where it is stated that Jeremiah is accused for speaking in the name of Yahweh. Interestingly, we notice that in the accusation, the protasis (of vv. 4–5) is completely negated making Jeremiah's message a direct judgment. This signifies the nature of human polemics where only partial statements of the opponent are focused so as to fabricate the whole truth and magnify the accusation. The trial proper begins at v. 10, where the שָׂרִים (officials) join the audience at the "New Gate" of the house of the Lord.[79] Here the officials act as the judges. In v. 11 the priests and the prophets bring their accusation to the officials who sit as judges. Once again, the prosecutors omit information to amplify the charges against the accused. This time they omit "this house" and mention only "this city." In doing this they foster political motives against the accused. Thus, the charge appears to be that Jeremiah has undermined the state by speaking against the city which in turn is a blasphemy against Yahweh as Jerusalem is

---

[78] The infinitive absolute is a verbal noun of action or of state. One of the uses of infinitive absolute in biblical Hebrew is that it may intensify a finite verb. Thus, the infinitive absolute plus finite verb of the same root is translated with an emphatic word such as certainly, surely, indeed, definitely. Therefore in v. 8 תמות (*qal* imperfect second person masculine singular) מות (*qal* infinitive absolute) is translated, "You shall surely die." Many languages do not have this grammatical feature. Paul Joüon and T. Muraoka state, "This linguistic process allows Hebrew to express certain emphatic nuances in a subtle way" (*A Grammar of Biblical Hebrew* [Rome: Pontifical Biblical Institute, 2006], 390-92; cf. also Bruce K. Waltke and M. O'Connor, *An Introduction to Biblical Hebrew Syntax* [Winona Lake, IN: Eisenbrauns, 1990], 580).

[79] The location is defined as a temple gate, the "New Gate," which is often equated with the "upper gate" built or rebuilt by Jotham (2 Kgs 15:35; cf. Jer 36:10) and is probably to be identified with the "Upper Benjamin Gate" on the north side of the temple in Jer 20:2.

the dwelling place of Yahweh. Therefore, the punishment for this blasphemy is death (Exod 22:27; Lev 24:10–16).[80]

So, then, after the prosecutors presented their case, the defense continues the case (vv. 12–15). Jeremiah speaks for himself. His defense includes three parts. First, Jeremiah claims that he was sent (שלח) by Yahweh himself to prophesy (v. 12) and thus challenges the prosecutor's charge that he prophesied in the name of the Lord.[81] Second, he paraphrases the oracle of Yahweh. Notice that in his paraphrasing he mentions that both "the house" and "the city" await Yahweh's judgment (v. 12), yet this also provides some aspect of hope within the message (v. 13). And third, Jeremiah skillfully argues for his personal innocence co-relating him as the divine agent. In doing this he warns the court of blood guilt which would result from his unfair death (vv. 14–15).[82] Jeremiah's claim that "in truth he was sent by Yahweh" squarely made this case about the issue of true and false prophecy.[83]

Verse 16 unfolds the verdict; the judges did not find the prosecutor's charges against Jeremiah justifiable. Interestingly, the prosecutor's point that Jeremiah deserves death because he prophesied in the name of Yahweh is used to reach the final conclusion. That is, Jeremiah does not deserve to die because he prophesied in the name of Yahweh. Perhaps the judges heard the prophecy in the defense given by Jeremiah. However, Allen has

---

[80] Holladay, *Jeremiah*, 2:107. See also Allen, *Jeremiah*, 300.

[81] This verb שלח is used in the commissioning of Moses by Yahweh. However, it has to be noted that the verse alone does not have a semantic meaning of its own. Rather the meaning of the verb has to be translated in the "cultural" relationship between the subject and the object. In other words, in the context of true and false prophecy, the mere usage of this verb does not verify a prophet to be either true or false. See C. John Collins, "שלח," *NIDOTTE* 4:119–23.

[82] Allen, *Jeremiah*, 300.

[83] See Lundbom, *Jeremiah 21–36*, 293.

argued strongly for an alternative view of the verdict. He contends that, "A deafening silence is maintained about the deeper issue of the content of Jeremiah's prophesying, now that its divine source was granted."[84] Jeremiah, indeed, was acquitted; but, his message of repentance was also completely ignored. Little wonder that Jeremiah will continue to face similar opposition from the same group of people.

Furthermore, the attitude of the people (כל־העם) has to be looked at differently given that they have already sided with the priests and the prophets earlier that Jeremiah must die. Interestingly, the people's response to Jeremiah's message is recorded twice. The first response is in v. 8 where they, along with the priests and the prophets, approve of sentencing Jeremiah to death. The second response is in v. 16 where they do not approve Jeremiah's death sentence. The reason for the change of people's verdict could be their incapacity to discern who actually was right. Was it the priests and the prophets? Was it Jeremiah? The fact that Jeremiah prophesied in the name of Yahweh obfuscates their ability to discern and, perhaps, sheds light on their unclear conscience.

In v. 17 another group of people surfaces in the narrative. This group is the elders of the land, and as indicated above, they might have been a group among the common people present in the temple that day. As a way of confirming the verdict of the judges, the elders deliver a speech (vv. 17–19).[85] It is only appropriate for the elders to bring up the name of the prophet Micah and his

---

[84] Allen, *Jeremiah*, 300.

[85] The elders' speech in vv. 17–19 can either be construed as a defense statement or as a confirmation of the verdict. However, the former construal will have slight problem in terms of the order of events as it follows the verdict. Therefore, the logical understanding of the speech of the elders should be as a confirmation of the verdict; and yet the crucial aspect of this speech is that it betrays that the elders were supporters of the prophet Jeremiah.

incident with King Hezekiah (cf. Mic 3:12). It is argued that the prophet Micah might have been an elder himself from the village of Moresheth and that these elders belonged to the larger Yahwistic group known as the "People of the Land."[86] The presence of this group suggests that Jeremiah was not functioning alone, although this does not preclude the courage to deliver the message of Yahweh in the center of his opponents. In line with this, the narrative also alludes to another prophet by the name of Uriah son of Shemiah from Kiriath-jearim (vv. 20–24).[87] Uriah too delivered a similar message to that of Jeremiah. When Jehoiakim attempted to kill him, Uriah escaped to Egypt. However, he was caught easily by Jehoiakim's official, Elnathan and returned to Judah where Jehoiakim personally executed him. The apparent ease with which Elnathan did this suggests that this event might have happened when Judah was a vassal of Egypt—that is, before the Carchemish event 605 BCE.[88]

This narrative of the prophet Uriah accentuates the courage of prophet Jeremiah, and also suggests, once again, that Jeremiah's

---

[86] See my discussion on the "people of the land" in ch. 4.

[87] Kiriath-jearim is identified with tell *al-'azar*, near *qaryat el-'inab*, also known as *abu gaws*, about thirteen kilometers west-northwest of Jerusalem. See Francis T. Cooke, "The Site of Kirjath-jearim," *AASOR* 5 (1925): 105-20. Note that many scholars think that the narrative of Uriah son of Shemiah is a secondary addition or a mere appendix—see J. Philip Hyatt, "Introduction and Exegesis, Jeremiah," *IB* 5 (1956): 775–1142]. However, Holladay argues cogently that vv. 20–23 conform to the whole narrative by means of the diction of the narrative—see *Jeremiah*, 2:102.

[88] Elnathan son of Achbor is mentioned in Jer 36:12, 25. Elnathan was present among others when Baruch read Jeremiah's scroll in 604 BCE. He then urged Jehoiakim not to burn the scroll. Elnathan might also be the same person mentioned in 2 Kgs 24:8. In which case, Elnathan was the father-in-law of Jehoiakim. Numerous seals, ostraca, and inscriptions of the period have been excavated with the name "Elnathan" and "Achbor"—see Lundbom, *Jeremiah 21–36*, 297.

opposition to the royal administration and its ideology was not an isolated event.

Chapter 26 ends by providing another window on the encounter with the larger group of supporters of the Yahwistic tradition. In v. 24 it is said that Jeremiah did not meet the end of the prophet Uriah because of the presence of Ahikam son of Shaphan. Lundbom states, "Prophets are never authenticated on the basis of their own witness alone. Their witness has to be corroborated at some point by the witness of others."[89] Is Ahikam the witness? He was a man of high rank, a supporter of Josiah's reform, and perhaps he was the son of Shaphan who was the scribe of Josiah (2 Kgs 22:12) and father of Gemariah and Elasah. Ahikam might have been old enough to work along with his father Shaphan during Josiah's reform around 622 BCE (2 Kgs 22:12, 14). In that case, by this period (609–601 BCE) he must have been relatively old to actively participate in social activism and perhaps for that reason he is not mentioned again in the rest of the book. Yet, certainly, he was still an influential person.[90] The other two brothers of Ahikam—Gemariah and Elasah—and his son Gedaliah, however, played important roles in the life of Jeremiah. For instance, Gemariah urged Jehoiakim not to burn Jeremiah's scroll (Jer 36:25), Elasah carried Jeremiah's letter to exiles in Babylon (Jer 29), and Gedaliah, who was appointed governor at Mizpah by the Babylonians, took charge of Jeremiah after the fall of Jerusalem in 587 BCE (Jer 39:14).[91] Besides the Shaphanite clan, Jeremiah had Baruch the scribe, and Delaiath, too (Jer 36:25).

---

[89] Lundbom, *Hebrew Prophets*, 144.

[90] Cf. Holladay, *Jeremiah*, 2:110. The name of Ahikam has shown up on the Arad ostraca and bullae contemporary with Jeremiah. See Nahman Avigad, *Hebrew Bullae from the Time of Jeremiah: Remnants of a Burnt Archive* (Michigan: University of Michigan, 1986), 34–35.

[91] Cf. J.A. Thomson, *The Book of Jeremiah* (NICOT; ed. R.K. Harrison; Grand Rapids: Eerdmans, 1980), 528.

5.4.2. Jer 27–28:[92] Jeremiah versus Hananiah

Chapters 27–28 form the core of the prophetic conflict. In this section, Jeremiah encounters direct confrontation with another Yahwistic prophet, Hananiah son of Azzur from Gibeon.[93] The confrontation between these two prophets occurred around 595/4 BCE, three or four years after Jehoiakim's death (cf. Jer 28:1) and the surrendering of Jerusalem by Jehoiachin in 598 BCE. As a result, Jehoiachin and many Judeans were taken into exile (598 BCE), and Zedekiah had been installed by Nebuchadnezzar as the king of Judah.[94] So then, in a way, Jeremiah's prophecy of Babylonian supremacy over the region was partially fulfilled.

The political context of the conflict between Jeremiah and Hananiah is apropos to our discussion. Zedekiah was appointed by

---

[92] Jeremiah 27 can be broadly divided into three divisions: vv. 2–11, 12–15, and 16–22. But all these sections contain similar negative exhortation: "Do not listen to your prophets…for they are prophesying a lie" (vv. 9–10, 14, 16). The first section comprises Yahweh's instruction for the prophet Jeremiah and has limited space for false prophecy. The emphasis on the issue of true and false prophecy is increased in the second section and becomes dominant in the final section. The final section, in fact, acts as the preparatory section for Jeremiah 28 which focuses solely on the prophetic conflict between prophet Jeremiah and Hananiah—see Allen, *Jeremiah*, 305. Chapters 27–28 are not only interconnected with the same subject matter of true and false prophecy, but also by the way two words are spelled. Normally Jeremiah is spelled ירמיהו; however, in these two chapters it is spelled ירמיה without the *waw*. This shorter form of the spelling of Jeremiah is also found in Ezra 1:1; Dan 9:2. The other word is the name of the king of Babylon. The king of Babylon is spelled as נבוכדראצר with *reš* in the rest of the book. However, in these chapters it is spelled נבוכדנאצר with *nun*. The spelling with *reš* occurs in the book of Ezekiel and with *nun* in 2 Kings, Chronicles, Ezra, Nehemiah, Esther, and Daniel.

[93] Both Gibeon and Anathoth (Jeremiah's place) was located in Benjamin. In fact, Gibeon was just five and a half kilometers northwest of Anathoth—see James B. Pritchard, "Gibeon," *IDB* 2:391–93.

[94] Nebuchadnezzar ransacked the Temple and exiled 7000 army and 1000 craftsmen. The prophet Ezekiel was also exiled to Babylon on this occasion.

the Babylonians in 598 BCE but he easily succumbed to the pressure of the partisan court system.[95] During this time Nebuchadnezzar was facing some internal crises in Babylon and concurrently, the Egyptians, under Pharaoh Psammetichus II (595–589 BCE), were showing their interest once again in Syria-Palestine.[96] Taking advantage of this political situation and, in spite of Zedekiah being installed by Nebuchadnezzar, Judah initiated a revolt in the region against Babylon.

Jer 27:1 states that the event mentioned in the passage took place in the beginning of the reign (בראשית ממלכות) of Zedekiah.[97] However, as discussed above, this phrase is not a reference to the technical accession year—i.e., the time of the king's accession to the first new year.[98] The text indicates that many foreign envoys were present in Jerusalem to discuss and conspire against Babylon (27:3). During this period Yahweh's revelation came to Jeremiah commanding him (עשׂה—note the *qal* imperative form) to make and wear yoke of מוסרה (straps) and מוטה (bars) round his neck[99]

---

[95] See Shimon Bakon, "Zedekiah: Last King of Judah," *JBQ* 36 (2008): 93–101.

[96] This is recorded in the Babylonian Chronicle: "In the tenth year the king of Akkad was in his own land; from the month of Kislev to the month of Tebet there was rebellion in Akkad…with arms he slew many of his own army. His own hand captured his enemy" (British Museum 21946, rev. 21–22; cf. also D.J. Wiseman trans., *Chronicles of Chaldean Kings, [626–556 B.C] in the British Museum* [London: British Museum, 1956], 72–73).

[97] In many manuscripts including MT the king's name is written Jehoiakim instead of Zedekiah. However, it is agreed that the translator made mistake while translating. For more on this, see above (155–56).

[98] See footnote no. 67.

[99] The MT and LXX read ושלחתם in 29:3 as "send them," meaning send "the straps and bars" to all the kings. However, NIV and NAS translate this as "send word to the king of Edom" under the influence of v. 4, "and command them to say to their master." This discrepancy in translation does not distort the meaning of the content but if we follow MT and LXX translations (which is also followed by JPS and NKJ) then the prophet Jeremiah was not only to send instruction to

and to send instructions to the kings of Edom, Moab, Ammon, Tyre, and Sidon through their envoys who traveled to Jerusalem to submit themselves to Babylon (Jer 27:2–9).[100]

Verses 5–11 contain the first oracle of the chapter. It contains two main themes: the sovereignty of Yahweh, and the role of Nebuchadnezzar. There is also a warning against false prophecy.[101] The oracle begins with God as the creator. Jeremiah based his argument on the notion of Yahweh as the creator of the universe and, therefore, not only Judah, but all the surrounding nations must submit themselves to Babylon. Yahweh has given his creation for a time to be ruled by Nebuchadnezzar until Babylon itself would be subdued by Yahweh (27:7).[102] Allen claims that this indicates that

---

the foreign kings through their envoys but also make the straps and bars for each king and transport them through the envoys.

[100] This is a symbolic action representing Yahweh's message. Prophetic symbolism was used frequently by Yahweh's prophets to provide powerful impetus to the message they were delivering. For instance, Ahijah the Shilonite, before announcing the break-up of the Solomonic kingdom, tears a new garment into twelve pieces and gives ten of them to Jeroboam son of Nebat, king-designate of the northern tribes. The ten tribes thus go on to follow Jeroboam (1 Kgs 11:29–39); Isaiah, for three years before Assyria took Ashdod at the close of the eighth century, went naked and barefoot in Jerusalem to dramatize the fate of Egyptian captives and Ethiopian exiles (Isa 20:2; see also other examples Jer 13:1–11; 2 Kgs 4:32–27; 1 Kgs 18:42–44; Ezek 3:22–27). Here the symbol of straps and bar must have been something common in an agrarian society. For instance, the farmers in an agrarian society, where modern machineries have not been introduced, use some kind of bar and straps to tie on to the neck of the oxen to till the ground effectively. In the same manner, perhaps, Jeremiah was instructed to tie the straps and bar as a yoke upon his neck to deliver the message of Yahweh—see Lucian Turkowski, "Peasant Agriculture in the Judaean Hills," *PEQ* 202 (1969): 21–33.

[101] See Osuji, *Where is the Truth?*, 172.

[102] Allen avers that the temporal limitation ועתה ("for now") in v. 6 provides a hint concerning the long term "agenda that the MT redaction in this chapter is concerned to promote: the eventual expiration of Babylon's leasehold" (Allen, *Jeremiah*, 307).

the message from Yahweh is not grounded on political factors but in the divine will.[103]

The oracle touches the traditional understanding of creation as well as that of exodus motifs (בכחי הגדול ובזרועי הנטויה—"my great power" and "outstretched arm;" Deut 4:34).[104] We should also note the emphatic אנכי ("I") in v. 5 which suggests that Yahweh is in control of all the nations and humanity. This emphatic אנכי is well supported by the phrase, ונתתיה לאשר ישר בעיני which can be translated as "and I will give to whomever is right in my eyes." Having declared the sovereignty of Yahweh, Jeremiah moves on to identify Nebuchadnezzar, the king of Babylon, as Yahweh's servant and to whom Yahweh has given all the lands and even the beasts of the field (v. 6). Interpreting vv. 5–6 within the context of Jeremiah (c. 594 BCE) would mean that Nebuchadnezzar, against whom the nations were conspiring to revolt, was actually the servant of Yahweh the creator of the universe. This indeed might have been a shocking message to the hearers of Jeremiah's oracle.

Verse 7 further declares that all the nations should serve Nebuchadnezzar as well as his son and grandson. However, there is a twist here and that is that Babylon will also become a slave to many nations. Many commentators have argued that this verse is *vaticinium ex eventu* and thus interrupts the flow from v. 6 to v. 7.[105] However, Lundbom argues this verse should be retained because hope accompanies every doom message.[106] Besides this,

---

[103] *Ibid.*, 306.

[104] Von Rad had argued that creation theme is late development in Israel history and therefore, it is argued that this verse might be late addition (see *Old Testament Theology* [OTL; 2 vols; Louisville: John Knox, 2001], 1:138). However, there are scholars who argue that the idea of Yahweh as the creator predates Jeremiah (see H.W. Saggs, *The Encounter with the Divine in Mesopotamia and Israel* [London: Athlone, 1978], 42–49).

[105] For instance, see Holladay, *Jeremiah*, 2:121.

[106] Lundbom, *Jeremiah 21–36*, 315.

the theme of Yahweh's sovereignty fits this verse as even Babylon will be obliterated by Yahweh when he decides. Simply put, the message that Yahweh is in control of his creation, which is the theme of this oracle, is well expounded through this verse.

Verses 8 and 11 provide for the nations two possibilities in relation to Babylon. In between 8–11, vv. 9–10 warn the nations about false prophecy. In v. 8, Jeremiah continues his oracle stating that those nations who do not submit to Babylon will face famine, war, and pestilence. Then in vv. 9–10, interestingly, Jeremiah also commands the foreign envoys not to listen to their prophets, diviners, dreamers, soothsayers, and sorcerers who were saying, "You shall not serve the king of Babylon."[107] Just as Judah's prophets and priests were denouncing submission to Babylon, these mediums were doing the same. Thus, the royal priests and the prophets were no different than their counterparts in the surrounding nations. Judah has become a nation just like the other nations (cf. 1 Sam 8:20). Jeremiah points out that the nations should not listen to their prophets, diviners, dreamers, and soothsayers who were encouraging the nations to rebel against Babylon. Jeremiah accuses them all of proclaiming falsehood.

In v. 11 Jeremiah delivers the second possibility for the nations. Jeremiah proclaims that if they submit and serve (עבד) Babylon, they will be restored in their land, where they can till (עבד) and live.[108] In other words, Yahweh is proposing peace to the nations if they submit to his plan—a peace procured through limited nationhood.

---

[107] In Israel mediums such as sorcerers, soothsayers, dreamers were banned in principle (see Deut 18:9–14).

[108] The argument is rhetorically stated by employing a wordplay that uses the same verb עבד which means both "serve" and "till."

Verses 12–15 represent the second oracle. Here Jeremiah turns his attention to King Zedekiah and Judah.[109] The message is similar to vv. 8–11, as indicated in v. 12: Jeremiah delivers a similar message to Zedekiah as he had delivered it to the neighboring nations. The message includes submission to Babylon and a warning against false prophets who were prophesying for rebellion against Babylon. Jeremiah accuses Judah's prophets of lying. Jeremiah's pro-Babylonian message by this time was pragmatic politics as much as it was Yahweh's revelation. However, the pro-Egyptian faction was still staunchly clinging to its ideology and, given that Zedekiah was a weak monarch, he was easily threatened and persuaded to listen to his royal administrators.[110] Here the pro-Egyptian faction might appear to be nationalistic in their fervor but

---

[109] Note that Jeremiah addresses the audience in plural indicating Zedekiah's officials and nation in general.

[110] King Zedekiah's attitude and behavior toward the prophet Jeremiah is fascinating. He appears to be as fickle as the "people" in the Temple Sermon (chapter 26). The author depicts Zedekiah as a person entangled between his royal counselors and his moral consciousness. For instance, he was installed by the Babylonians as the king but was motivated to rebel against Babylon by his court advisors. Even so, he inquires of Jeremiah what Yahweh has planned for him and Judah. In Jeremiah 37–38 we see that Jeremiah was put in the dungeon for being pro-Babylon. Interestingly, Zedekiah sent for him and questioned him secretly in his palace: "Is there any word from the Lord?" (37:17). Jeremiah's response was the same: "You shall be delivered into the hands of the king of Babylonia." In spite of this truthful response, Zedekiah did not put Jeremiah back into the dungeon but in a prison compound where he was given food daily. But later when his officials demanded Jeremiah's execution, he responded: "Behold, he is in your hands, for the king can do nothing against you" (38:5). The irony is his lack of integrity. On the one hand, he acts according to the advice of the royal counselors; on the other hand, he has sympathetic feelings for Jeremiah and seeks him out to discover God's will. The fact that he was sympathetic to Jeremiah is also suggestive within the context of true and false prophecy.

if their pro-Egyptian stance was opportunistic, so too was their nationalistic outlook, which was ill-conceived.

Verses 16–22 represent the third oracle which was delivered to the priests and the people. Once again Jeremiah warns both the priest and the people against false prophesy. Here Jeremiah identifies another issue relating to false prophecy, namely, the return of the vessels in two years' time. In a way, Jeremiah's message does not contradict the prophecy that the vessels will be returned from Babylon but that it will only take time (v. 22). For Jeremiah the issue of when the vessels will return to Judah concerns only Yahweh. The oracle, however, offers hope as Yahweh will indeed bring back the vessels.

Interestingly, the pro-Egyptian prophets were prophesying that the temple's vessels that were taken away to Babylon along with the other exiles in 598 BCE would be returned within two years. They derived their confidence about this message from the internal conflict that Nebuchadnezzar was facing in Babylon, as well as the enthusiasm shown by Pharaoh Psammatichus II in dominating Syria-Palestine. Such a message built false confidence among the people. Jeremiah, on the other hand, exhorted the priest and the prophets by declaring that, if anything, they should pray that the remaining vessels in the royal palace and temple might not be taken away (27:18–22). For Jeremiah the patience of Yahweh for Judah has come to an end and they must face judgment by submitting to Babylon. However, Jeremiah's message was not entirely bleak. He prophesies that Yahweh will bring Judah back and restore them, just not yet (27:22). As we shall see, Jeremiah's message of hope becomes clearer in chapter 29.

In chapter 28 the scene shifts from the royal court of Jerusalem to the Temple.[111] We should note that this activity occurs during

---

[111] Chapter 28 is built on a disputation between the prophet Jeremiah and Hananiah. Verses 1–4 represent Hananiah's message of salvation; vv. 5–9

the fifth month of the fourth year of King Zedekiah's reign. The significance of this date becomes important at the end of the chapter with regard to the death of prophet Hananiah. Hananiah dies within two months of the confrontation with Jeremiah. Although an accused prophet, Hananiah's name carries symbolic importance because it means "God is gracious." In the presence of the priests and all the people, Hananiah proclaims, "Thus says the Lord of hosts, the God of Israel: I have broken the yoke of the king of Babylon." We note that the verb שברתי is a *perfectum propheticum* (prophetic past) indicating that Hananiah is certain that the future is already fulfilled. Indeed, this message of Hananiah is confusing because the prophet is accused of false prophecy even though he had given it in the name of Yahweh.

Was Hananiah inspired to make this prophesy? Or did he intentionally prophesy falsehood? Hananiah was no doubt inspired to make his prophesy, but the fact that inspiration can be relative says nothing about Hananiah's source of prophecy. It can be assumed that he did not consider himself to be a false prophet, or that he thought his prophesy was falsehood. In fact, his message was the popular message that circulated even among the neighboring nations of Judah. In this case, Jeremiah's message of submission to Babylon was one belonging to a minority voice. So, what made Hananiah believe that his message was the truth? To answer this, one must explore the dynamics of worldview.

As discussed earlier in chapter two, a worldview dictates one's reasoning and way of life. Once a person is committed to a certain worldview it becomes his or her lens through which everything is interpreted. It has to be noted that Hananiah's worldview of

---

contain Jeremiah's response; vv. 10–11 deal with Hananiah's action toward Jeremiah's message; and vv. 12–17 consist of Jeremiah's further revelation from Yahweh in relation to Hananiah's message and action which also brings the disputation to resolution.

"absolute monarchy" (as opposed to "limited monarchy") has been around since the time of King Solomon.[112] Leon Festinger's theory of dissonance can shed light on the construction or formation of one's worldview.[113]

The dissonance theory is a psychological description of how people react when there is a conflict between their belief and practice. For instance, a person might *believe* the ethical instruction "do not steal or bribe," but if that person takes a bribe and extorts others, he or she is *behaving* contrary to his or her belief. In such an act dissonance is created. Now this person has two obvious ways to resolve the dissonance: (1) by changing his or her behavior according to the belief system; or (2) by modifying the belief system to rationalize his or her actions (e.g., distinguishing clandestine robbery from authoritative extortion, or

---

[112] See my discussion in chapter 3 (above).

[113] Carroll utilized Festinger's theory of dissonance to argue that failed prophecies of the OT prophets were made acceptable by the supporters of the prophets by resorting to dissonance theory—see R.P. Carroll, *When Prophecy Failed: Reactions and Response to Failure in the Old Testament Prophetic Traditions* [London: SCM, 1979]; cf. idem., "Ancient Israelite Prophecy and Dissonance Theory," in *"The Place is Too Small for Us": The Israelites Prophets in Recent Scholarship* (ed. Robert P. Gordon; SBTS 5; Winona Lake, IN: Eisenbrauns, 1995), 377–91. In fact, Carroll also adopted the title of his book from Festinger et al.—see Leon Festinger, Henry Riecken, and Stanley Schachter, *When Prophecy Fails* (Minneapolis: University of Minnesota Press, 1956). However, Festinger-Riecken-Schachter's argument (on which Carroll based his) has recently been criticized as a reductionist understanding of prophecy. Benton Johnson argues, "The model's treatment of belief as consisting solely of the prophecy itself obscures the fact that prophecies are invariably embedded within a larger matrix of cognitive elements that cohere in the minds of the followers" ("Revisiting *When Prophecy Fails*," in *How Prophecy Lives* [ed. Diana G. Tumminia and William H. Swatos; Leiden: Brill, 2011], 9–20). With that said, I think dissonance theory can be helpful in shedding light on the gradual formation of worldview and the commitment to it by the so-called prophet.

calling a bribe a gift). If someone modifies a belief system to adjust to his or her behavior and to reduce the dissonance, that belief system becomes his or her point of view in due time. Subsequently, such a changed view becomes the rationale or lens through which everything is interpreted. The prophet Hananiah and his associates changed their Yahwistic tradition so as to conform it to their lifestyle. Jeremiah and his supporters, however, were acting as agents to change the behavior of the Judeans in order to turn them back to their original belief system. Thus, irrespective of Hananiah's thoughts, from the perspective of the Yahwistic tradition he was indeed a false prophet, receiving inspiration not from Yahweh but from his support group. In this case, Robert Wilson's argument that the prophets prophesy according to the need and demand of his or her support group is correct.[114]

In vv. 3–4, Hananiah prophesies that King Jehoiachin along with the vessels of the temple and the other Judeans would be brought back from exile within two years. It is an intriguing prophecy because Zedekiah was the incumbent king installed by the Babylonians and to bring back Jehoiachin would create the problem of having two kings at once. Hananiah's prophecy of Jehoiachin's return does not suggest much, other than the fact that Zedekiah was a king who did not have the respect of his court administrator.

Jeremiah's response to Hananiah (in v. 6) is worthy of attention: אמן כן יעשה יהוה יקם יהוה את־דבריך ("Amen! May the Lord do so; may the Lord fulfill the words that you have prophesied"). It is here that the theme of true and false prophecy reaches its climax. Quell argues that Jeremiah's response to Hananiah points out the dilemma of Jeremiah's conviction.[115] Similarly, Childs contends that one expects Jeremiah's response to Hananiah to be explosive

---

[114] See my discussion on Wilson's view in ch. 1 (above).
[115] Quell, *Wahre und Falsche Propheten*, 46.

with "fiery denunciation."[116] This meek reply, however, suggests that Jeremiah was uncertain as to whether Yahweh had changed his own mind. In favor of this suggestion, Childs reduces prophecy and divine revelation to mere *ad hoc* concepts. Yet, I myself agree with Holladay, who argues that Jeremiah's response is colored with sarcasm or irony.[117] It has to be noted that Jeremiah had been preaching his message for some time now and his prophesy to Jehoiakim had also been partly fulfilled by the invasion of Judah by Babylon in 597 BCE. Moreover, Jeremiah's message was based on the covenantal relationship between Yahweh and his people. Thus, it is highly unlikely that Jeremiah would believe Yahweh had a fickle mind with regard to this issue. The word אמן literally means "it is true," however, the sentence construction of this verse contains optative imperfects (יעשה—may the Lord do) and these, along with an ironic tone, would mean, "Be it true (even though it is not true!)."[118]

In v. 7 Jeremiah further countered Hananiah in the presence of everyone. This is denoted by an adversative particle אך (variously translated as "yet, however, but, only, nevertheless"). As a way of reminding them of the past prophets, Jeremiah avers that former prophets have all prophesied judgment and doom rather than peace and salvation (v. 8). Perhaps Jeremiah has in mind prophets such as Micah, Amos, *et al.* However, reminding the doom message of the past prophets does not mean that a true prophet always prophesies doom. Rather, this means that Yahweh has sent his prophets to change Israel's evil paths resulting from covenant unfaithfulness. Therefore, it is only logical for Yahweh's prophets to proclaim messages of repentance and judgment.[119] Then he goes

---

[116] Childs, *Old Testament Theology*, 135–36.
[117] Holladay, *Jeremiah*, 2:128.
[118] See Lundbom, *Jeremiah 21–36*, 334.
[119] Allen, *Jeremiah*, 316.

on to argue that peace prophecy has to be fulfilled in order for it to be true.[120] These words of Jeremiah resemble Deut 18:21–22, where it is asserted that a true prophecy has to be substantiated with fulfillment (v. 22). Perhaps, Jeremiah is aware that a doom prophecy might not necessarily need fulfillment because usually that kind of prophecy comes with a condition. If the condition is heeded then the doom prophecy might be cancelled.[121] Osuiji also argues that, "The isolated prophet does not enjoy the benefit and protection of tradition and so has to undergo a proof for accreditation."[122] Osuji has a point here: if the message of the prophetic tradition is that of doom then a message like Hananiah's needs to be further tested.

Furthermore, Holladay points out that Jeremiah uses the imperfect ינבא ("the prophet who shall prophesy peace"), and not the participle ("the prophet who prophesies peace"), implying that Jeremiah's statement is related to a specific situation and not general statement.[123] It is imperative to acknowledge the premise of the prophecy, that is, the covenantal relationship between Yahweh and Judah. In other words, a peace prophecy in an appropriate context is not a false prophecy, just as a doom prophecy in an appropriate context is a true prophecy.

Concerning this, Hananiah broke the yoke from around Jeremiah's neck, declaring that the Lord would break Babylon's yoke from Judah in a similar way (v. 10). In breaking the yoke from the neck of Jeremiah, Hananiah too performs a symbolic action that represents his message. At this point Jeremiah went away (v. 11). We do not know the exact reason why Jeremiah

---

[120] These words of Jeremiah resemble Deut 18:21–22. I will deal on the text of Deuteronomy below in an excursus.

[121] Dearman, *Jeremiah and Lamentations*, 254–55.

[122] Osuji, *Where is the Truth?*, 205.

[123] See Holladay, *Jeremiah*, 2:128.

simply walked away. Lundbom contends that Jeremiah might have been roundly put to shame; Thompson thinks Jeremiah was taken by surprise; whereas Clements avers that Jeremiah might have been confused.[124] Whichever is the case, Wiesel criticizes Jeremiah for not retaliating against Hananiah. Specifically, Wiesel contends, "if he [Jeremiah] is sure [of his prophecy], he is obliged to confront Hananiah and tell him the truth."[125] However, in this confrontation, Hananiah appears to be out to prove Jeremiah's message was incorrect. McKane asserts:

> [T]he unflappable prophet who does not rush his fences and was unruffled by the circumstance that he had no immediate riposte to make to Hananiah's theatrical gesture. He judged that reason would not prevail and refused to engage in a slanging match. He left the field and bided his time before he returned to reassert his prophetic authority, and deal finally with Hananiah.[126]

Jeremiah's quiet composure indicates that he was indeed not the imposter.[127]

Again, Jeremiah's quiet retirement from the scene also suggests something about the dynamic of Yahweh and his prophets in relation to divine revelation. Prophecy does not simply have to do with the reaction to a situation but rather it is about contemplation and understanding Yahweh. Thus, it was only when Jeremiah received a fresh revelation that he returned to deliver Yahweh's message (v. 12). Jeremiah returned to reaffirm that

---

[124] Lundbom, *Jeremiah 21–36*, 341; cf. Thompson, *Book of Jeremiah*, 540; R.E. Clements, *Jeremiah* (Atlanta: John Knox, 1988), 166.

[125] Elie Wiesel, *Five Biblical Portraits* (Notre Dame: University of Notre Dame Press, 1981), 116.

[126] McKane, *Jeremiah*, 2:720.

[127] See also Duhm, *Buch Jeremia*, 226.

message and to pronounce judgment against Hananiah (vv. 13–16). Jeremiah announced that Hananiah would die because he let the people believe שֶׁקֶר a "lie."[128] Jeremiah once again depended upon Deuteronomy (Deut 13:2–6 [13:1–5 (Eng.)]) which articulates that a prophet who prophesies in the name of Yahweh and yet says, "Let us follow other gods" and "let us serve them" is a false prophet (v. 2–3). Such a prophet should be put to death (v. 6). In Jeremiah's thinking Hananiah falls under this category of prophets who prophesy in the name of Yahweh but lead people to other gods. Hananiah prophesied in the name of Yahweh but he led Judah to revolt against the Lord and, in the process, misled the masses away from Yahweh and toward falsehood. Thus, Jeremiah was warranted in pronouncing a judgment of death upon him. The verb מְשַׁלֵּחֲךָ, used in pronouncing the judgment of Hananiah, is a declarative Piel meaning "dispatch or remove." Thus, "the one who prophesied without being sent would in reprisal be sent away—to his doom."[129] Just as Jeremiah pronounced the death judgment of Hananiah from Yahweh, Hananiah died the same year in the seventh month.

Excursus: Deut 13:2–6 (13:1–5 [Eng.]) and 18:21–22

Deut 13:2–6 (13:1–5 [Eng.]) and 18:21–22 provide criteria for determining true and false prophecy.[130] These two texts are the

---

[128] This is strong word in Hebrew with a negative connotation, meaning falsehood. See my discussion in chapter 1 (above).

[129] Allen, *Jeremiah*, 318.

[130] Both the passages Deut 13:2–6 (13:1–5 [Eng.]) and 18:21–22 fall within the broader section in the book of Deuteronomy: the specific stipulations of the covenant (12:1–26:15). These stipulations were given in anticipation of living in the Promised Land. Perhaps these covenant stipulations help fueled Josiah's reform. See Eugene H. Merrill, *Deuteronomy* (NAC 4; Nashville: Broadman and Holman, 1994), 217–336; J.G. McConville, *Deuteronomy* (AOTC; Nottingham: Apollos, 2002), 21–32.

only legal passages in the OT that deal with prophets and prophecy.[131] The former articulates that a prophet or dreamer who gives a "wonder or sign" and it comes to pass and uses that to lead the people to follow other gods is a false prophet (v. 2–3). Such a prophet deserves capital punishment (v. 6). The latter asserts that a prophecy given in Yahweh's name has to be substantiated with fulfillment to be considered true (18:22).

Both criteria (as discussed above) are utilized by Jeremiah *mutatis mutandis* in his confrontation with the so-called false prophets. Jeremiah pronounces the death penalty over Hananiah, (and later Ahab, Zedekiah, and Shemaiah in 29:21; 32). However, we must notice that in the confrontation between Jeremiah and Hananiah, unlike the legislation in Deuteronomy, both the prophets are Yahweh's prophets. Yet Jeremiah pronounces the death penalty on Hananiah because, according to him, Hananiah led the people astray from Yahweh (Jer 28:15). Still one can ask: how is Hananiah, a prophet of Yahweh just like Jeremiah, leading the people astray from Yahweh?

Likewise, the criterion of fulfillment (Deut 18:22) looks problematic. In his defense against Hananiah, Jeremiah avers that a "peace" prophecy has to be proven in order to be true (Jer 28:9). However, Deut 18:22 does not specify the type of prophecy but states in general that any prophecy prophesied in Yahweh's name should be fulfilled in order to be truthful. These criteria appear to be vague and problematic. Lundbom states, "But this test requiring fulfillment of the prophetic word, even when combined with the credential test of 13:2–6 (1–5 [Eng.]), falls short of being a complete measurement of false (and true) prophecy."[132] These

---

[131] Jack R. Lundbom, *Deuteronomy: A Commentary* (Grand Rapids: Eerdmans, 2013), 450.
[132] *Ibid.*, 560.

criteria are doubtless difficult to understand and have led some scholars to argue that they are meaningless.¹³³

But perhaps they are not supposed to be used as categorical statements across different milieus. J. Todd Hibbard states in his comments on Deut 18: 22, "This is the only real criterion given in the passage but the evaluative framework it provides is obvious at best and nugatory at worst."¹³⁴ Hibbard is pessimistic about the feasibility of these criteria; however, his reference to the "evaluative framework" is intriguing. Perhaps it might be helpful to consider these criteria in conjunction with the fluidity of the development of Yahwistic tradition with specific reference to covenantal relationship between Yahweh and Israel. In other words, what I am suggesting is that the covenant between Yahweh and his people can be the evaluative framework to understand and utilize these criteria meaningfully.

The book of Deuteronomy, which literally means second law, concerns with the covenantal relationship between Yahweh and his people.¹³⁵ It expounds the covenant in which Israel's society was to be established. It is only right, therefore, to look into the legal legislation of the prophets and prophecy (Deut 13:2–6; 18:21–22) from the perspective of covenant relationship between Yahweh and Israel. The crux of the covenant relationship is that this covenant is based on the חסד character of Yahweh, and that obedience fosters blessings and disobedience incurs Yahweh's wrath. Translating this covenant premise within the context of prophets and their prophecy would mean that a prophet can actually prophesy both peaceful/blessings as well as doom/judgment messages. However,

---

¹³³ For instance see Crenshaw, *Prophetic Conflict*, 47.

¹³⁴ J. Todd Hibbard, "True and False Prophecy: Jeremiah's Revision of Deuteronomy," *JSOT* 35.3 (2011): 339–58.

¹³⁵ See S. Dean McBride, "Polity of the Covenant People: The Book of Deuteronomy," in *A Song of Power and the Power of Song* (ed. Duane L. Christensen; SBTS 3; Winona Lake, IN: Eisenbrauns, 1993), 62–77.

it is true that in many instances Yahweh's prophet prophesies doom and judgment messages because of the recalcitrant nature of Israel. Thus, in a way, Yahweh's persistent and perpetual sending of his prophets implies his חסד for his people.

Jeremiah's recounting that past prophets prophesied doom and judgment and that peace prophecy has to be aided by fulfillment (Jer 28:8–9) can be understood as a commentary on Deut 18:22 within his own context.[136] The criterion of Deut 18:22, that is, that true prophecy has to be substantiated by fulfillment, is thus more nuanced in its meaning. In other words, this criterion has to be understood generally from the Yahwistic tradition and specifically from the חסד character of Yahweh. Yahweh's prophets are the manifestation of Yahweh's חסד. Their role was largely to guide the Israelites away from evil paths. Thus, their messages came with a condition: Repent or face Yahweh's judgment. In this case their prophecy was contingent on the response of the audience.

Therefore, on the one hand, if the audience receives the message and repents, then Yahweh's wrath is averted; on the other hand, if the audience ignores the message, then Yahweh's wrath is enforced. In the case of Jeremiah, the audience did not avail themselves of Yahweh's message and thus Jeremiah's prophecy was fulfilled in the fall of Jerusalem in 587 BCE. Similarly, one should understand the issue of doom prophecy from this perspective. As noted above, there is truth in Jeremiah's statement that Yahweh's prophets have more often than not prophesied doom messages but there is also a scope and space within the Yahwistic tradition for true Yahwistic prophets to prophesy peace or salvation messages. Thus, Jeremiah could also prophesy a peace prophecy (see Jer 30–33). However, if a prophet prophesies peace without acknowledging the covenantal premise, namely, the right

---

[136] Hibbard argues that Jeremiah modifies the legal legislation of Deut 18:22. See Hibbard, "True and False Prophecy," 347–49.

relationship between Yahweh and his people, such prophecy becomes utterly false. It should also be noted that, in fact, a deeper reading of the so-called doom prophecy is closely related to the salvation message, provided the audience takes the message to heart.[137]

Deut 13:2–6, as already noted, is less problematic. It relates specifically to the second commandment (Deut 5:7) of the Decalogue: "you shall have no other gods before me." It states that if a prophet prophesies something that does occur and yet leads the people away to other gods, that prophet is a false prophet. It has to be noted, however, that this passage does not specify in whose name the prophet speaks. As noted above, in the confrontation of Jeremiah and Hananiah (Jer 28) we have two Yahweh prophets; thus, the issue of true and false prophecy becomes more complicated. In other words, the passage is concerned with whose message is right and whose message is leading the people astray from Yahweh. Again, the covenantal premise becomes crucial in adjudicating true and false prophecy.

However, one must acknowledge that very often adjudicating criteria are fabricated by the ideology of the support system. In other words, it all really comes down to the support group of the prophet. There is a certain truth in the contention that true and false prophecy is a matter of the clash of ideology between differing

---

[137] Claus Westermann labels these as the conditional oracles of salvation—see *Prophetic Oracles of Salvation in the Old Testament* (trans. Keith Crim; Louisville: John Knox, 1991), 195–226. Although it has to be noted that for Westernmann this conditional oracle of salvation is not proper prophecy *per se* but derived from the exhortatory style of later Deuteronomistic editors during the exilic period. I have, however, argued above that the Deuteronomistic editors and the prophet Jeremiah might have been contemporaries and have shared common vision in Yahwistic tradition. Thus this conditional oracle of salvation is not necessarily an exclusive product of the exilic editors but intrinsic to Yahwistic tradition itself.

groups. Although, one needs to be careful about this type of remark. Jeremiah, as Yahweh's prophet, had his support group in the people of the land. But it is important to emphasize that the *modus operandi* of both Jeremiah and his support group were the covenant, the received tradition, and the perpetual revelation of Yahweh in the light of that tradition. Jeremiah was not merely prophesying according to the whims and wishes of his support group. False prophecy arises once the prophet becomes the mouthpiece of his or her support group. In most of Israelite history the (Yahwistic) ideology of Jeremiah and his support group held a minority status even though it gained major momentum during the times of Asa, Josiah, and Hezekiah. Still, it persisted and acted as the watchtower in Israel's society. However, as discussed above in chapter four, there were institutions and groups that modified the Yahwistic tradition and depended on their own hidden agenda instead of the illumination of the divine revelation. Unfortunately, Hananiah appears to have been this type of prophet.

5.4.3. Jer 29: The Spillover of Prophetic Conflict to the Exilic Community

Chapter 29 continues recounting the prophetic conflict within the exilic community, particularly with regard to those who were exiled to Babylon in 598 BCE.[138] This text contains two letters, one sent from Jeremiah to the exilic community (vv. 1–23), and the second a rejoinder by Jeremiah to Shemaiah of Nehelam, who had earlier written asking the priest Zephaniah to take action against Jeremiah (vv. 24–32).

The letter from Jeremiah was sent through Elasah son of Shaphan and Gemariah son of Hilkiah, who were official envoys

---

[138] Dearman writes: "Chapter 29 is linked with the previous chapter by literary proximity, historical context, and common vocabulary" (*Jeremiah and Lamentations*, 261).

of Zedekiah to Nebuchadnezzar (29:1–3).[139] It was a pastoral letter as much as it was a letter to denounce false prophecy. Since the letter contained a harsh word for Zedekiah (vv. 16–20), it might be assumed that the letter was smuggled without the knowledge of the king.[140] The letter was addressed to the יתר (remnant) of the elders of the people along with the priests, prophet, and to all the people.[141] In the letter Jeremiah exhorts the exilic community to בנו (build), שבו (live), נטעו (plant), and הולידו (multiply), because this was the will of Yahweh (v. 5–6, 28). In line with this, he also urges the exiled Judeans to pray for Babylon so that in the שלום (shalom or welfare) of Babylon they might fulfill their own שלום (v. 7). To seek welfare for Babylon, especially in the given context, also means not to rebel or incite revolt against Babylon.

This message of Jeremiah is consistent with what he has been saying all along: it would take time (seventy years) before the

---

[139] It is unknown why Zedekiah sent his official envoys to Babylon. Perhaps, they went to pay annual tribute as a vassal of Babylon, or it might be to make peace after the Jerusalem conference mentioned in 27:3 ended in a failure. As noted earlier Elasah might be the brother of Ahikam son of Shaphan (Jer 26:24). Gemariah's father Hilkiah might have been the high priest who discovered the book of the law during the reign of Josiah—see Holladay, *Jeremiah*, 2:140. This letter also inspired the later "Epistle of Jeremiah," an apocryphal work from the Hellenistic period (Lundbom, *Jeremiah 21–36*, 348).

[140] Since vv. 16–20 concerns negative judgment of Zedekiah, it is argued that these verses are a secondary addition by the redactor. This conclusion is also supported by the omission of these verses in the LXX. However, Holladay argues that the LXX translator has the tendency of committing haplography and, moreover, some important vocabularies used in these verses are related to those used throughout the chapter. For more discussion on this see Holladay, *Jeremiah*, 2:135.

[141] The word יתר can mean two things. It can mean "remnant/left over" (Exod 10:5; 1 Kgs 11:41) or "preeminent" (Isa 56:2; Ps 31:24). Here יתר could potentially have both the meanings—the elders who survived 597 BCE invasion of Nebuchadnezzar, and the elders as the preeminent guardian of the exilic community.

exiled community would return to their homeland (v. 10).¹⁴² Yet, Jeremiah encourages the exilic community by reminding them that Yahweh is gracious and that they will be restored to their homeland (vv. 11–14).¹⁴³ However, his opposition has also penetrated the exilic community by painting a more optimistic early return (vv. 8–9, 15).¹⁴⁴ In vv. 16–19, against the optimistic

---

¹⁴² Verse 10 specifically mentions that the exile will be seventy years. However, this is a symbolic number that envisages completeness or wholeness (Gen 46:27; 50:3; Deut 10:22; Judg 1:7; 1 Sam 6:19; 2 Sam 24:15)—see Lundbom, *Jeremiah 21-36*, 352. In Ps 90:10 human lifespan is purports to be seventy years and Jeremiah might seemingly mean that it would take a life time before the Jews return from the exile—a message completely opposite from Hananiah's who have predicted that the exile will return in two years time—see Osuji, *Where is the Truth?*, 249.

¹⁴³ Verses 10–11 epitomize the חסד of Yahweh for his people. Yahweh declares that he will visit his people after the seventy years. The emphatic אנכי (I) in v. 11 indicates that Yahweh is in charge of the whole situation. He will initiate the recovery and restoration of his people. In v. 13 the word "seek" or "search" occurs twice, which is actually the translation of two Hebrew בקש and דרש verbs. The meanings of these two words simply do not imply seeking as in inquiring something but "an attitude of actively desiring to live in fellowship with God." The meaning of "seek" is more of a fact, something that will happen; rather than conditional ("if")—see Hetty Lalleman, *Jeremiah and Lamentations* (TOTC; Downers Grove: IVP Academic, 2013), 220. Also notice the cognate accusative construction in v. 14: ושבתי את־ שביתכם (which can be translated as "I will restore your fortunes" or "I will turn your captivity"). This expression occurs eleven times in Jeremiah (29:14; 30:3, 18; 31:23; 32:44; 33:7, 11, 26; 48:47; 49:6, 39). When the noun, having the same root as the verb and is directly controlled by the verb, it is used to describe the intensity of the verbal idea—see Christo H.J. van der Merwe, Jackie A. Naudé and Jan H. Kroeze, *A Biblical Hebrew Reference Grammar* (Sheffield: Sheffield Academic, 2000), 241–45. Lalleman contends, "God's initiatives and promises of return are certain, and there is a sense of God's unconditional love for his people" (*Jeremiah*, 220).

¹⁴⁴ Besides the prophets, Jeremiah also mentions another groups namely, the diviners (קסמיכם—Qal participle masculine plural plus second person masculine plural suffix) who interpret the dreams of the Judean people. Diviners were prohibited in Judah and therefore, Holladay comments that the Jewish exiles

message, Jeremiah declares that Jerusalem, its king, and its inhabitants will be punished because of their unfaithfulness. Jeremiah identifies two prophets, namely, Ahab son of Kolaiah, and Zedekiah, son of Maaseiah, who were prophesying a lie akin to Hananiah's (vv. 20–23). Besides prophesying a lie, Jeremiah accuses them of adultery and as such both of them are condemned to death.[145] Interestingly, these two prophets will die at the hands of Nebuchadnezzar because it is only logical for the Babylonian king to execute anyone who incites rebellion.

In vv. 24–32, Jeremiah deals with another optimistic prophet: Shemaiah the Nehelamite. Jeremiah is writing a rejoinder to Shemaiah's letter to the high priest of Jerusalem, that is, Zephaniah the son of Maaseiah. Apparently, Shemaiah has written a letter to Zephaniah (which the latter read to Jeremiah—see v. 29) accusing Jeremiah of being a mad man for the message he was delivering. For Jeremiah, exile is a means of rebuilding the broken covenantal relationship between Israel and Yahweh; for the opponents of Jeremiah, such a message was total madness (cf. v. 26).[146] Subsequently, Shemaiah calls Zephaniah to punish Jeremiah. Jeremiah in his rejoinder accuses Shemaiah of leading the people to trust in lies (v. 31) and as a result he and his descendants will not see the good things Yahweh has restored for his people (v. 32).

5.4.4. Summary of the Prophetic Conflict

The analysis of this text culminates the arguments I have made in the last three chapters: central to understanding the conflict

---

were in danger of becoming pagans (*Jeremiah*, 2:141); whereas Lundbom contends that even though diviners were prohibited in Judah they still existed covertly and now that they were in foreign land the diviners might have become openly active (*Jeremiah 21–36*, 352).

[145] The law of Moses sanctions death penalty for both false prophecy and adultery (see Deut 18:20; 22:22).

[146] See also Lalleman, *Jeremiah*, 40.

between true and false prophecy is a hermeneutic of critical realism. This hermeneutic is used to better understand divine revelation, the development of Yahwistic tradition, and the sociological elements of ancient agrarian Israelite society. Along with these items, the study of the late seventh and early sixth centuries BCE enabled us to understand afresh the prophetic conflict found in Jer 26–29. Israel's prophetic conflict, although supernatural phenomenon and a subjective enterprise, can also be an objective subject matter if one considers its development of tradition in history. In other words, Israel's prophetic conflict has to be interpreted contextually. This does not mean that Israel's prophets were unique vis-à-vis other ANE prophetic movements. From a phenomenological perspective, in fact, they were similar— e.g., the occasional experience of ecstasy, and the prophets' status and role within society. However, every prophet, ancient or present, prophesies from the worldview he or she has been born into and nurtured in. Therefore, it is imperative to study Israelite prophetic conflict contextually and to note that every specific context brings different specific challenges and requirements which have to be wisely monitored and studied in order to provide a semblance of understanding of the prophetic conflict.

In the context of ancient Israelite society, the prophetic movement was strongly connected to Yahweh not just because he was their national God, but more so because he manifested himself in history through his divine revelations. Thus, in ancient Israel the prophetic conflict arose not just because of the misinterpretation of history or tradition but also because of the broken covenantal relationship between Israel and Yahweh. This broken covenantal relationship was related to the inability of the kings and their administration to live within a limited monarchy. Yahweh's response to this could have been instant judgment, but because of his חסד for his people, Yahweh decided to send prophet after prophet. Some monarchs in Judah did respond to Yahweh's חסד (for instance, Asa, Hezekiah and Josiah), however, many ignored it and incurred inevitable judgment.

By the time of the prophets Jeremiah and Hananiah, the tension within covenantal relationship between Yahweh and his chosen people had reached a climax. Jeremiah's message and his specific interpretation of history were the outcome of his commitment to and critical reading of the covenantal law. In contrast to Jeremiah, Hananiah's message and interpretation of history were the result of the political crisis with Babylon, political activism of Egypt, and an institutionalized reading of Yahweh's covenant.

In such a scenario, one can argue that distinguishing true and false prophecy does not necessarily work by following specific criteria in a dogmatic manner. This does not mean that criteria for adjudicating true and false prophecy are worthless. To be sure, it is not as straightforward as we would like at times; however, adequate and meaningful construal of the criteria can be navigated within the Yahwistic tradition and provide us with helpful results. It is in the fluidity of the development of Yahwistic tradition that one sees the mark of true prophecy. It is also true that such criteria depend, to a certain extent, on the support system of the prophet under scrutiny. However, it is one thing to have the prophet prophesy according to the agenda of his or her support group, and a completely different thing to have both the prophet and his support system subjected to a tradition and divine revelation. In the former, the prophet prophesies to gratify the support group, whereas in the latter the prophet can even prophesy against the support system, especially if the covenantal relationship is broken. In other words, just as Yahweh's prophets aspired to live within his משפטים, so also an exemplification of such an aspiration is required on the part of the adjudicator in order to determine true and false prophecy. For Jeremiah, such an adjudicator was found in the "people of the land," who shared a common vision and imagination based on Yahwistic tradition.

5.5. Conclusion

In this chapter, I analyzed Jer 26–29 by utilizing insights gained from the overall study, namely, appreciating divine revelation from a critical realist perspective, the development of the Yahwistic tradition, the sociology of ancient Israel agrarian society, and the history of Judah in the seventh and early sixth centuries BCE. Prophetic conflict, though a supernatural phenomenon, stands in conflict within history. In ancient Israel prophetic conflict was deeply rooted in the development of Yahwistic tradition. From this perspective it can be argued that ancient Israel had a rubric in its Yahwistic tradition to adequately distinguish true from false prophecy. Jeremiah and his supporters guarded the Yahwistic tradition and interpreted history from that perspective. Jeremiah's opponents, however, interpreted history from the perspective of political opportunism. This picture surfaces vividly when one analyzes the conflict against the background of ancient agrarian society, as I have shown.

This chapter also dealt briefly, in an excursus, with how to understand the criteria of true and false prophecy as found in Deut 13:2–6; 18:21–22. These criteria are not without meaning and value. However, they should not be interpreted as a fixed and final set of principles but rather should be evaluated in light of an evolving ancient Yahwistic tradition.

Chapter 6
CONCLUSIONS

In this study, I endeavored to determine whether ancient Israel had a rubric for distinguishing between true and false prophecy in its Yahwistic tradition. The investigation employed a synthetic analysis through the lens of critical realism. The synthetic analysis is the cultural, social, political, and religious study of ancient Israel. I began the study with a selective literature review in conjunction with the scholars' views on the issue of true and false prophecy in the OT. The literature review was broadly divided within the timeline of pre-modern, modern, and postmodern. This division, while it appears to be chronological in nature, is also pregnant with philosophical hermeneutics. Therefore, a person living in the period of the so-called post-modern world can still harbor the pre-modern or modern mind. With that said, this division of the timeline was required to depict that the discussion of true and false prophecy in OT studies has been enveloped within the dominant hermeneutical trajectory of the interpreters' milieu.

Understandably the topic of revelation, which is intrinsic to prophecy, played a crucial role in the scholars' discussion of true and false prophecy. In the pre-modern milieu, interpretation was done through the doctrinal lens; however, beginning with the European Renaissance the seed of modern scientific and objective hermeneutics was sowed. Such a hermeneutical enterprise does not acknowledge revelation as a legitimate source of knowledge since it could not be verified. When this type of hermeneutics is applied to the discussion of true and false prophecy, prophecy becomes unintelligible, haphazard, and exclusively ethereal.

Along with this, I also emphasized the attempts to marry this hermeneutical lens with metaphysics, especially during the Biblical theology movement. However, the outcome was either an awkward and disjointed theology (for instance, von Rad's understanding of *Heilsgeschichte*) or forceful attempts to prove the biblical texts are scientific history. Such interpretations complicate the already complex issue of distinguishing true and false prophecy. Some of the conclusions that scholars arrived at were: only a prophet can adjudicate another prophet's prophecy (Quell); prophetic conflict is merely a conflict between differing groups which thrived on the ideologies of the opposing factions (Wilson); the capricious character of God completely makes adjudication of prophecy impossible (Crenshaw); the prophetic fulfillments recorded in the OT are prophecy *ex eventu* (De Jong). Moreover, the postmodern interpretation, with its emphasis on reader-response, has only relativized the parameters in adjudicating true and false prophecy. Therefore, a need to understand afresh prophecy/revelation, development of tradition, and history becomes imperative if there is to be a better construal of Israelite prophetic conflict.

In the epistemology of critical realism, I argued that such a need is met. Critical realism is not necessarily a methodological hermeneutic. In other words, it does not have any specific tenets of interpretation; rather critical realism espouses a perspective through which to analyze and interpret texts and issues. Critical realism, therefore, provides a point of view from which one can look at reality. In critical realism, knowledge is articulated and sustained through the process of experience, understanding, and judgment. Unlike critical realism, knowledge in naïve realism is based on sense data or experience, whereas in idealism human understanding is the basis of knowledge. It is from this perspective of critical realism one can argue that objective truth is not just about the transmission of information, but the transmission of authentic subjectivity. Critical realism understands that objective knowledge cannot be attained apart from one's subjective experience, motivation, and worldview. Such epistemology opens vistas for theological inquiries as an important and necessary element in the quest for objective truth. Thus, history is understood not just as a neutral and objective study, but as bias and open to subjective experience; albeit, it has to go through the grinding process of judgment in order to arrive at authentic knowledge.

Closely related to this is the issue of the redaction process in the formation of the literature of the OT. There is no doubt that OT is an outcome of a very long redaction process. The process, in fact, began with the oral culture until they slowly found their ways into written forms that again went through the process of revision and edition. One of the crucial questions that one should ask concerning the redactional process is: how was the process conducted? Some scholars have argued that the OT contains fictive, ideological materials written from the perspective of the few elites. Contrary to this, I contended that the redaction process was carried out with utmost care by the guardians of the Yahwistic tradition and with an overarching intention to depict the relationship between Yahweh and his people.

From a critical realist perspective, prophecy and revelation, although a supernatural phenomenon, or private experience, are not without any frame of reference. Rather, prophecy and its essence, divine revelation, can be intelligible, studied, and deliberated upon to verify its authenticity. Such claims could be made possible with a nuanced understanding of tradition and its development. From a critical realist perspective, tradition is embedded in social context. In fact, rationality is tradition-bound. In other words, the tradition of a society is a historically extended and socially embodied argument. Thus, tradition is at once both dynamic as well as referential in its character.

It is within such understanding of tradition one should examine Israel's Yahwistic tradition. For ancient Israel, their Yahwistic tradition was believed to have its origin in Yahweh's divine revelation, chiefly, the exodus event and the covenantal law. In due course of time, these divine revelations of Yahweh became the *depósitum fidei*—the referential point. Tradition, however, is never an anemic dogma but a living and dynamic entity. Such an understanding enables one to envisage Israel's prophets as receivers of divine revelation within the framework of Yahwistic tradition even as her tradition evolved and developed according to the changes and needs of the social context. It has to be emphasized that Israel's prophets were Yahweh's prophets because of their close relationship with him. It is only in the repentance and faithfulness of the prophets that they received perpetual divine revelation from Yahweh.

In the third chapter, I explored the content of the Yahwistic tradition and its development. Yahwistic tradition has its genesis in Yahweh's revelation, first to the forefathers of the Israelite people group, but later and more concretely to the Israelite people in the exodus event. This event led to the establishment of the covenant relationship between Yahweh and Israel. This relationship was based on the covenant stipulations (משפטים). These משפטים concentrated on themes such as, who Israel should worship and how they should be faithful to Yahweh. Furthermore, the משפטים relate to how Israel should co-exist with one another and deal with the poor, widows, aliens and orphans. The core intention of this covenantal stipulation is to establish Yahweh's righteousness and justice in the Promised Land and exalt the name of Yahweh. Observing משפטים would provide life to Israel, but breaking משפטים means judgment and punishment from Yahweh. Basically, this was the message of Yahweh's prophets. Put another way, although Yahweh's prophets received fresh revelation according to the need of the time and circumstances, it was never at the expense of the core message of the Yahwistic tradition, and was always with the context of that tradition.

I also argued that Israel's Yahwistic tradition was not against the monarchy, but it only supported a certain form of monarchy namely, "limited monarchy." In this form of the monarchial system, even the human king was expected to rule within the requirement of covenant stipulations. In fact, Yahweh's prophets were sent to ensure that Israel's rulers were functioning within the concept of limited monarchy.

Another issue that I discussed relating to Yahwistic tradition was the Davidic covenant. Many have argued that the Davidic covenant was a royal propagandistic ideology that eventually gave birth to the Judean tradition and created friction with the Yahwistic tradition that was preserved in the northern kingdom of Israel (so Wilson's Ephraimite tradition). However, I argued that the Davidic covenant was not a royal programmatic project but rather a necessary development in the evolution of Yahwistic tradition. In fact, Jeroboam the first king of the northern kingdom of Israel was also given the chance to enter into a similar kind of covenant relationship with Yahweh by the prophet Ahijah, but he ruined his opportunity. The Davidic covenant did not supersede the Sinaitic covenant, but it complemented and functioned within the Sinaitic covenant. It is not the Davidic covenant that led to the downfall of Judah, rather it was the inability of the monarchy and its administration to live within the system of limited monarchy that led to the downfall of Judah. In fact, this is even true for the northern kingdom of Israel. It is within this broader context of Yahwistic tradition and its development that the relevancy of Yahweh's prophets and prophecies is found.

The inability of the monarchy and its administration to function within the requirement of limited monarchy is exposed when ancient Israel's agrarian society is analyzed utilizing the macro sociology of Gerhard Lenski and Patrick Nolan (chapter four). The agrarian economy in ancient Israel during the Iron Age II provided the impetus for the acceleration of urbanization as well as for centralization and expansion of the royal monarchy and its administration. However, the resources for survival were limited, which means for the royal establishment to maintain their status and privilege, they had to exploit and extort the poor peasant. Within such a context, the priests and the prophets interestingly found themselves in the higher echelon of the social stratification. This was because they appealed to a power higher than the ruler himself. However, many of the priests and the prophets were perceived to have been motivated for their personal status and privileges by distorting the Yahwistic tradition of justice and righteousness. In other words, the Yahwistic tradition was manipulated to enable the royal administrative system to thrive in its ill-intentions. Such a distortion gave rise to an institutionalized form of Yahwistic tradition that was signified by an outward expression of worship and sacrifices without any hint of inward rejuvenation. Not only this, but institutionalized Yahwism did not have any problem in embracing other cultic gods and their different forms of worship. This was because Yahwistic tradition had become a dead faith of the living. This distortion of Yahwistic faith also affected the faith of the general masses whose economic condition was in dire straits. Such circumstances made many of them easy prey to magic and fatalism. This condition—where people's faith was weak and shaky—was fertile ground for the false prophets to not only exist but thrive and excel.

This does not, however, suggest that false prophecy was a straightforward intentional enterprise. Every society is a composition of a complex network of factors and within this complexity it is not always easy to reflect on one's perspective and walks of life. No doubt some individual prophets were driven by personal ambition over and against the altruistic concerns of the Yahwistic tradition, but for some it might have been a case of inability to understand and read the complexity of the situation. This conclusion on the false prophets could be reached because there were Yahweh's prophets who, in spite of the complexity of the social context, remain rooted in his or her old Yahwistic tradition and yet remained open to Yahweh's further illumination. I also argued that false prophecy is not exclusively about misreading the tradition and the historical context, but it is most importantly about degeneration of morality in relation to the covenant relationship with Yahweh.

There is truth in the assertion that prophets do not function alone, but that they survive and are sustained through their support group. However, it is one thing to have the prophet prophesy according to the agenda of his or her support group, and completely another proposition to have both the prophet and his support system subjected to a tradition and divine revelation. In the case of Israel's Yahwistic prophets, the true prophets did not prophesy to the penchant of their support group but prophesied on the basis of their shared tradition and vision. It was the Yahwistic tradition that brought together the true prophets and their supporters and provided them with common moral imagination. In the "people of the land" Israel's prophets had a strong support group. This "people of the land" consisted of people from different walks of life such as landed gentries, priests, Levites, prophets, elders, scribes, and even royal officials. These people were those who persisted in keeping the Yahwistic tradition alive, and sought to make this tradition the norm of their society. It is this group that played a vital role in delineating true and false prophecy.

In chapter five I applied these findings to the analysis of Jer 26–29. This text represents the *locus classicus* of the prophetic conflict in the OT. The study shows that Jeremiah, as Yahweh's prophet, prophesied as and when he received divine revelation from Yahweh. Jeremiah operated within the concept of Yahweh's חסד. The fact that Yahweh sent the prophet Jeremiah to the recalcitrant Judeans manifests the חסד character of Yahweh. In other words, Yahweh loved his people, in spite of their stubbornness, and he wanted them to repent from their evil paths. Jeremiah might not have been necessary as Yahweh's prophet had the Judeans observed the משפטים of Yahweh. Thus, Jeremiah's overarching message was that of repentance and judgment. Note that while Yahweh's חסד is endless, his patience is not, for his wrath comes inevitably when his persistent love is continuously ignored. Such an understanding of Yahweh puts Jeremiah's prophetic ministry in perspective.

Jeremiah prophesied from the Yahwistic perspective and was supported by the "people of the land." In contradistinction to Jeremiah, Hananiah prophesied to please his support group, and in accordance with the fluctuation of the political circumstances in relation to Babylon and Egypt. As a result, Jeremiah's prophecy was vindicated in the fall of Jerusalem in 586 BCE; as for Hananiah, he received Yahweh's judgment for his falsehood. Tracking the Yahwistic tradition and its development does provide a scope to understand the prophetic conflict as presented in the OT.

A synthetic study permits us to analyze ancient Israel's prophetic conflict in a contextual manner. In line with this, I discussed briefly in an excursus how to construe the criteria found in Deut 13:2–6 (13:1–5 [Eng.]) and 18:21–22. These criteria are not straightforward but at the same time, they are also not meaningless. Taking these criteria at face value would lead to the risk of distorting their meanings. These criteria are to be understood against the backdrop of the whole Yahwistic tradition—the covenant relationship between Israel and Yahweh, and the חסד character of Yahweh—and not as a wooden dogma that fit across the milieu. Only then these criteria will make sense; anything short of such analysis would only lead to reductionism.

The study of true and false prophecy is contentious by nature. In this dissertation, I endeavored to provide a perspective through which to analyze the prophetic conflict in the OT. Thus, I argued that a synthetic analysis through the lens of critical realism provides "a" scope whereby, one can suggest that ancient Israel had a rubric for distinguishing between true and false prophecy in its Yahwistic tradition.

BIBLIOGRAPHY

Abraham, William J. *Crossing the Threshold of Divine Revelation*. Grand Rapids: Eerdmans, 2006.

———. *Divine Revelation and the Limits of Historical Criticism*. Oxford: Oxford University Press, 1982.

———. *The Divine Inspiration of Holy Scripture*. Oxford: Oxford University Press, 1981.

Aharoni, Yohanan. "Excavations at Ramat Raḥel." *Biblical Archaeology* 24 (1961): 98–118.

Albertz, Rainer. "Why a Reform Like Josiah's Must Have Happened." Pages 27–46 in *Good Kings and Bad Kings*. Library of Hebrew Bible/Old Testament Studies 393. Edited by Lester L. Grabbe. London: T&T Clark, 2005.

Albright, William. F. *Archaeology and the Religion of Israel*. 5th edition. Baltimore: Johns Hopkins Press, 1969.

———. *From the Stone Age to Christianity: Monotheism and the Historical Process*. 2nd edition. New York: Doubleday, 1957.

Allen, Leslie C. *Jeremiah: A Commentary*. Old Testament Library. John Knox: Louisville, 2008.

Alt, Albrecht. "Die Staatenbildung der Israeliten in Palästina." *Kirjath-Sepher* II (1930): 1–65.

Alter, Robert. *The Art of Biblical Narrative*. New York: Basic Books, 1981.

Arnold, Bill T. *Introduction to the Old Testament*. New York: Cambridge University Press, 2014.

———. "Old Testament Eschatology and the Rise of Apocalypticism." Pages 23–39 in *The Oxford Handbook of Eschatology*. Edited by Jerry L. Walls. Oxford: Oxford University Press, 2008.

_____. "The Neo-Babylonian Chronicle Series." Pages 407–26 in *The Ancient Near East: Historical Sources in Translation*. Edited by Mark W. Chavalas. Malden: Blackwell, 2006.

_____. *1 & 2 Samuel: The NIV Application Commentary*. Grand Rapids: Zondervan, 2003.

_____. "Religion in Ancient Israel." Pages 391–420 in *The Faces of Old Testament Studies: A Survey of Contemporary Approaches*. Edited by David W. Baker and Bill T. Arnold. Grand Rapids: Baker, 1999.

Arnold, Bill T. and John H. Choi, *A Guide to Biblical Hebrew Syntax*. Cambridge: Cambridge University Press, 2003.

_____ and Bryan E. Beyer. *Reading from the Ancient Near East: Primary Sources for Old Testament Study*. Grand Rapids: Baker Academic, 2002.

Avigad, Nahman. *Hebrew Bullae from the Time of Jeremiah: Remnants of a Burnt Archive*. Michigan: University of Michigan, 1986.

Bakon, Shimon. "Zedekiah: Last King of Judah." *Jewish Bible Quarterly* 36 (2008): 93–101.

Barbour, Ian. *Myths, Models and Paradigms: A Comparative Study in Science and Religion*. New York: Harper & Row, 1974.

Bar-Efrat, S. *Narrative Art in the Bible*. Bible and Literature Series 17. Sheffield: Almond, 1989.

Barkay, G. "The Iron Age II-III." Pages 302–73 in *The Archaeology of Ancient Israel*. Edited by Amnin Ben-Tor. Translated by R. Greenberg. New Haven: Yale University Press, 1992.

Barr, James. *History and Ideology in the Old Testament: Biblical Studies at the End of a Millennium*. The Hensley Henson Lectures for 1997 delivered to the University of Oxford. Oxford: Oxford University Press, 2000.

_____. *The Concept of Biblical Theology: An Old Testament Perspective*. Minneapolis: Fortress, 1999.

_____. *Fundamentalism*. London: SCM, 1977.

Barton, John. "The Day of Yahweh in the Minor Prophets." Pages 279–88 in *The Old Testament: Canon, Literature and Theology: Collected Essays of John Barton*. Hampshire: Ashgate, 2007.

_____. "Natural Law and Poetic Justice in the Old Testament." *Journal of Theological Studies* 30 (1979): 1–4.

Bendor, S. *The Social Structure of Ancient Israel: The Institution of the Family (beit 'ab) from the Settlement to the End of the Monarchy*. Jerusalem: Simor, 1996.

Berlin, Adele. *Poetics and Interpretation of Biblical Narrative*. Bible and Literature Series 9. Sheffield: Almond, 1983.

Beyerlin, Walter. *Die Kultraditionen Israels in der Verkündigung des Propheten Micah*. Forschungen zur Religion und Literatur des Alten und Neuen Testament 62. Göttingen: Vandenhoeck & Ruprecht, 1959.

Bhaskar, Roy. *A Realist Theory of Science*. 2nd edition. New York: Verso, 1997.

_____. *The Possibility of Naturalism: A Philosophical Critique of the Contemporary Human Sciences* Atlantic Highlands: Humanities, 1979.

_____. *Scientific Realism and Human Emancipation*. New York: Verso, 1986.

_____. *Dialectic: The Pulse of Freedom*. New York: Verso, 1993.

Bloesch, Donald G. *Holy Scripture: Revelation, Inspiration & Interpretation*. Downers Grove: InterVarsity, 1994.

Boda, Mark J. and J. Gordon McConville, eds. *Dictionary of the Old Testament: Prophets*. Downers Grove: IVP Academic, 2012.

Bordreuil, Pierre, F. Israel, and D. Pardee. "King's Command and Widow's Plea: Two New Hebrew Ostraca of the Biblical Period." *Near Eastern Archaeology* 61 (1998): 2–13.

Botterweck, G.J. and H. Ringgren, eds. *Theological Dictionary of the Old Testament*. 15 vols. Translated by David E. Green and Douglas W. Scott. Grand Rapids: Eerdmans, 2006.

Brenneman, James E. *Canons in Conflict: Negotiating Texts in True and False Prophecy*. Oxford: Oxford University Press, 1997.

Bright, John. *A History of Israel*. 4th edition. Louisville: Westminster John Knox, 2000.

Broshi M and I. Finkelstein. "The Population of Palestine in Iron Age II." *Bulletin of the American Schools of Oriental Research* 287 (1992): 47–60.

Brueggemann, Walter. *A Commentary on Jeremiah: Exile and Homecoming*. Grand Rapids: Eerdmans, 1998.

Buber, Martin. "False Prophets (Jeremiah 28)." Pages 166–71 in *Biblical Humanism: Eighteen Studies*. Edited by Nahum N. Glatzer. London: Macdonald, 1968.

_____. *On the Bible: Eighteen Studies by Martin Buber*. Edited by Nahum N. Glatzer. Introduction by Harold Bloom. New York: Schocken Books, 1982.

Carr, David M. *The Formation of the Hebrew Bible: A New Reconstruction*. Oxford: Oxford University Press, 2011.

Carroll R, Mark Daniel. *Contexts for Amos: Prophetic Poetics in Latin American Perspective*. Journal for the Study of Old Testament Supplement Series 132. Sheffield: Sheffield Academic, 1992.

Carroll, R.P. "Ancient Israelite Prophecy and Dissonance Theory." Pages 377–91 in *The Place is Too Small for Us: The Israelite Prophets in Recent Scholarship*. Sources for Biblical and

Theological Sources 5. Edited by Robert P. Gordon. Winona Lake, IN: Eisenbrauns, 1995.

———. *Jeremiah: A Commentary*. Old Testament Library. Philadelphia: Westminster, 1986.

———. *When Prophecy Failed: Reactions and Response to Failure in the Old Testament Prophetic Traditions*. London: SCM, 1979.

Carter, Charles E. "A Discipline in Transition: The Contributions of the Social Sciences to the Study of the Hebrew Bible." Pages 3–36 in *Community, Identity, and Ideology: Social Science Approaches to the Hebrew Bible*. Edited by Charles E. Carter and Carol L. Meyers. Sources for Biblical and Theological Study. 8 vols. Winona Lake, IN: Eisenbrauns, 1996.

Chaney, Marvin L. "The Bible, the Economy, and the Poor." *Journal of Religion & Society Supplement Series* 10 (2014): 34–60.

———. "Systemic Study of the Israelite Monarchy." *Semeia* 37 (1986): 53–76.

Childs, Brevard S. *Biblical Theology of the Old and New Testaments: Theological Reflection on the Christian Bible*. Minneapolis: Fortress, 1993.

———. *Old Testament Theology in a Canonical Context*. Philadelphia: Fortress, 1985.

———. *Introduction to the Old Testament as Scripture*. Philadelphia: Fortress, 1979.

———. *The Book of Exodus: A Critical, Theological Commentary*. Old Testament Library. Philadelphia: Westminster, 1974.

Clark, Gordon R. *The Word Hesed in the Hebrew Bible*. Journal for the Study of the Old Testament Supplementary Series 157. Sheffield: Sheffield Academic, 1993.

Clements, R.E. *Jeremiah*. Interpretation: A Bible Commentary for Teaching and Preaching. Atlanta: John Knox, 1988.

Cogan, M. "Into Exile: From the Assyrian Conquest of Israel to the Fall of Babylon." Pages 242–75 in *The Oxford History of the Biblical World*. Edited by Michael D. Coogan. Oxford: Oxford University Press, 1998.

_____. *Imperialism and Religion: Assyria, Judah, and Israel in the Eight and Seventh Centuries B.C.E*. Society of Biblical Literature Monograph Series 19. Missoula: Scholars Press, 1974.

_____. "A Technical Term for Exposure." *Journal of Near Eastern Studies* 27 (1968): 133–35.

Coggins, Richard J. "Prophecy—True and False." Pages 80–90 in *Of Prophets' Visions and the Wisdom of Sages: Essays in Honour of R. Norman Whybray on his Seventieth Birthday*. Edited by Heather A. McKay and David J.A. Clines. Journal for the Study of the Old Testament Supplement Series 162. Sheffield: Sheffield Academic, 1993.

Coogan, M. D. *Stories from Ancient Canaan*. Philadelphia: Westminster Press, 1978.

Cook, Stephen L. "The Levites and Sociocultural Change in Ancient Judah: Insights from Gerhard Lenski's Social Theory." Pages 41–58 in *Social Theory and the Study of Israelite Religion: Essays in Retrospect and Prospect*. Edited by. Saul M. Olyan; Atlanta: SBL, 2012.

_____. *The Social Roots of Biblical Yahwism*. Studies in Biblical Literature 8. Atlanta: SBL, 2004.

Cooke, Francis T. "The Site of Kirjath-jearim." *Annual of the American Schools of Oriental Research* 5 (1925): 105–20.

Collier, Andrew. *Critical Realism: An Introduction to Roy Bhaskar's Philosophy*. New York: Verso, 1994.

Cox, Harvey. *The Secular City: Secularization and Urbanization in Theological Perspective* New York: Macmillan, 1965.

Crenshaw, James L. *Prophetic Conflict: Its Effect Upon Israelite Religion*. Beihefte zur Zeitschrift für die altestmentliche Wissenschaft 124. Berlin: de Gruyter, 1971.

Cross, F.M. *Canaanite Myth and Hebrew Epic: Essays in the History of the Religion of Israel*. Cambridge: Harvard University Press, 1973.

———. "The Fallacy of 'True and False' in Prophecy Illustrated by Jer 28:8–9." *Journal of Hebrew Scripture* 12.10 (2012): 1–29.

Darby, Erin. *Interpreting Judean Pillar Figurines: Gender and Empire in Judean Apotropaic Ritual*. Forschungen zum Alten Testament 2.69. Tübingen: Mohr Siebeck, 2014.

Day, John. "Inner-biblical Interpretation in the Prophets." Pages 230–46 in *The Place is Too Small for Us: The Israelite Prophets in Recent Scholarship*. Sources for Biblical and Theological Studies 5. Edited by Robert P. Gordon. Winona Lake, IN: Eisenbraums, 1995.

Dearman, J. Andrew. *Jeremiah and Lamentation: The NIV Application Commentary*. Grand Rapids: Zondervan, 2002

De Jong, Matthijs J. *Isaiah among the Ancient Near Eastern Prophets: A Comparative Study of the Earliest Stages of the Isaiah Tradition and the Neo-Assyrian Prophecies*. Leiden: Brill, 2007.

Denton, Donald L. *Historiography and Hermeneutics in Jesus Studies: An Examination of the Work of John Dominic Crossan and Ben F. Meyer*. London: T&T Clark, 2004.

Derrida, J. *Positions*. Translated by Alan Bass. Chicago: University of Chicago Press, 1980.

Dever, William G. *Did God have a Wife? Archaeological and Folk Religion in Ancient Israel*. Grand Rapids: Eerdmans, 2005.

———. "Social Structure in Palestine in the Iron II Period on the Eve of Destruction." Pages 416–31 in *The Archaeology of*

Society in the Holy Land. Edited by Thomas E. Levy. London: Leicester University Press, 1995.

De Vaux, R. "Le roi d'Israel vassel de YHWH." Pages 119–33 in *Mélanges Eugene Tisserant*. Vatican City: Biblioteca Apostolica Vaticana, 1964.

Davies, Philip R. *In Search of 'Ancient Israel.'* Journal for the Study of Old Testament Supplement Series 148. Sheffield: Sheffield Academic, 1992.

Dietrich, M., O. Loretz, and J. Sanmartin, eds. *Die Keilalphabetischen Texte aus Ugarit*. AOAT 24/1. Kevelaer: Neukirchen-Vluyn, 1976.

_____. *The Cuneiform Alphabetic Texts from Ugarit, Ras Ibn Hani, and Other Places*. Münster: Ugarit-Verlag, 1995.

Dietrich, W. *Prophetie und Geschichte*. Forschungen zur Religion und Literatur des Alten und Neuen Testament 108. Göttingen: Vanderhoeck & Ruprecht, 1972.

Drake, Durant and Arthur Lovejoy, et al. *Essays in Critical Realism*. London: Macmillan, 1921.

Duhm, B. *Das Buch Jeremia*. Kurzer Hand-Commentar zum Alten Testament 11. Tübingen: Mohr, 1901.

Durand, Jean-Marie. *Archives épistolaires de Mari* I/1. Archives royales de Mari 26. Paris: Editions Recherche sur les Civilizations, 1988.

Dutcher-Walls, P. "The Social Location of the Deuteronomists: A Sociological Study of Factional Study of Factional Politics in Late Pre-Exilic Judah," *Journal for the Study of Old Testament* 52 (1991): 77–94.

Eissfeldt, Otto. *The Old Testament: An Introduction*. Translated by P.R. Ackroyd. New York: Harper & Row, 1965.

Epp-Tiessen, Daniel. *Concerning the Prophets: True and False Prophecy in Jeremiah 23:9–29:32*. Eugene, OR: Pickwick, 2012.

Faust, Avraham. *The Archaeology of Israelite Society in Iron Age II*. Translated by Ruth Ludlum. Winona Lake, IN: Eisenbrauns, 2012.

_____. "Settlement and Demography in Seventh Century Judah and the Extent and Intensity of Sennacherib's Campaign." *Palestine Exploration Quarterly* 140.3 (2008): 168–94.

_____. "Rural Community in Ancient Israel during the Iron Age II." *Bulletin of the American Schools of Oriental Research* 317 (2000): 17–39.

Faust, Avraham and Ehud Weiss. "Judah, Philistia, and the Mediterranean World: Reconstructing the Economic System of the Seventh Century B.C.E." *Bulletin of the American Schools of Oriental Research* 338 (2005): 71–92.

Festinger, Leon, Henry Riecken and Stanley Schachter. *When Prophecy Fails*. Minneapolis: University of Minnesota Press, 1956.

Finkelstein, Israel. "The Archaeology of the Days of Manasseh." Pages 169–87 in *Scripture and Other Artifacts: Essays on the Bible and Archaeology in Honor of Philip J. King*. Edited by M.D. Coogan, J.C. Exum, and L.E. Staeger. Louisville: Westminster John Knox, 1994.

_____. "The Emergence of the Monarchy in Israel: The Environmental and Socio-Economic Aspects." *Journal for the Study of the Old Testament* 44 (1989): 43–74.

Finkelstein, Israel and Neil Asher Silberman. *The Bible Unearthed: Archaeology's New Vision of Ancient Israel and the Origin of its Sacred Text*. New York: Free, 2001.

Finkelstein, Louis. "Introductory Study to Pirke Abot." *Journal of Biblical Literature* 57 (1938): 13–50.

Fishbane, Michael. *Biblical Interpretation in Ancient Israel*. Oxford: Oxford University Press, 1985.

Flanagan, Joseph. "Lonergan's Epistemology." *The Thomist* 36 (1972): 75–97.

Fleming, Daniel E. *The Legacy of Israel in Judah's Bible: History, Politics, and the Reinscribing of Tradition.* Cambridge: Cambridge University Press, 2012.

Franken, H.J. and M.L. Steiner. *Excavations in Jerusalem 1961–1967: The Iron Age Extramural Quarter on the South-East Hill.* Vol II/V. Oxford: Oxford University Press, 1990.

Freedman, David Noel, ed. *The Anchor Bible Dictionary.* 6 vols. New York: Doubleday, 1992.

Freedman, David Noel and Frey, Rebecca. "False Prophecy is True." Pages 82–87 in *Inspired Speech: Prophecy in the Ancient Near East.* Essays in Honor of Herbert B. Huffmon. Edited by John Kaltner and Louis Stulman. London: T&T Clark International, 2004.

Frick, Frank S. "Norman Gottwald's *The Tribes of Yahweh* in the Context of 'Second-Wave' Social-Scientific Biblical Criticism." Pages 17–34 in *Tracking "The Tribes of Yahweh:" On the Trail of a Classic.* Edited by Roland Boer. London: Sheffield Academic, 2002.

Friebel, Kelvin. Review of Epp-Tiessen, *Concerning the Prophets: True and False Prophecy in Jeremiah 23:9–29:32. Review of Biblical Literature,* 2013.

Galling, K. "Die israelitische Staatsverfassung in ihrer vorderorientalischen Umwelt." *Der Alte Oreint* 28 (1929): 5–64.

Geertz, Clifford. "Ideology as a Cultural System." Pages 193–233 in *The Interpretation of Cultures: Selected Essays.* New York: Basic Books, 1973.

Genry Peter J. and Stephen J. Wellum. *Kingdom through Covenant: A Biblical–Theological Understanding of the Covenants.* Wheaton: Crossway, 2012.

Gerstenberger, Erhard S. *Theologies in the Old Testament.* Translated by John Bowden. Minneapolis: Fortress, 2002.

Glueck, N. *Ḥesed in the Bible.* Translated by A. Gottschalk. Cincinnati: Hebrew Union College, 1967.

Gordon, C.H. *Ugaritic Textbook.* Rome: Pontifical Biblical Institute Press, 1965.

Gorringe, T.J. *Discerning Spirit: A Theology of Revelation.* London: SCM Press, 2001.

Gossai, Hemchand. *Justice, Righteousness and the Social Critique of the Eighth–Century Prophets.* New York: Peter Lang, 1993.

Gottwald, Norman K. *All the Kingdoms of the Earth: Israelite Prophecy and International Relations in the Ancient Near East.* New York: Harper & Row, 1964.

Grabbe, Lester L. "Jeremiah among the Social Anthropologist." Pages 80–88 in *Prophecy in the Book of Jeremiah.* Beihefte zur Zeitschrift für die alttestamentliche Wissenschaft 388. Edited by Hans M. Barstad and Reinhard G. Kratz. Berlin: de Gruyter, 2009.

_____. *Ancient Israel: What Do We Know and How Do We Know It?* London: T&T Clark, 2007.

_____. *Priests, Prophets, Diviners, Sages: A Socio-Historical Study of Religious Specialists in Ancient Israel.* Valley Forge: Trinity, 1995.

Grayson, A.K. *Assyrian and Babylonian Chronicles.* Winona Lake, IN: Eisenbrauns, 2000.

Greenberg, M. "Religion: Stability and Ferment." Pages 79–124 in *The Age of the Monarchies: Culture and Society.* 5 vols. Edited by Abraham Malamat. Jerusalem: Massada, 1979.

Grenz, Stanley J. *A Primer on Postmodernism.* Grand Rapids: Eerdmans, 1996.

Gunneweg, A.H.J. "'AM HA'ARES—A Semantic Revolution." *Zeitschrift für die alttestamentliche Wissenschaft* 95 (1983): 437–40.

———. "Sinaibund und Davidsbund." *Vetus Testamentum* 10 (1960): 335–41.

Gunton, Colin E. *A Brief Theology of Revelation: The 1993 Warfield Lectures*. Edinburgh: T&T Clark, 1995.

Hackett, Jo Ann. "'There was no King in Israel:' The Era of the Judges." Pages 132–64 in *The Oxford History of the Biblical World*. Edited by Michael D. Coogan. Oxford: Oxford University Press, 1998.

Hallo, William W. "Compare and Contrast: The Contextual Approach to Biblical Literature." Pages 1–30 in *Bible in the Light of Cuneiform Literature*. New York: Edwin Mellen, 1990.

Halpern, B. "Jerusalem and the Lineages in the Seventh Century BCE: Kinship and the Rise of Individual Moral Liability." Pages 11–107 in *Law and Ideology in Monarchic Israel*. Journal for the Study of the Old Testament Supplement 124. Edited by Baruch Halpern and Deborah W. Hobson. Sheffield: Sheffield Academic, 1991.

———. *The Constitution of the Monarchy in Israel*. Harvard Semitic Monographs 25. Chicago: Scholars Press, 1981.

Hanson, Paul D. *The People Called: The Growth of Community in the Bible*. New York: Harper & Row, 1987.

Healey, Joseph P. "AM HA'AREZ." Pages 168–69 in of *The Anchor Bible Dictionary*. Vol. 1. Edited by David Noel Freedman. 6 vols. New York: Doubleday, 1992.

Herion, Gary A. "The Impact of Modern and Social Science Assumptions on the Reconstruction of Israelite History." Pages 78–108 in *Social-Scientific Old Testament Criticism*. The

Biblical Seminar 47. Edited by David J. Chalcraft. Sheffield: Sheffield Academic, 1997.

Hess, Richard S. *Israelite Religions: An Archaeological and Biblical Survey*. Grand Rapids: Baker Academic, 2007.

Hibbard, J. Todd. "True and False Prophecy: Jeremiah's Revision of Deuteronomy." *Journal for the Study of Old Testament* 35.3 (2011): 339–58.

Hiebert, Paul G. *Missiological Implications of Epistemological Shifts: Affirming Truth in a Modern/Postmodern World*. Harrisburg: Trinity, 1999.

Hiebert and Meneses. *Incarnational Ministry: Planting Churches in Band, Tribal, Peasant, and Urban Societies*. Grand Rapids: Baker Academic, 1995.

Holladay, J. S. "The Kingdoms of Israel and Judah: Political and Economic Centralization in the Iron Age II A-B (ca. 1000–750 B.C.E)." Pages 368–98 in *The Archaeology of Society in the Holy Land*. Edited by T.E. Levy. London: Leicester University Press, 1995.

_____. "Religion in Israel and Judah under the Monarchy: An Explicitly Archaeological Approach." Pages 249–309 in *Ancient Israelite Religion*. Edited by Patrick D. Miller, Paul D. Hanson, and S. Dean McBride. Philadelphia: Fortress, 1987.

Holladay, W. *Jeremiah*. 2 vols. Hermeneia. Minneapolis: Fortress, 1989.

House, Paul R. "The Day of the Lord." Pages 179–223 in *Central Themes in Biblical Theology: Mapping Unity in Diversity*. Edited by Scott J. Hafemann and Paul R. House. Grand Rapids: Baker Academic, 2007.

Houston, Walter J. "Exit the Oppressed Peasant? Rethinking the Background of Social Criticism in the Prophets." Pages 101–06 in *Prophecy and Prophets in Ancient Israel: Proceedings of the Oxford Old Testament Seminar*. Library of Hebrew Bible/Old

Testament Studies 531. Edited by John Day. New York: T&T Clark, 2010.

Huffmon, Herbert B. "A Company of Prophets: Mari, Assyria, Israel." Pages 47–70 in *Prophecy in its Ancient Near Eastern Context: Mesopotamian, Biblical, and Arabian Perspectives*. Edited by Martti Nissinen. Society of Biblical Literature Symposium Series 13. Atlanta: SBL, 2000.

Huyssteen, Wentzel van. *Essays in Postfoundationalist Theology*. Grand Rapids: Eerdmans, 1997.

———. *The Realism of the Text: A Perspective on Biblical Authority*. Pretoria: University of Pretoria Press, 1987.

———. *The Shaping of Rationality*. Grand Rapids: Eerdmans, 1999.

———. *Theology and the Justification of Faith: Constructing Theories in Systematic Theology*. Translated by H.F. Snijders. Grand Rapids: Eerdmans, 1989.

Hvidt, Niels Christian. *Christian Prophecy: The Post-Biblical Tradition*. Oxford: Oxford University Press, 2007.

Ishida, T. *The Royal Dynasties in Ancient Israel*. Beihefte zur Zeitschrift für die Alttestamentliche Wissenschaft 104. Berlin: Walter de Gruyter, 1977.

———. "'The People of the land' and the Political Crisis in Judah." *Annual of the Japanese Biblical Institute* 1 (1975): 23–38.

Jacob, E. "Quelques remargues sur les faux prophetes." *Theologische Zeitschrift* 13 (1957): 479–86.

Jenni, Ernst, and Claus Westernmann, eds. *Theological Lexicon of the Old Testament*. Translated by Mark E. Biddle. 3 vols. Peabody, Mass.: Hendrickson, 1997.

Jenson, Philip Peter. *Obadiah, Jonah, Micah: A Theological Commentary*. New York: T&T Clark, 2008.

Johnson, Benton. "Revisiting *When Prophecy Fails.*" Pages 9–20 in *How Prophecy Lives*. Edited by Diana G. Tumminia and William H. Swatos. Leiden: Brill, 2011.

Joüon, Paul and T. Muraoka. *A Grammar of Biblical Hebrew*. Rome: Pontifical Biblical Institute, 2006.

Kant, Immanuel. *Critique of Practical Reason and Other Works on the Theory of Ethics*. Translated by T.K. Abbott. London: Longmans, Green, and Co., Ltd., 1927.

Kaufmann, Y. *The Religion of Israel*. Translated by M. Greenberg. Chicago: University of Chicago Press, 1960.

Keener, Craig S. *Miracles: The Credibility of the New Testament Accounts*. 2 vols. Grand Rapids: Baker Academic, 2011.

Kelle, Brad E. "Judah in the Seventh Century: From the Aftermath of Sennacherib's Invasion to the Beginning of Jehoiakim's Rebellion." Pages 350–82 in *Ancient Israel's History: An Introduction to Issues and Sources*. Edited by Bill T. Arnold and Richard S. Hess. Grand Rapids: Baker Academic, 2014.

King Philip J. and Lawrence E. Stager. *Life in Biblical Israel*. Library of Ancient Israel. Edited by Douglas A. Knight. Louisville: Westminister John Knox, 2001.

Kitchen, K. A. *On the Reliability of the Old Testament*. Grand Rapids: Eerdmans, 2003.

_____. *The Third Intermediate Period in Egypt, 1100–650 B.C.* 2nd edition. Warminster: Aris & Phillips, 1986.

Kletter, Raz. "Between Archaeology and Theology: The Pillar Figurines from Judah and the Asherah." Pages 179–216 in *Studies in the Archaeology of the Iron Age in Israel and Jordan*. Journal for the Study of Old Testament: Supplement Series 331. Edited by Amihai Mazar. Sheffield: Sheffield Academic, 2001.

Knight, Henry H. *A Future for Truth: Evangelical Theology in a Postmodern World*. Nashville: Abingdon, 1997.

Knoppers, Gary N. "Ancient Near Eastern Royal Grants and the Davidic Covenant: A Parallel?" *Journal of the America Oriental Society* 116.4 (1996): 670–97.

_____. "David's Relation to Moses: The Contexts, Content and Conditions of the Davidic Promises." Pages 91–118 in *King and Messiah in Israel and the Ancient Near East: Proceedings of the Oxford Old Testament Seminar*. Journal for the Study of the Old Testament Supplement Series 270. Edited by John Day. Sheffield: Sheffield Academic, 1998.

Koch, Klaus. *The Prophets: The Assyrian Period*. Vol. 1. Philadelphia: Fortress, 1983.

Kuenen, Abraham. *De Profeten en de Profetie onder Isräel: Historisch-dogmatische studie*. 2 vols. Leiden: P. Engels, 1875.

Kutsch, Ernst. *Verheißung und Gesetz: Untersuchungen zum Sogenannten "Bund" im Alten Testament*. Beihefte zur Zeitschrift für die alttestamentliche Wissenschaft 131. Berlin: De Gruyter, 1973.

Lalleman-de Winkel, H. *Jeremiah and Lamentations*. Tyndale Old Testament Commentaries. Downers Grove: IVP Academic, 2013.

_____. *Jeremiah in Prophetic Tradition: An Examination of the Book of Jeremiah in the Light of Israel's Prophetic Tradition*. Leuven: Peeters, 2000.

Lang, B. "The Social Organization of Peasant Poverty in Biblical Israel." Pages 83–99 in *Anthropological Approaches to the Old Testament*. Edited by B. Lang. Philadelphia: Fortress, 1985.

Lange, Armin. *Vom prophetischen Wort zur prophetischen Tradition: Studien zur Traditions-und Redaktionsgeschichte innerprophetischer Konflikte in der Hebräischen Bibel*. Forschungen zum Alten Testament 34; Tübingen: Mohr Siebeck, 2002.

Lemaire, André. "Toward a Redactional History of the Book of Kings." Pages 446–61 in *Reconsidering Israel and Judah: Recent Studies on the Deuteronomistic History*. Sources for Biblical and Theological Study 8. Edited by Gary N. Knoppers and J. Gordon McConville. Winona Lake, IN: Eisenbrauns, 2000.

Lemche, N.P. *Early Israel: Anthropological and Historical Studies on the Israelite Society before the Monarchy*. Leiden: Brill, 1985.

_____. "The Greek Amphictyony: Could it be a Prototype for the Israelite Society in the Period of the Judges?" *Journal for the Study of the Old Testament* 4 (1977): 48–59.

Lenski, Gerhard E. *Power and Privilege: A Theory of Social Stratification*. Chapel Hill: University of North Carolina Press, 1984.

Lenski Gerhard and Patrick Nolan. *Human Societies: An Introduction to Macrosociology* Boulder: Paradigm Publishers, 2009.

Levenson, Jon D. "Historical Criticism and the Fate of the Enlightenment Project." Pages 106–26 in *The Hebrew Bible, the Old Testament, and Historical Criticism*. Louisville: John Knox, 1993.

_____. *Sinai and Zion: An Entry into the Jewish Bible*. Minneapolis: Winston, 1985.

_____. "The Davidic Covenant and its Modern Interpreters." *Catholic Biblical Quarterly* 41 (1979): 205–20.

Lindblom, J. *Prophecy in Ancient Israel*. Philadelphia: Muhlenberg, 1962.

Lipschits, Oded. *The Fall and Rise of Jerusalem: Judah under Babylon Rule*. Winona Lake, IN: Eisenbrauns, 2005.

Lonergan, B. *Insight: A study of Human Understanding*. London: Longmans, 1957.

_____. *Method in Theology.* New York: Herder and Herder, 1972.

_____. "The Future of Thomism." Pages 49–53 in *A Second Collection.* Edited by W.F. Ryan and B.J. Tyrrell. Philadeiphia: Westminster, 1974.

_____. *Collected Works of Bernard Lonergan: Understanding and Being.* Edited by Elizabeth A. Morelli and Mark D. Morelli. 5 vols. Toronto: University of Toronto Press, 1990.

Long, Burke O. "Social Dimensions of Prophetic Conflict." Pages 308–31 in *The Place is Too Small for Us: The Israelite Prophets in Recent Scholarship.* Sources for Biblical and Theological Studies 5. Edited by Robert P. Gordon. Winona Lake, IN: Eisenbrauns, 1995.

Long, V. Philips. "Historiography of the Old Testament." Pages 145–75 in *The Faces of Old Testament Studies: A Survey of Contemporary Approaches.* Edited by David W. Baker and Bill T. Arnold. Grand Rapids: Baker Books, 1999.

Lowery, R. *The Reforming Kings: Cults and Society in First Temple Judah.* Journal for the Study of Old Testament Supplement 120. Sheffield: Sheffield Academic, 1991.

Lundbom, Jack R. *Deuteronomy: A Commentary.* Grand Rapids: Eerdmans, 2013.

_____. *The Hebrew Prophets: An Introduction.* Minneapolis: Fortress, 2010.

_____. *Jeremiah 21–36: A New Translation with Introduction and Commentary.* Anchor Bible 21B. New York: Doubleday, 2004.

_____. *The Early Career of the Prophet Jeremiah.* Lewiston: Edwin Mellen, 1993.

Matthews Victor H. and Don C. Benjamin, *Social World of Ancient Israel 1250–587 BCE.* Peabody, MA:
Hendrickson, 1993.

MacIntyre, Alasdair. *After Virtue.* Notre Dame: University of Notre Dame Press, 1981.

_____. *Whose Justice? Which Rationality?* Notre Dame: University of Notre Dame Press, 1988.

Malamat, Abraham. "The Years of the Kingdom of Judah." Pages 205–21 in *The World History of the Jewish People.* Vol IV/I. Jerusalem: Massada, 1979.

_____. "The Historical Background of the Assassination of Amon, King of Judah." *Israel Exploration Journal* 3 (1953): 26–29.

Margaret Archer, et al., eds. *Critical Realism: Essential Readings.* New York: Routledge, 1998.

Mason, R. "The Prophets of the Restoration." Pages 137–54 in *Israel's Prophetic Tradition: Essays in Honor of Peter Ackroyd.* Edited by Richard Coggins, Anthony Phillips, and Michael Knibb. Cambridge: Cambridge University Press, 1982.

Mazar, Amihai. *Archaeology of the Land of the Bible 10,000–586 B.C.E.* New Haven: Yale University Press, 2009.

McBride, S. Dean. "Polity of the Covenant People: The Book of Deuteronomy." Pages 62–77 in *A Song of Power and the Power of Song.* Sources for Biblical and Theological Studies 3. Edited by Duane L. Christensen. Winona Lake, IN: Eisenbrauns, 1993.

McCarthy, D.J. *Treaty and Covenant: A Study in Form in the Ancient Oriental Documents and in the Old Testament.* Analecta Biblica 21. Rome: Biblical Institute, 1963.

McConville, J. Gordon. *Deuteronomy.* Abingdon Old Testament Commentaries. Nottingham: Apollos, 2002.

McEvenue, Sean. *Interpretation and Bible: Essays on Truth in Literature.* Collegeville: Michael Glazier Book, 1994.

McEvenue, Sean and Ben F. Meyer, eds. *Lonergan's Hermeneutics: Its Development and Application.* Washington: Catholic University Press, 1989.

McGrath, Alister E. *The Science of God: An Introduction to Scientific Theology*. London: T&T Clark, 2004.

McKane, William. *A Late Harvest: Reflections on the Old Testament*. Edinburgh: T&T Clark, 1995.

———. *A Critical and Exegetical Commentary on Jeremiah*. International Critical Commentary. 2 vols. Edinburgh: T&T Clark, 1986–1996.

McKay, J. W. *Religion in Judah under the Assyrians, 732–609 BC*. Studies in Biblical Theology 2/26. London: SCM, 1973.

McMahon, Christopher. "The Relevance of Historical Inquiry for the Christian Faith: A Comparative Study of the Historical Methodologies of J.P. Meier and N.T. Wright." Ph.D. Diss., The Catholic University of America, 2003.

McNutt, Paula. *Reconstructing the Society of Ancient Israel*. London: SPCK, 1999.

Mead, James K. "The Biblical Prophets in Historiography." Pages 262–85 in *Ancient Israel's History: An Introduction to Issues and Sources*. Edited by Bill T. Arnold and Richard S. Hess. Grand Rapids: Baker Academic, 2014.

Megill, Allan. *Prophets of Extremity: Nietzsche, Heidegger, Foucault, Derrida*. Berkeley: University of California Press, 1985.

Mendenhall, G.E. "Covenant Forms in Israelite Tradition." *Biblical Archaeology* 17 (1954): 50–76.

Merrill, Eugene H. *Deuteronomy*. New American Commentary 4. Nashville: Broadman and Holman, 1994.

Merwe, Christo H.J. van der, Jackie A. Naudé and Jan H. Kroeze. *A Biblical Hebrew Reference Grammar*. Sheffield: Sheffield Academic, 2000.

Meyer, Ben F. *Reality and Illusion in New Testament Scholarship: A Primer in Critical Realist Hermeneutics*. Collegeville: Liturgical Press, 1994.

_____. *Critical Realism and New Testament*. Allison Park: Pickwick, 1989.

_____. *Christus Faber: The Master Builder and the House of God*. Allison Park: Pickwick, 1992.

Meyer, Raymond. "An Evangelical Analysis of the Critical Realism and Corollary Hermeneutics of Bernard Lonergan with Application for Evangelical Hermeneutics." Ph.D Diss., Southeastern Baptist Theological Seminary, 2007.

Miller, Daniel R. "The Shadow of the Overlord: Revisiting the Question of Neo-Assyrian Imposition on the Judean Cult during the Eighth-Seventh Centuries BCE." Pages 146–68 in *From Babel to Babylon: Essays on Biblical History and Literature in Honour of Brian Peckham*. Edited by Joyce R. Wood, John E Harvey, and Mark Leuchter. Library of Hebrew Bible/Old Testament Studies 455. New York: Clark, 2006.

Miller, James. *The Passion of Michel Foucault*. New York: Simon & Schuster, 1993.

Moberly, R.W.L. *Prophecy and Discernment*. Cambridge: Cambridge University Press, 2006.

Morgan, R. "Troeltsch and Christian Theology." Pages 203–33 in *Ernst Troeltsch: Writings on Theology and Religion*. Edited and translated by R. Morgan and M. Pye. Louisville: Westminster, 1990.

Moritz, Thorsten. "Critical Realism." Pages 147–50 in *Dictionary for Theological Interpretation of the Bible*. Edited by Kevin J. Vanhoozer, Craig G. Bartholomew, and Daniel J. Treier. Grand Rapids: Baker, 2005.

_____. "Critical but Real: Reflecting on N.T. Wright's Tool for the Task." Pages 172–97 in *Renewing Biblical Interpretation*. Edited by Craig Bartholomew, Colin Greene and Karl Möller. Grand Rapids: Zondervan, 2000.

Morris, L.L. *Testament of Love*. Grand Rapids: Eerdmans, 1981.

Mowinckel, S. *Zur Komposition des Buches Jeremia*. Kristiania: J. Dybwad, 1914.

Negev, Avraham, ed. "Astarte; Ashtoreth." Pages 39–40 in *The Archaeological Encyclopedia of the Holy Land*. Nashville: Thomas Nelson, 1986.

Nelson, Richard. "Realpolitik in Judah (687–609 B.C.E)." Pages 177–90 in *Scripture in Context II: More Essays on the Comparative Method*. Edited by William W. Hallo, James C. Moyer, and Leo G. Perdue. Winona Lake, IN: Eisenbrauns, 1983.

Nicholson, E. W. *Preaching to the Exiles: A Study of the Prose Tradition in the Book of Jeremiah*. Oxford: Blackwell, 1970

_____. "The Meaning of the Expression 'am ha'arez in the Old Testament." *Journal of Semitic Studies* 10 (1965): 59–66.

Niditch, Susan. *Oral World and Written Word: Ancient Israelite Literature*. Louisville: Westminster, 1996.

Nietzsche, F. "On Truth and Lie in an Extra-Moral Sense." Pages 44–46 in *The Portable Nietzsche*. Edited and translated by Walter Kaufmann. New York: Penguin Books, 1976.

Nissinen, Martti, ed. *Prophecy in its Ancient Near Eastern Context: Mesopotamian, Biblical, and Arabian Perspectives*. SBL Symposium Series 13. Atlanta: Society of Biblical Literature, 2000.

Noth, Martin. *Überlieferungsgeschichtliche Studien: Die sammelnden und bearbeitenden Geschichtswerke im Alten Testament*. Schriften der Königsber Gelehrten Gesellschaft Geisteswissenschaftliche Klasse 18. Jh. H. 2 Bd. 1. Tübingen: Max Niemeyer, 1943.

_____. *Exodus: A Commentary*. Old Testament Library. Philadelphia: Westminster, 1962.

_____. *A History of Pentateuchal Traditions.* Edited and Translated by B.W. Anderson. Englewood Cliffs, NJ.: Prentice-Hall, 1972.

Nunez, Theodore W. "Rolston, Lonergan, and the Intrinsic Value of Nature," *Journal Religious Ethics* 27.1 (Spring 1999): 105–28.

Oded, B. "Judah and the Exile." Pages 435–88 in *Israelite and Judaean History*. Old Testament Library 39. Edited by John H. Hayes and J. Maxwell Miller. Philadelphia: Westminster, 1977.

O'Keefe, John J. "'A Letter that Killeth': Toward a Reassessment of Antiochene Exegesis, or Diodore, or Theodore, and Theodoret on the Psalms." *Journal of Early Christian Studies* 8 (2000): 83–104.

Olyan, Saul M., ed. *Social Theory and the Study of Israelite Religion: Essays in Retrospect and Prospect*. Society of Biblical Literature 71; Atlanta: Society of Biblical Literature, 2012.

Oppenheim, A. Leo. *Ancient Mesopotamia: Portrait of a Dead Civilization*. Revised and Edited by Erica Reiner. Chicago: Chicago University Press, 1977.

Osuji, Anthony Chinedu. *Where is the Truth?: Narrative Exegesis and the Question of True and False Prophecy in Jer 26–29 (MT)*. Leuven: Uitgeverij Peeters, 2010.

Oswalt, John N. *The Bible among the Myths: Unique Revelation or Just Ancient Literature?* Grand Rapids: Zondervan, 2009.

Overholt, Thomas W. *Channels of Prophecy: The Social Dynamics of Prophetic Activity*. Minneapolis: Fortress, 1989.

_____. *Cultural Anthropology and the Old Testament.* Minneapolis: Fortress, 1996.

_____. *Prophecy in Cross-Cultural Perspective: A Sourcebook for Biblical Researchers*. Society of Biblical Literature Sources for Biblical Study 17. Edited by Burke O. Long. Atlanta: Scholars Press, 1986.

_____. *The Threat of Falsehood: A Study in the Theology of the Book of Jeremiah.* Studies in Biblical Theology 2.16. Naperville, Ill.: Alec R. Allenson Inc., 1970.

Peacocke, Arthur. *Intimations of Reality: Critical Realism in Science and Religion.* Mendenhall Lectures 1983. Notre Dame: University of Notre Dame Press, 1984.

_____. *Theology for a Scientific Age.* Theology and Sciences. Minneapolis: Fortress, 1993.

Pelikan, Jaroslav. *The Vindication of Tradition: The 1983 Jefferson Lecture in the Humanities.* New Haven: Yale University Press, 1984.

Perlitt, L. *Bundestheologie im Alten Testament.* Wissenschaftliche Monographien zum Alten und Neuen Testament 36. Neukirchen-Vluyn: Neukirchener Verlag, 1969.

Philips, Anthony. "Prophecy and law." Pages 217–32 in *Israel's Prophetic Tradition: Essays in Honor of Peter Ackroyd.* Edited by Richard Coggins et al. Cambridge: Cambridge University Press, 1982.

Pleins, J. David. *Social Visions of the Hebrew Bible: A Theological Introduction.* Louisville: Westminster John Knox, 2001.

Porter, Jean. "Tradition in the Recent Work of Alasdair MacIntyre." Pages 38–69 in *Alasdair MacIntyre.* Cambridge: Cambridge University Press, 2003.

Postgate, J.N. *Taxation and Conscription in the Assyrian Empire.* Rome: Pontifical Biblical Institute, 1974.

Premnath, D.N. *Eighth Century Prophets: A Social Analysis.* St Louis: Chalice, 2003.

Pritchard, James B., ed. *Ancient Near Eastern Texts: Relating to the Old Testament.* 3rd edition. Princeton: Princeton University Press, 1969.

———. "Gibeon." Pages 391–93 in vol. 2 of *Interpreter's Dictionary of the Bible*. Edited by G.A. Buttrick. 4 vols. Nashville: Abingdon, 1962.

Propp, William H. C. *Exodus 19–40: A New Translation with Introduction and Commentary*. Anchor Bible 2A. New York: Doubleday, 2006.

Quell, Gottfried. *Wahre und Falsche Propheten: Versuch einer Interpretation*. Beitrage zur Forderung christlicher Theologie 46. Band 1. Heft. Guetersloh: C. Bertelsmann Verlag, 1952.

Quesnell, Quentin. "Mutual Misunderstanding: The Dialectic of Contemporary Hermeneutics." Pages 19–37 in *Lonergan's Hermeneutics: Its Development and Application*. Edited by Sean McEvenue and Ben F. Meyer. Washington DC: Catholic University of America Press, 1989.

Rahner, Karl. *Visions and Prophecies*. London: Burns and Oats, 1963.

Reviv, H. *The Elders in Ancient Israel: A Study of a Biblical Institution*. Jerusalem: Magnes, 1989.

———. "The Structure of Society." Pages 125–46 in *The Age of the Monarchies: Culture and Society*. Edited by Abraham Malamat. 5 vols. Jerusalem: Massada, 1979.

Richter, Sandra L. *The Epic of Eden: A Christian Entry into the Old Testament*. Downers Grove: IVP Academic, 2008.

Roberts, J.J.M. "In Defense of the Monarchy: The Contribution of Israelite Kingship to Biblical Theology." Pages in 377–97 in *Ancient Israelite Religion: Essays in Honor of Frank Moore Cross*. Edited by Patrick D. Miller, Paul D. Hanson, and S. Dean McBride. Philadelphia: Fortress, 1987.

Robinson, H. Wheeler. *Inspiration and Revelation in the Old Testament*. Oxford: Clarendon, 1946.

Rose, M. *Deuteronomist und Jahwist: Untersuchungen zu den Berührungspunkten beider Literaturwerke*. Abhandlungen zur

Theologie des Alten und Neuen Testaments 67. Zürich: Theologischer Verlag, 1981.

Ross, Allen and John N. Oswalt. *Genesis, Exodus*. Cornerstone Biblical Commentary. Carol Stream, IL: Tyndale, 2005.

Routledge, Robin. *Old Testament Theology: A Thematic Approach*. Downers Grove: IVP Academic, 2008.

Saggs, H.W. *The Encounter with the Divine in Mesopotamia and Israel*. London: Athlone, 1978.

Sakenfeld, K.D. *The Meaning of Hesed in the Hebrew Bible: A New Enquiry*. Harvard Semitic Museum 17. Missoula: Scholars Press, 1978.

Sanders, James A. "Hermeneutics in True and False Prophecy." Pages 21–41 in *Canon and Authority: Essays in Old Testament Religion and Theology*. Edited by George W. Coats and Burke O. Long. Philadelphia: Fortress, 1977.

_____. "Adaptable for Life: The Nature and Function of Canon." Pages 531–60 in *Magnalia Dei, The Mighty Acts of God: Essays on the Bible and Archaeology in Memory of G. Ernest Wright*. Edited by Frank Moore Cross, Werner E. Lemke, and Patrick D. Miller, Jr. Garden City: Doubleday & Company, 1976.

Sarna, Nahum M. *Exodus: The JPS Torah Commentary*. Philadelphia: Jewish Publication Society, 1991.

Schniedewind, W.M. *How the Bible Became a Book*. Cambridge: Cambridge University Press, 2004.

Schmid, Hans Heinrich. *Der sogenannte Jahwist: Beobachtungen und Fragen zur Pentateuchforschung*. Zürich: Theologischer Verlag, 1976.

Seitz, Christopher R. *Theology in Conflict: Reactions to the Exile in the Book of Jeremiah*. Beihefte zur Zeitschrift für die Alttestamentliche Wissenschaft 176. Berlin: de Gruyter, 1989.

Selms, van A. *Jeremia III*. De Prediking van het Oude Testament. Nijkerk: Callenback, 1980.

Seybold, K. *Das davidischen Konigtum im Zeugnis der Propheten*. Forschungen zur Religion und Literatur des Alten und Neuen Testament 107. Gottingen: Vanderhoeck & Ruprecht, 1972.

Sheppard, Gerald T. "True and False Prophecy within Scripture." Pages 262–84 in *Canon, Theology, and Old Testament Interpretation: Essays in Honor of Brevard S. Childs*. Edited by Gene M. Tucker, David L. Petersen, and Robert R. Wilson. Philadelphia: Fortress, 1988.

Sherratt, Susan and Andrew Sherratt. "The Growth of the Mediterranean Economy in the Early Millennium BC." *World Archaeology: Ancient Trade New Perspectives* 24 (1993): 361–78.

Simkins, Ronald and Stephen L. Cook. "Introduction: Case Studies from the Second Wave of Research in the Social World of the Hebrew Bible." *Semeia* 87 (2001): 1–14.

Smend, R. *Die Enstehung des Alten Testaments*. 4th edition. Stuttgart: Kohlhammer, 1989.

Smith, Mark S. *The Memoirs of God: History, Memory, and the Experience of the Divine in Ancient Israel*. Minneapolis: Augsburg Fortress, 2004.

_____. *The Origins of Biblical Monotheism: Israel's Polytheistic Background and the Ugaritic Texts*. Oxford: Oxford University Press, 2001.

_____. "Yahweh and Other Deities in Ancient Israel: Observations on Old Problems and Recent Trends." Pages 197–234 in *Ein Gott allein? JHWH-Verehrung und biblischer Monotheismus im Kontext der israelitischen und altorientalischen Religionsgeschichte*. Edited by W. Dietrich and M.A. Klopfenstein. Orbis biblicus et orientalis 139. Göttingen: Vanderhoeck & Ruprecht, 1994.

_____. *The Early History of God: Yahweh and the Other Deities in Ancient Israel*. San Francisco: Harper & Row, 1990.

Smith, W. Robertson. *Lectures on the Religion of the Semites: First Series, The Fundamental Institutions*. 3rd edition. New York: Macmillan, 1927.

Soggin, J.A. "Der judäische 'am-ha'ares und das Königtum in Juda." *Vetus Testamentum* 13 (1963): 187–95.

Solomon, Robert C. *Continental Philosophy Since 1750: The Rise and Fall of the Self*. Oxford: Oxford University Press, 1988.

Spalinger, Anthony J. "History of Egypt (3d Intermediate-Saite Period [Dyn. 21-26])." Pages 353–64 in vol. 2 of *The Anchor Bible Dictionary*. Edited by David Noel Freedman. 6 vols. New York: Doubleday, 1992.

_____. "Egypt and Babylonia: A Survey (c. 620 B.C.–550 B.C.)." in *Studien zur Altägyptischen Kultur* 5 (1977): 221–44.

Sparks, Kenton L. *Ethnicity and Identity in Ancient Israel: Prolegomena to the Study of Ethnic Sentiments and Their Expression in the Hebrew Bible*. Winona Lake, IN: Eisenbrauns, 1998.

Spieckermann, H. *Juda unter Assur in der Sargonidenzeit*. Forschungen zur Religion und Literatur des Alten und Neuen Testaments 129. Göttingen: Vandenhoeck & Ruprecht, 1982.

Spinoza, Benedict de. *Theological-Political Treatise*. Translated by Samuel Shirley. 2nd edition. Indianapolis: Hackett Publishing Co., 2001.

Sprinkle, Joes M. *'The Book of the Covenant': A literary Approach*. Journal for the Study of the Old Testament Supplement Series 174. Sheffield: JSOT, 1994.

Stager, L. "The Archaeology of the Family in Ancient Israel." *Bulletin of the American Schools of Oriental Research* 260 (1985): 1–35.

Steiner, Margreet. "Jerusalem in the Tenth and Seventh Centuries BCE: From Administrative Town to Commercial City." Pages 280–88 in *Studies in the Archaeology of the Iron Age in Israel and Jordan*. Journal for the Study of Old Testament Supplement 331. Edited by Amihai Mazar. Sheffield: Sheffield Academic, 2001.

Stern, Ephraim. *Archaeology of the Land of the Bible: The Assyrian, Babylonian, and the Persian Periods 732–332 BCE*. Vol 2. New York: Doubleday, 2001.

Sternberg, Meir. *The Poetics of Biblical Narrative: Ideological Literature and the Drama of Reading*. Indiana Literary Biblical Series. Bloomington: Indiana University Press, 1985.

Stohlmann, Stephen. "The Judean Exile of 701 B.C.E." Pages 147–75 in *Scripture in Context II: More Essays on the Comparative Method*. Edited by William W. Hallo, James C. Moyers, Leo G. Perdue. Winona Lake, IN: Eisenbrauns, 1983.

Stocking, George W. *Victorian Anthropology*. New York: Free, 1987.

Stulman, Louis. *Jeremiah*. Abingdon Old Testament Commentaries. Nashville: Abingdon, 2005.

Sulzberger, M. *The AM HA-ARETZ: The Ancient Hebrew Parliament*. Philadelphia: Julius H. Greenstone, 1910.

Sweeney, Marvin A. "The Truth in True and False Prophecy." Pages 9–26 in *Truth: Interdisciplinary Dialogues in a Pluralist Age*. Edited by Christine Helmer and Kristin De Troyer. Leuven: Peeters, 2003.

Tadmor, Hayim. "Treaty and Oath in Ancient Near East: A Historian's Approach." Pages 127–52 in *Humanizing America's Iconic Book: Society of Biblical Literature Centennial Addresses 1980*. Edited by Gene M. Tucker and Douglas A. Knight. Chicago: Scholars Press, 1980.

Talmon, Shemaryahu. "Kingship and the Ideology of the State." Pages 3–26 in *The Age of the Monarchies: Culture and Society*. Vol 5. Edited by Abraham Malamat; Jerusalem: Massada, 1979.

⸻. "The 'Comparative Method" in Biblical Interpretation—Principles and Problems," *Vetas Testamentum Supplement* 29 (1978): 320–56.

Tarrer, Seth B. *Reading with the Faithful: Interpretation of True and False Prophecy in the Book of Jeremiah from Ancient Times to Modern*. Journal of Theological Interpretation Supplement 6. Winona Lake, IN: Eisenbrauns, 2013.

Thiel, W. *Die deuteronomistische Redaktion von Jere 1–25*. Wissenschaftliche Monographien zum Alten und Neuen Testament 41. Neukirchener-Vluyn: Neukirchener Verlag, 1973.

Thiele, Edwin R. *The Mysterious Numbers of the Hebrew Kings: A Reconstruction of the Chronology of the Kingdoms of Israel and Judah*. 3rd edition. Grand Rapids: Eerdmans, 1983.

Thiselton, Anthony. *New Horizons in Hermeneutics: The Theory and Practice of Transforming Biblical Reading*. Grand Rapids: Zondervan, 1992.

Thompson, J.A. *The Book of Jeremiah*. New International Commentary of Old Testament. Edited by R.K. Harrison. Grand Rapids: Eerdmans, 1980.

Tigay, Jeffrey H. *You Shall Have No Other Gods: Israelite Religion in the Light of Hebrew Inscriptions*. Harvard Semitic Studies 31. Atlanta: Scholars Press, 1986.

Tov, Emmanuel. "Some Aspects of the Textual and Literary History of the Book of Jeremiah." Pages 145–67 in *Le Livre de Jérémie: Le Prophéte et Son Milieu, les Oracles et Leur Transmission*. Edited by P.M. Bogaert. Bibliotheca Ephemeridum Theologicarum Lovaniensium 54. Leuven: Peeters, 1981.

Troesltsch, Ernst. "Historiography." Pages 716–23 in *Encyclopedia of Religion and Ethics*. Vol. 6. Edited by James Hastings. Edinburgh: T&T Clark, 1914.

Turkowski, Lucian. "Peasant Agriculture in the Judaean Hills." *Palestinian Exploration Quarterly* 202 (1969): 21–33.

Van Der Toorn, Karel. *Scribal Culture and the Making of the Hebrew Bible*. Cambridge: Harvard University Press, 2007.

VanGemeren, Willem A. *New International Dictionary of Old Testament Theology and Exegesis*. 5 vols. Grand Rapids: Zondervan, 1997.

Van Seters, John. *Abraham in History and Tradition*. New Haven: Yale University Press, 1975.

_____. *In Search of History: Historiography in the Ancient World and the Origins of Biblical History*. New Haven: Yale University Press, 1983.

_____. *Prologue to History: The Yahwist as Historian in Genesis*. Louisville: John Knox, 1992.

_____. *The Life of Moses: The Yahwist as Historian in Exodus-Numbers*. Louisville: John Knox, 1994.

Vaux, R. de. *Ancient Israel: Its Life and Institutions*. New York: McGraw Hill, 1965.

Varughese, Alex. "The Royal Family in the Jeremiah Tradition." Pages 319–29 in *Inspired Speech: Prophecy in the Ancient Near East-Essays in Honor of Herbert B. Huffmon*. Edited by John Kaltner and Louis Stulman. New York: T&T Clark, 2004.

Veijola, T. *Das Königtum in der Beuteilung der deuteronomistischen Historiographie*. Annalae Academiae Scientiarum Fennicae 198. Helsinki: Suomalainen Tiedeakatemia, 1977.

Volken, Laurent. *Visions, Revelations and the Church*. New York: Kenedy, 1963.

Von Rad, Gerhard. "The Form-Critical Problem of the Hexateuch." Pages 1–78 in *The Problem of the Hexateuch and Other Essays*. Translated by E.W. Trueman Dicken. New York: McGraw-Hill, 1966.

_____. *Wisdom in Israel*. Translated by James D. Martin. Nashville: SCM, 1972.

_____. *Old Testament Theology: The Theology of Israel's Prophetic Tradition*. 2 vols. Translated by D.M.G. Stalker. New York: Harper & Row, 1965.

_____. "The Origin of the Concept of the Day of Yahweh." *Journal of Semitic Studies* (1959): 97–108.

_____. *Studies in Deuteronomy*. Translated by D. Stalker. Studies in Biblical Theology 9. Chicago: Regnery 1953.

_____. "Die Falschen Propheten." *Zeitschrift für die altestmentliche Wissenschaft* 51 (1933): 109–20.

Vorländer. H. *Die Entstehungszeit des jehowistischen Geschichtswerkes*. Frankfurt am Main: Peter Lang, 1978.

Vries, Simon J. de. *Prophet Against Prophet: The Role of the Micah Narrative (1 Kings 22) in the Development of Early Prophetic Tradition*. Grand Rapids: Eerdmans, 1978.

Waltke, Bruce K. and Michael P. O'Connor. *An Introduction to Biblical Hebrew Syntax*. Winona Lake, IN: Eisenbrauns, 1990.

Weinfeld, M. "Ancient Near Eastern Patterns in Prophetic Literature." Pages 32–49 in *The Place is Too Small for Us: The Israelite Prophets in Recent Scholarship*. Sources for Biblical and Theological Study 5. Edited by Robert P. Gordon. Winona Lake, IN: Eisenbrauns, 1995.

_____. *Deuteronomy and the Deuteronomic School*. Oxford: Oxford University Press, 1972.

_____. "The Covenant of Grant in the Old Testament and in the Ancient Near East," *Journal of the America Oriental Society* 90 (1970): 184–203.

Weinstein, J.R. *On MacIntyre*. Belmont: Wadsworth, 2003.
Weippert, H. *Die Prosareden des Jeremiabuches*. Beihefte zur Zeitschrift für die Alttestamentliche Wissenschaft 132. Berlin: de Gruyter, 1973.
Wellhausen, Julius. *Prolegomena to the History of Israel*. Translated by J.S. Black and Allan Menzies. Edinburgh, 1885.
Westermann, Claus. *Prophetic Oracles of Salvation in the Old Testament*. Translated by Keith Crim. Louisville: John Knox, 1991.
Westphal, Merold. *Suspicion and Faith: The Religious Uses of Modern Atheism*. Grand Rapids: Eerdmans, 1993.
Whybray, R.N. *The Making of the Pentateuch: A Methodological Study*. Reprint. Sheffield: Sheffield Academic, 1994.
Wiesel, Elie. *Five Biblical Portraits*. Notre Dame: University of Notre Dame Press, 1981.
Wilson, Robert R. "Social Theory and the Study of Israelite Religion: A Retrospective on the Past Forty Years of Research." Pages 7–18 in *Social Theory and the Study of Israelite Religion: Essays in Retrospect and Prospect*. Society of Biblical Literature 71. Edited by Saul M. Olyan. Atlanta: Society of Biblical Literature, 2012.
_____. "Interpreting Israel's Religion: An Anthropological Perspective on the Problem of False Prophecy." Pages 332–44 in *The Place is Too Small for Us: The Israelite Prophets in Recent Scholarship*. Sources for Biblical and Theological Study 5. Edited by Robert P. Gordon. Winona Lake, IN: Eisenbrauns, 1995.
_____. *Prophecy and Society in Ancient Israel*. Philadelphia: Fortress, 1980.
Wiseman, D.J., trans. *Chronicles of Chaldean Kings, (626–556 B.C) in the British Museum*. London: British Museum, 1956.

Witherington, Ben. *Jesus the Seer: The Progress of Prophecy*. Peabody: Hendrickson, 1999.

Wolff, Hans Walter. "Micah the Moreshite—The Prophet and His Background." Pages 77–84 in *Israelite Wisdom: Theological and Literary Essays in Honor of Samuel Terrien*. Edited by J. Gammie, et al. Missoula: Scholars Press, 1978.

Wolin, Sheldon S. "On the Theory and Practice of Power." Pages 179–202 in *After Foucault: Humanistic Knowledge, Postmodern Challenges*. Edited by Jonathan Arac. New Brunswick: Rutgers University Press, 1988.

Wood, Laurence W. *God and History: The Dialectical Tension of Faith and History in modern Thought*. Lexington: Emeth, 2005.

Wright, Christopher J.H. *Old Testament for the People of God*. Downers Grove: InterVarsity, 2004.

Wright, G. Ernest. "The Nations in Hebrew Prophecy." *Encounter* 26.2 (1965): 225–37.

_____. *Biblical Archaeology*. Philadelphia: Westminster, 1962.

Wright, N.T. *The New Testament and the People of God*. Minneapolis: Fortress Press, 1992.

Young, Frances M. *Biblical Exegesis and the Formation of Christian Culture*. Cambridge: Cambridge University Press, 1997.

Zvi, Ehud Ben. "A Deuteronomistic Redaction in/among 'The Twelve?' A Contribution from the Standpoint of the Books of Micah, Zephaniah and Obadiah." Pages 232–61 in *Those Elusive Deuteronomists: The Phenomenon of Pan Deuteronomism*. Journal for the Study of Old Testament Supplement 269. Edited by S.L. McKenzie. Sheffield: Sheffield Academic, 1999.

Primary Sources

Gen 1–11, *15*
Gen 4:26, *94*
Gen 12–50, *15*
Gen 15:2, *94*
Gen 21:23, *1*
Gen 23:7, *157*
Exod 3:4–6, 10, *69*
Exod 6:2–8, *94*
Exod 6:7, *95*
Exod 10:1–2, *79*
Exod 12:26, *79*
Exod 13:8, 14, *79*
Exod 15, *95*
Exod 15:1–5, *96*
Exod 15:1–12, *96*
Exod 15:11, *96*
Exod 15:13, *96*
Exod 15:13–18, *96*
Exod 15:14–15, *97*
Exod 19, *99*
Exod 19:4, *98*
Exod 19:5–6, *98*
Exod 19-20, *87*
Exod 20:1–17, *98–100*
Exod 20:18–21, *99*
Exod 20:3–23:33, *100–101*

Exod 20:3–17, *101*
Exod 20:22–23:33, *99, 102–3*
Exod 20:23–26, *103*
Exod 21:1–11, *103*
Exod 21:18–23:33, *98*
Exod 22:15–16, *135*
Exod 22:21, *104*
Exod 22:22–24, *104*
Exod 22:25–27, *104*
Exod 22:27, *193*
Exod 24, *99*
Lev 19:11, *1*
Lev 19:31, *7*
Lev 20:6, *7*
Lev 24:10–16, *193*
Lev 26, *148*
Num 22, *143*
Num 27, *105*
Num 27:21, *102*
Deut 4:2, *188*
Deut 5:20, *183*
Deut 5:22, *87*
Deut 6:4–9, *79*
Deut 6:20–24, *15*
Deut 11:13–21, *79*
Deut 13:1, *188*

Deut 13:2–6, *3, 4, 162–63, 210–15*
Deut 16:18–20, *183*
Deut 17:14–20, *110*
Deut 18:10–13, *7*
Deut 18:21–22, *163, 210–15*
Deut 18:22, *3*
Deut 19:10, *183*
Deut 19:16–21, *2*
Deut 21:8, *183*
Deut 22:28–29, *135*
Deut 26:5–6, *15*
Deut 27–28, *148*
Deut 28, *99*
Deut 33:17, *146*
Josh 4:21, *79*
Josh 11:23, *105*
Josh 13:23, *105*
Josh 14:13–14, *105*
Josh 15:20, *105*
Josh 17:3–4, *105*
Josh 19:49–50, *105*
Judg 5, *108*
Judg 7, *148*
Judg 19–21, *109*
1 Sam 4:11, *190*
1 Sam 8:5, *37, 109*
1 Sam 8:7, *110*
1 Sam 8:11–12, *136*
1 Sam 8:14–15, *136*
1 Sam 13, *112*
1 Sam 13:5–14, *113*

1 Sam 15:1–35, *113, 120*
1 Sam 15:29, *1*
1 Sam 16–2 Sam 8, *55*
1 Sam 16:1–2 Sam 5:10, *115*
2 Sam 2:4, *130*
2 Sam 3:12, 17, 21, *130*
2 Sam 5:1–3, *130*
2 Sam 5:10, *115*
2 Sam 6–8, *115*
2 Sam 7, *118, 121*
2 Sam 7:1, 143
2 Sam 7:1–3, *114*
2 Sam 7:1–7, *114*
2 Sam 7:1–29, *113*
2 Sam 7:4–11a, *114*
2 Sam 7:4–17, *120*
2 Sam 7:11b–17, *114*
2 Sam 7:13, 15, 16, *114*
2 Sam 7:14, *115*
2 Sam 7:18–29, *114*
2 Sam 8:18, *130*
2 Sam 8:15–18, *130*
2 Sam 8:16, *131*
2 Sam 8:18, *139*
2 Sam 9–1 Kgs 2, *115*
2 Sam 12:1–14, *111*
2 Sam 12:1–15, *143*
2 Sam 12:1–7, *147*
2 Sam 15:24, 29, 35, *139*
2 Sam 19:12, *139*
2 Sam 20:23, *131*
2 Sam 20:23–26, *130*

2 Sam 20:24, *136*
2 Sam 20:25, *139*
2 Sam 24:11, *143*
2 Sam 24:25, *105*
1 Kgs 4:7–19, *130*
1 Kgs 5:13–18, *136*
1 Kgs 8:25, *121*
1 Kgs 9:4–5, *121*
1 Kgs 9:20–22, *140*
1 Kgs 11:5, *140*
1 Kgs 11:7, *140*
1 Kgs 11:26–38, *122*
1 Kgs 11:28, *136*
1 Kgs 12:31, *139*
1 Kgs 13:2, *19*
1 Kgs 14:7–11, *112*
1 Kgs 14:24, *121*
1 Kgs 15:3, *121*
1 Kgs 15:22, *136*
1 Kgs 15:34, *121*
1 Kgs 16:19, *121*
1 Kgs 16:24, *105*
1 Kgs 16:29–34, *145*
1 Kgs 16:32, *141*
1 Kgs 18:1–46, *145*
1 Kgs 18:16–18, *111*
1 Kgs 18:19, *141*
1 Kgs 20, *112*
1 Kgs 20:35, *142*
1 Kgs 21, *106*
1 Kgs 21:1–29, *145*
1 Kgs 21:20–24, *111*

1 Kgs 22:6–7, *112*
1 Kgs 22:8, *146*
1 Kgs 22:10, *147*
1 Kgs 22:16, *143*, *145–46*
1 Kgs 22:17, *146*
1 Kgs 22:19–23, *147*
1 Kgs 22:53, *121*
2 Kgs 3:11, *112*
2 Kgs 5:1–14, *143*
2 Kgs 5:22, *142*
2 Kgs 6:1, *143*
2 Kgs 6:1–7, *142*
2 Kgs 6:28, *160*
2 Kgs 9:1, *142*
2 Kgs 10, *112*
2 Kgs 11, *159*
2 Kgs 11:14, *157*
2 Kgs 11:18, *141*
2 Kgs 17:26, *102*
2 Kgs 19:6–7, *164*, *167*
2 Kgs 21, *141*, *171*
2 Kgs 21:3–4, *165*
2 Kgs 21:16, *173*
2 Kgs 21:20–21, *173*
2 Kgs 21:23, *173*
2 Kgs 21:24, *157*
2 Kgs 22, *19*
2 Kgs 22:12, *196*
2 Kgs 22-23, *158–59*, *174*
2 Kgs 23:4–14, *171*
2 Kgs 23:12, *171*
2 Kgs 23:13, *140*

2 Kgs 23:30, *157, 175*
2 Kgs 23:32, 37, *121*
2 Kgs 23:35, *176*
2 Kgs 24:8, *195*
2 Kgs 24: 9, 19, *121*
2 Kgs 24:13–16, *178*
2 Kgs 25:19, *157*
2 Kgs 25:27, *187*
2 Kgs 32-34, *164*
1 Chr 10:13, 14, *7*
1 Chr 17:1–15, *121*
1 Chr 18:15, *131*
1 Chr 27:25, *131*
2 Chr 13:9, *157*
2 Chr 23, *157*
2 Chr 29:25, *143*
2 Chr 33:11–16, *165*
2 Chr 34–35, *174*
Ezra 9:1, 11, *157*
Neh 13:23, *157*
Ps 18:1–2, *97*
Ps 21-22, *61, 83, 146*
Ps 27:7–13, *2*
Ps 44:17, *1*
Ps 78:5–8, *79*
Ps 78:60, *190*
Ps 89, *114*
Ps 89:33, *1*
Ps 118:14, *97*
Ps 132, *114*
Prov 30:6, *188*
Eccl 3:14, *188*

Isa 1:7, 21, *102*
Isa 1:9–10, 150
Isa 1:21–23, *138*
Isa 2:4, *29*
Isa 5:7, *102*
Isa 5:8, *139*
Isa 5:11–13, *138*
Isa 5:23, *138*
Isa 6:1–13, *69*
Isa 7, *149*
Isa 9:4, *148*
Isa 10:1–2, *138*
Isa 10:2, *102*
Isa 12:2, *97*
Isa 28:7, *2*
Isa 32:7, *138*
Isa 40:6, *69*
Isa 42:17, *152*
Isa 44:9–17, *152*
Isa 59:8–9, *102*
Isa 63:8, *1*
Jer 1:2, *163*
Jer 1:4–19, *69*
Jer 1:13–14, *70*
Jer 1:18, *156*
Jer 2–20, *163*
Jer 2:34, *183*
Jer 3:6, *163*
Jer 5:1, *102*
Jer 5:27–28, *170*
Jer 6:1, *177*
Jer 6:13, *1–2*

Jer 6:14, *2*
Jer 7:5, *102*
Jer 7:5–6, 9, *183*
Jer 7:6, *183*
Jer 8:8, *183*
Jer 8:10, *2*
Jer 8:11, *2*
Jer 9:4–9, *183*
Jer 13:20, *176*
Jer 14:13, *2*
Jer 14:14, *2*
Jer 22:3, *183*
Jer 22:11, *175*
Jer 22:13–19, *170*
Jer 22:13–23, *177*
Jer 23:9–40, *34*
Jer 23:17, *2*
Jer 23:18, *70*
Jer 23:21, *2*
Jer 23:25, *2*
Jer 23:30, *19*
Jer 23:9–29:23, *33–34*
Jer 25:1–9, *176–77*
Jer 25:3, *163*
Jer 26, *186*
Jer 26:1–16, *186*
Jer 26:1–24, *34*
Jer 26:3, *188*
Jer 26:4–6, *190*
Jer 26:7, *191*
Jer 26:7–8, 11, 16, *1*
Jer 26:8, *192*

Jer 26:9, *10, 11, 192*
Jer 26:12–17, *193*
Jer 26: 20–24, *195*
Jer 26:17–19, *167, 186*
Jer 26:20–23, *177*
Jer 26:20–24, *186*
Jer 26–29, *33, 36, 38, 162, 184–85*
Jer 26, 29, 36, *158, 159*
Jer 26–52, *185*
Jer 27, *179*
Jer 27:9, *1*
Jer 27:10, 16, *2*
Jer 27:1–28:17, *34*
Jer 27–28, *186, 197–210*
Jer 28, *16–18, 26–27*
Jer 28:1, *1*
Jer 28:1–9, *2*
Jer 28:2–3, *26*
Jer 28:8, 9, *3, 4, 30, 31*
Jer 28:15, *2*
Jer 28:15–16, *26*
Jer 28–29, *24*
Jer 29, *186, 215–18*
Jer 29:1, 8, *1*
Jer 29:1–19, *34*
Jer 29:7, *31*
Jer 29:9, *2*
Jer 29:30–32, *34*
Jer 34:19, *156*
Jer 36:1–8, *177*
Jer 36:2, *163*

Jer 36:11–19, *177*
Jer 36:12, 25, *195*
Jer 36:20–26, *177*
Jer 36:25, *196*
Jer 36:30–31, *177*
Jer 36:32, *177*
Jer 37:2, *156*
Jer 39:14, *196*
Jer 44:15–25, *152*
Jer 46:1–12, *176*
Jer 50, *181*
Ezek 7:27, *156*
Ezek 13:1–8, *2*
Ezek 22:29, *156*
Ezek 22:28, *2*
Hos 1–3, *151*
Hos 4:5, *2*
Hos 4:11–14, *151*
Hos 9:1–3, *138*
Joel 2:13, *190*
Joel 4:9–17, *29*
Joel 4:10, *29*
Amos 3:1, *151*
Amos 3:8, *69*

Amos 4:4–5, *151*
Amos 4:1–3, *138*
Amos 4:11, *150*
Amos 5:1–3, *151*
Amos 5:18–20, *148*
Amos 5:21–24, *151*
Amos 5:21–27, *148*
Amos 6:4–7, *138*
Amos 7:15, *69*
Amos 7–9, *70*
Amos 7:10–13, *140*
Mic 2:1–5, *138*
Mic 2–3, *19*
Mic 2:6–11, *143*
Mic 3:5, *143*
Mic 3:5–8, *2*
Mic 3:12, *195*
Mic 4:3, *29*
Mic 5:12–14, *151*
Mic 7:1–7, *151*
Hab 1:4, *102*
Zeph 3:4, *2*
Zech 13:2, *1*

MODERN AUTHORS

Abraham, W.J., *22, 71–75, 81, 85*
Ackroyd, P.R., *98*
Aharoni, Y., *177*
Albright, W.F., *10, 69, 89, 151*
Allen, L.C., *186, 191, 193–94, 197, 199, 207, 210*
Alt, A., *10, 110, 125*
Alter, R., *26*
Arnold, B.T., *1, 92, 121, 129, 142, 148, 175*
Arnold, B.T. and B.E. Beyer, *104*
Bacon, F., *41–42*
Baer, D.A. and R.P. Gordon, *97*
Bakon, S., *198*
Barbour, I., *46*
Bar-Efrat, S., *85*
Barkay, G., *140*
Barr, J., *11, 15, 25, 82, 119*
Barth, K., *10, 14*
Barton, J., *26, 148*
Bashkar, R., *47*
Bendor, S., *108, 134*
Benjamin, D.C., *126*
Berlin, A., *85*
Bird, A.P., *126*
Bloesch, D. *81*
Bordreuil, P., F. Isreal, and D. Pardee, *106*
Brenneman, J.E., *28–30*
Bright, J., *150–51*
Broshi, M., *131*
Brueggemann, W., *10, 11, 15, 25, 34, 185*
Buber, M., *17, 21, 27, 33*
Butterworth, M., *189*
Carpenter, E. and M.A. Grisanti, *2*
Carr, D., *86*
Carroll, R.M.D., *151*
Carroll, R.P., *33–34, 182, 205*
Carter, C., *38, 125*
Chaney, M.L., *38, 124, 137–38*
Childs, B., *11, 14–15, 25–28, 33, 35, 206–7*
Clark, G.R., *96*
Clements, R.E., *209*
Cogan, M., *168, 171, 187*
Collins, C.J., *193*

Comte, A., *42*
Coogan, M.D., *171*
Cook, S.L., *38, 109, 116, 126, 130, 144, 158-60*
Cook, S.L. and R. Simkins, *125*
Cooke, F.T., *195*
Cox, H., *119*
Crenshaw, J.L., *17-20, 149, 212, 223*
Cross, F.M., *89-90, 96, 110, 113-15*
Darby, E., *140*
Davies, P., *174*
Dawson, D., *9*
Day, J., *80*
De Jong, M.J., *6, 30-31, 34, 112, 223*
Dearman, J.A., *164, 185, 208, 215*
Deist, F.E., *11*
Denton, D.L., *47, 50-51, 55, 57, 59, 77*
Derrida, J., *46*
Descartes, R., *41-42*
Dever, W., *91, 129*
Dietrich, W., *113-14*
Drake, D., *46*
Duhm, B., *13-14, 181, 209*
Durand, J.M., *143*
Dutch-Walls, P., *38, 158, 160, 184*

Dyckman, D., *84*
Eichrodt, W., *10*
Enns, P., *102*
Epp-Tiessen, D., *33-34*
Faust, A., *130-32, 135, 137-38, 158, 169*
Faust, A. and E. Weiss, *165, 169*
Finkelstein, I., *109, 169*
Finkelstein, I. and M. Broshi, *131-32*
Finkelstein, I. and N.A. Silberman, *169-70*
Finkelstein, L., *84*
Fishbane, M., *80*
Flanagan, J., *50*
Foucault, M., *45*
Franken, H.J. and M.L. Steiner, *152*
Freedman, D.N. and R. Frey, *4*
Frick, F.S., *125*
Friebel, K., *34*
Friethem, T., *34*
Gabler, J.P., *10*
Galling, K., *157*
Geertz, C., *120*
Gentry, P. and S.J. Wellum, *116*
Gerstenberger, E.S., *116*
Glueck, N., *97*
Goldingay, J., *11*

Gordon, R.P., *13*
Gordon, R.P. and D.A. Baer, *97*
Gossai, H., *102*
Gottwald, N.K., *125, 146*
Grabbe, L.L., *6–7, 22, 92, 126, 154*
Grayson, A.K., *178*
Greenberg, M., *147*
Grenz, S.J., *41, 43, 45*
Grünwaldt, K., *1*
Gunneweg, A.H.J., *117, 157*
Gunton, C.E., *71*
Hackett, J.A., *108*
Hagedorn, A.C., *32*
Hallo, W.W., *6*
Halpern, B., *157, 166, 169–70*
Hanson, P.D., *37, 99, 101, 104, 111*
Hayes, J.H., *13*
Healey, J.P., *157*
Herion, G.A., *119*
Hess, R.S., *3*
Hibbard, J.T., *212–13*
Hiebert, P.G., *42*
Hillard, K.E., *1*
Hobbes, T., *12*
Holladay, J.S., *134, 136, 142, 158*
Holladay, W.L., *163, 181–82, 184, 186, 190–91, 193, 195–96, 200, 207–8, 216–17*
Horsley, R.A., *38, 126*
House, P.R., *148*
Houston, W.J., *38, 137*
Huffmon, H.B., *3, 111, 113*
Hume, D., *43, 48*
Huyssteen, W.V., *46–47*
Hyatt, J.P., *195*
Jeremias, J., *69*
Johnson, B., *102–03*
Joüon, P. and T. Muraoka, *192*
Kant, I., *43–44, 48*
Kaufmann, Y., *37, 93*
King, P.J. and L.E. Stager, *130*
Kitchen, K.A., *100, 174*
Kletter, R., *140, 152*
Knight III, H.H., *41*
Knohl, I., *85*
Knoppers, G.N., *117, 121–22*
Koch, K., *111*
Merwe, C.H.J., J.A. van der Naudé, and J.H. Kroeze, *217*
Kuenen, A., *14, 16*
Kutsch, E., *99*
Lalleman, H., *190, 217–18*
Lang, B., *134*
Lange, A., *32–34*
Lemaire, A., *113*

Lemche, N.P., *107, 134*
Lenski, G., *38, 126, 128, 144, 156*
Lenski, G. and P. Nolan, *37–38, 126–29, 133, 143, 160, 227*
Lenski, G., P. Nolan, and J. Lenski, *128*
Levenson, J.D., *116–18*
Lindblom, J., *5*
Lipschits, O., *165, 172, 175, 177–78, 180*
Lonergan, B., *47–61, 65, 67, 74–75, 77*
Long, B.O., *18, 23–25*
Long, V.P., *72*
Lovejoy, A.O., *46*
Lundbom, J.R., *68, 70, 164, 187, 191, 193, 195–96, 200, 207, 209, 211, 216–18*
MacIntyre, A., *78–80*
Malamat, A., *173, 175*
Martens, E.A. and J.A. Thompson, *189*
Matthews, V.H., *126*
Matthews, V.H. and D.C. Benjamin, *111*
Mazar, A., *141, 151*
McBride, S.D., *212*
McCarthy, D.J., *99*
McEvenue, S., *47, 54–56, 58, 76, 80, 118–19, 145*
McEvenue, S. and B.F. Meyer, *47, 54, 59*
McGrath, A., *79*
McKane, W., *14, 182–183, 209*
McKay, J.W., *170–171*
McMahon, C., *63*
McNutt, P., *108, 132*
Mead, J.K., *144*
Megill, A., *45*
Mendenhall, G.E., *99, 125*
Merrill, E.H., *210*
Meyer, B.F., *35, 47–49, 51–55, 57–59, 65, 74, 76–77, 119*
Meyer, R., *65*
Meyers, C., *38*
Miller, D.R., *171*
Miller, J., *45*
Miller, P.D., *34*
Moberly, R.W.L., *8, 17, 34, 35, 39, 146–47, 149*
Morgan, R., *72*
Moritz, T., *48, 59–60*
Mowinckel, S., *181*
Müller, H.P., *69*
Nelson, R., *172*
Nicholson, E.W., *156–57, 184*
Niditch, S., *87*
Nietzsche, F., *44–45*
Nissinen, M., *6*

Noth, M., *10, 14, 89, 95, 98, 108, 113-14, 125*
Nunez, T., *49*
O'Connor, M. and B.K. Waltke, *192*
O'Keefe, J.J., *9*
Oded, B., *159*
Oppenheim, A.L., *87*
Osuji, A.C., *33, 35, 183, 189, 199, 208, 217*
Oswalt, J.N., *11, 37, 69-70, 81, 92-93*
Oswalt, J.N. and A. Ross, *96, 98-100, 103*
Overholt, T.W., *6, 126*
Peacocke, A., *46*
Pelikan, J., *155*
Perdue, L.G., *10*
Perlitt, L., *99*
Petersen, D.L., *7*
Pleins, J.D., *136*
Porter, J., *79*
Postgate, J.N., *170*
Premnath, D.N., *138*
Propp, W.H.C., *98*
Quell, G., *17-18, 23, 206, 223*
Reimer, D.J., *103*
Reviv, H., *131, 135, 158*
Richter, S.L., *109-110*
Festinger, L., H. Riecken, and S. Schachter, *205*

Roberts, J.J.M., *6, 139*
Robinson, H.W., *82*
Rose, M., *86*
Sakenfeld, K.D., *97*
Saldarini, A.J., *38*
Sanders, J.A., *17, 20-23, 27-29, 39, 80, 149*
Santayana, G., *46*
Sarna, N.M., *94-96, 100-1*
Schmid, H.H., *86*
Schneiders, S.M., *81*
Schniedewind, W.M., *87, 167-68*
Schult, H., *189*
Seebass, H., S. Beyerle, and K. Gruwaldt, *1*
Seitz, C., *165, 173-74, 176*
Sellars, R.W., *46*
Seters, J.V., *86*
Seybold, K., *117*
Sheppard, G.T., *28*
Ska, J.L., *9*
Smith, M.S., *91-92*
Smith, W.R., *125*
Snell, D., *136*
Soggin, J.A., *158, 166, 189*
Solomon, R.C., *43*
Spalinger, A., *174, 176*
Sparks, K.L., *108, 167*
Spieckermann, H., *169-70*
Spinoza, B. de., *12*
Sprinkle, J.M., *98-99*

Stager, L.E., *130, 134, 152*
Steiner, M.L. and H.J. Franken, *152*
Steiner, M., *168*
Stern, E., *164–65, 168*
Sternberg, M., *85*
Stocking, G.W., *11, 42*
Stulman, L., *4, 185*
Sulzberger, M., *156*
Sweeney, M.A., *31, 34*
Tadmor, H., *99–100, 166*
Talmon, S., *6, 122*
Tarrer, S.B., *8, 12, 20, 32–33*
Thiel, W., *184*
Thiele, E.R., *165–66*
Thiselton, A., *63*
Thompson, J.A., *196, 209*
Thompson, J.A. and E. A. Martens, *189*
Toorn, K. v.d., *88*
Troeltsch, E., *72–73*
Turkowski, L., *199*
Vaux, R.D., *117, 125, 132, 156, 158*
Von Rad, G., *10, 14, 16, 100, 119, 145, 148, 159*
Vries, S.J.D., *162*

Waltke, B.K., *192*
Walton, J.H., *113*
Weinfeld, M., *85, 99, 111, 117*
Weinstein, J.R., *78*
Wellhausen, J., *13, 85*
Westermann, C., *214*
Westphal, M., *45*
Whitelam, K.W., *38*
Whybray, R.N., *25–26, 86*
Wiesel, E., *209*
Wilson, R.R., *6–7, 18, 23–25, 28, 39, 115–16, 125–26, 155, 206, 223, 226*
Wiseman, D.J., *198*
Witherington, B., *7*
Wolff, H.W., *167*
Wolin, S.S., *45*
Wood, L.W., *43*
Wright, C.J.H., *92–93*
Wright, G.E., *20, 69*
Wright, N.T., *8, 9, 20, 35, 47–48, 58–67, 71, 74, 76, 78, 85, 92, 152*
Young, F.M., *9*
Zimmerli, W., *27*

SUBJECTS

Archaeology, *92*
Canaanite Religion, *89–91, 93*
Critical Realism, *35, 46–48, 222*
  Horizon, *51–52, 57, 68*
  Inspiration, *80–82*
  Lonergan, B., *48–54*
  Meyer, B.F., *54–58*
  Revelation, *68–75*
  Subjectivity/Objectivity, *35, 51–54, 59–60, 64, 67–68*
  Tradition, *77–80*
  Worldview/Story, *60–61, 64–66, 92–94*
  Wright, N.T., *58–67*
Davidic Covenant, *113–22, 226*
  Ideology, *24–25, 114–15, 119–20, 132, 172, 224*
Deposit of Faith, *76–77, 79, 81, 225*
Dissonant Theory, *205–06*
History/Historiography, *3, 71–74, 85*
History of Biblical Interpretation
  Critical/Enlightenment, *10–28, 41–44*
  Post-Critical, *11–12, 28–30, 44–46*
  Pre-critical, *8–10, 12*
  Recent Trends, *30–35*
Macrosociology, *126*
  Adaptation of Tradition, *133–35*
  Agrarian Society, *124–28, 156, 171, 191, 199*
  Class Stratification, *128–29, 132–33, 135*
  Economy, *135, 137, 165, 227*
  Institutionalized Yahwism, *145–50, 188, 227*
  Vox Populi, *19, 37, 122, 150, 161*
Monarchy/Limited Monarchy, *37, 107–13, 115–16, 120–23, 142, 154–54, 159, 161, 180, 187, 205, 219, 226*
Prophetic Conflict in the Old Testament
  Criteria for Judging Prophetic Conflict, *3–5, 211–15*
  Definition of a Prophet, *5–7*
Redactors, *56, 86–89, 113, 183–84*

The Book of Jeremiah, *181–84*
The Prophet Jeremiah
  Context, *163–71*
  Internal Politics, *171–80*
  Conflict with Hananiah, *197–210*
Yahwistic Tradition, *84,* 89
  Exodus 15, *95–97*
  Ḥesed (חסד), *96–97, 100, 114, 189–90, 212–13, 217, 219–20, 229–30*
  Mispatim (משפטים), *102–6, 109, 112, 139, 142, 144, 156, 159, 162, 164, 191, 220, 225, 229*
  The Book of the Covenant (Exod 21:18–23:33), *102–04*
  The Covenant Relationship/The Decalogue (Exod 20:1–17), *98-102*
  The Land, *104–6*
  The People of the Land (עם־הארץ), *156–57, 159–60, 215*

www.ingramcontent.com/pod-product-compliance
Lightning Source LLC
Chambersburg PA
CBHW071726080526
44588CB00013B/1915